MW01625648

THE BEST OF WATERCOLOR

splash 15

creative solutions

EDITED BY RACHEL RUBIN WOLF

NORTH LIGHT BOOKS
CINCINNATI, OHIO
artistsnetwork.com

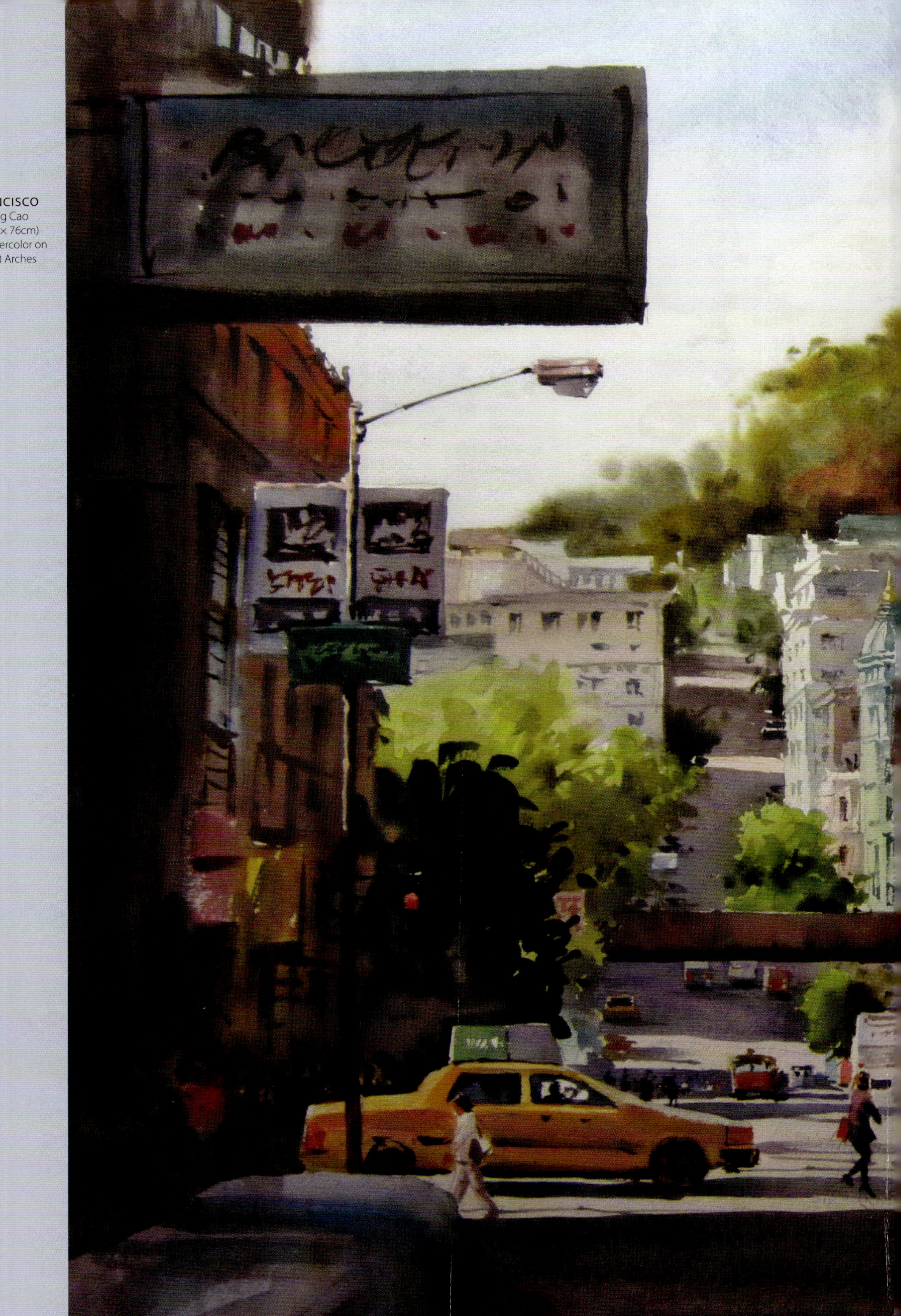

▶ **SAN FRANCISCO STREET** | Peng Cao
22" × 30" (56cm × 76cm)
Transparent watercolor on 140-lb. (300gsm) Arches

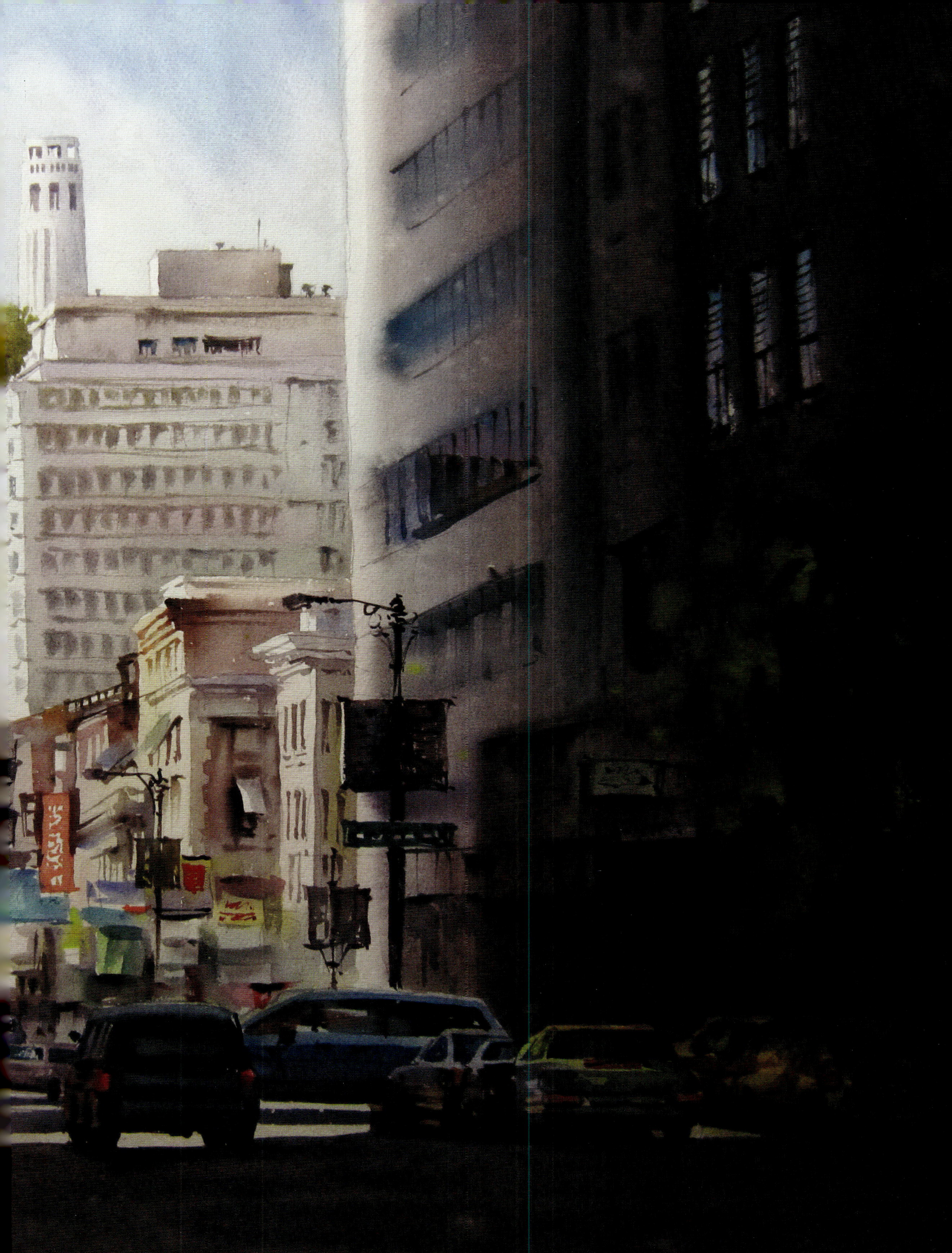

Contents

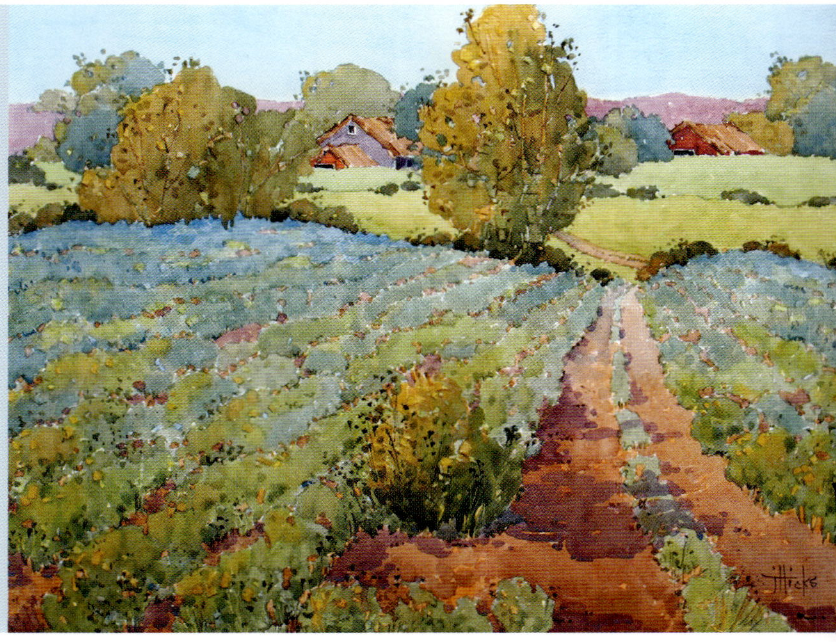

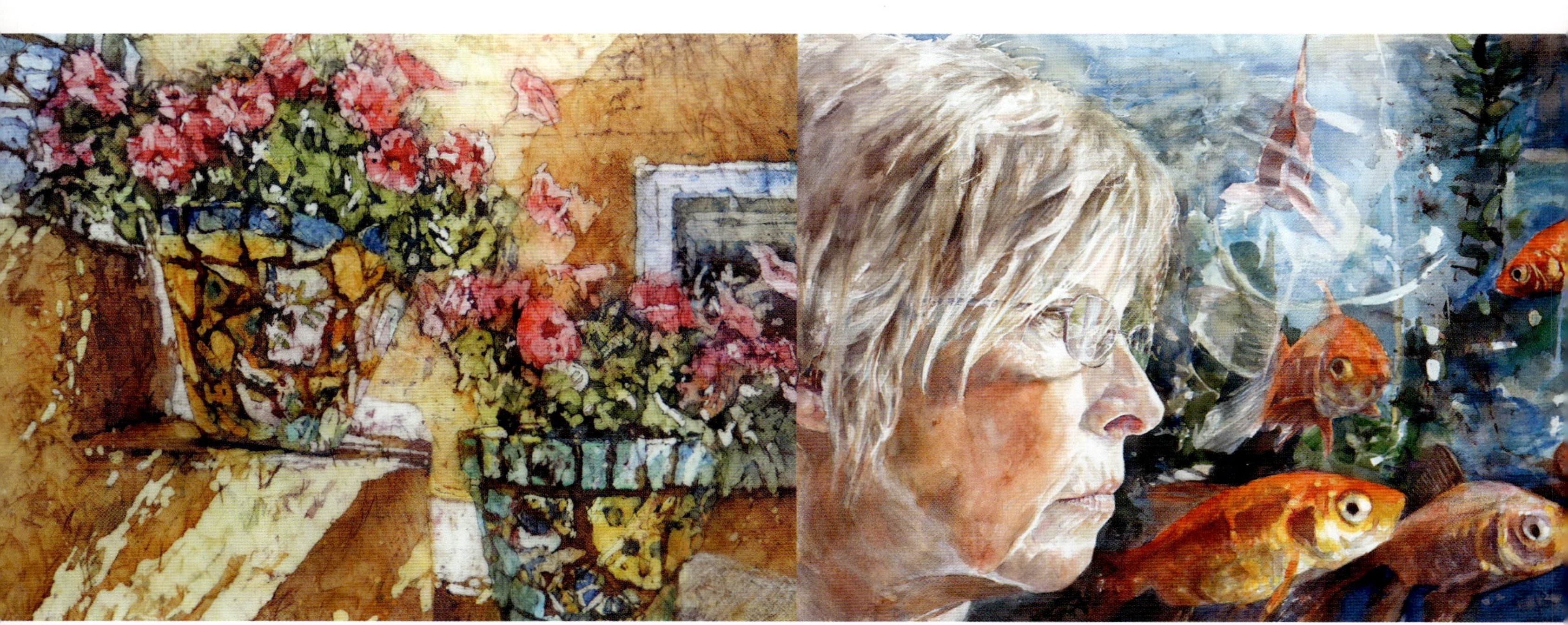

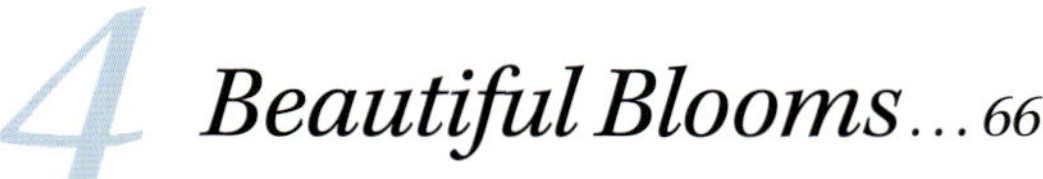

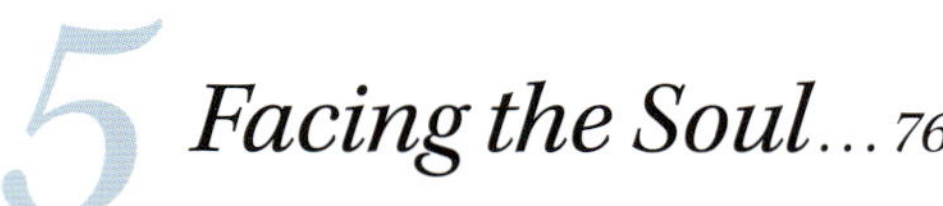

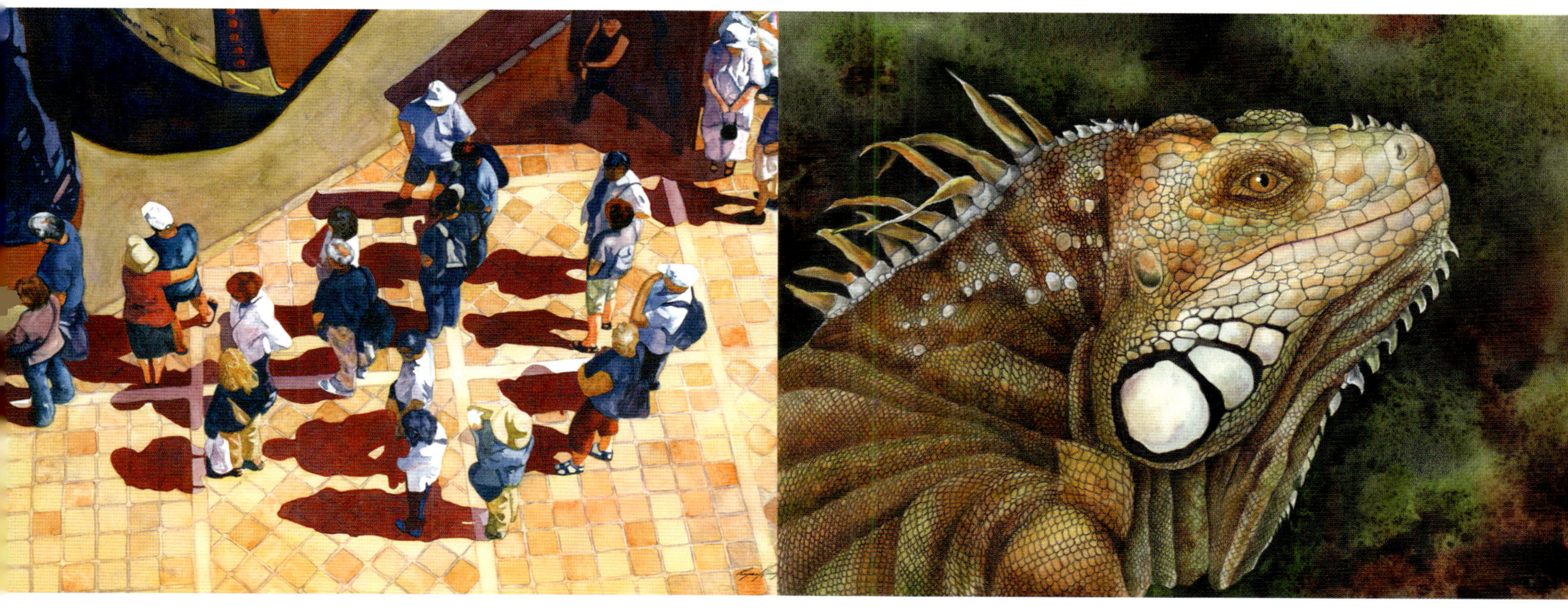

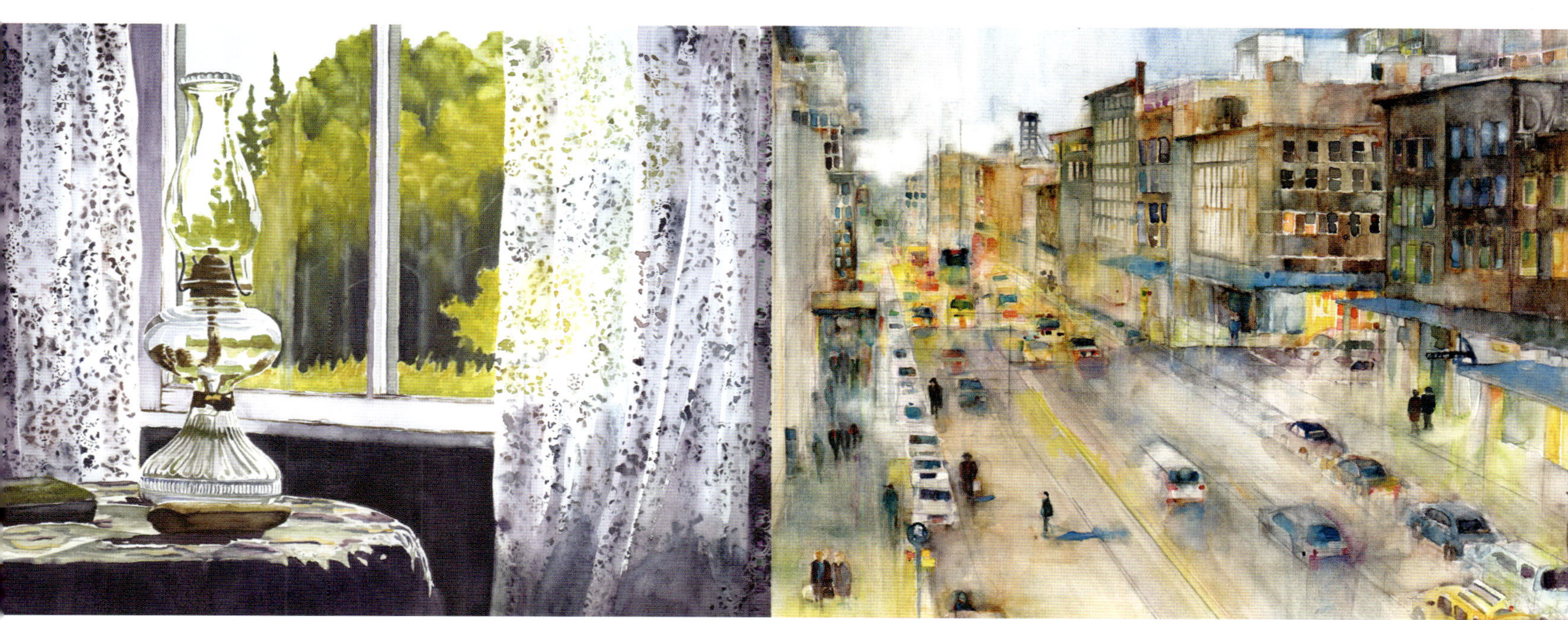

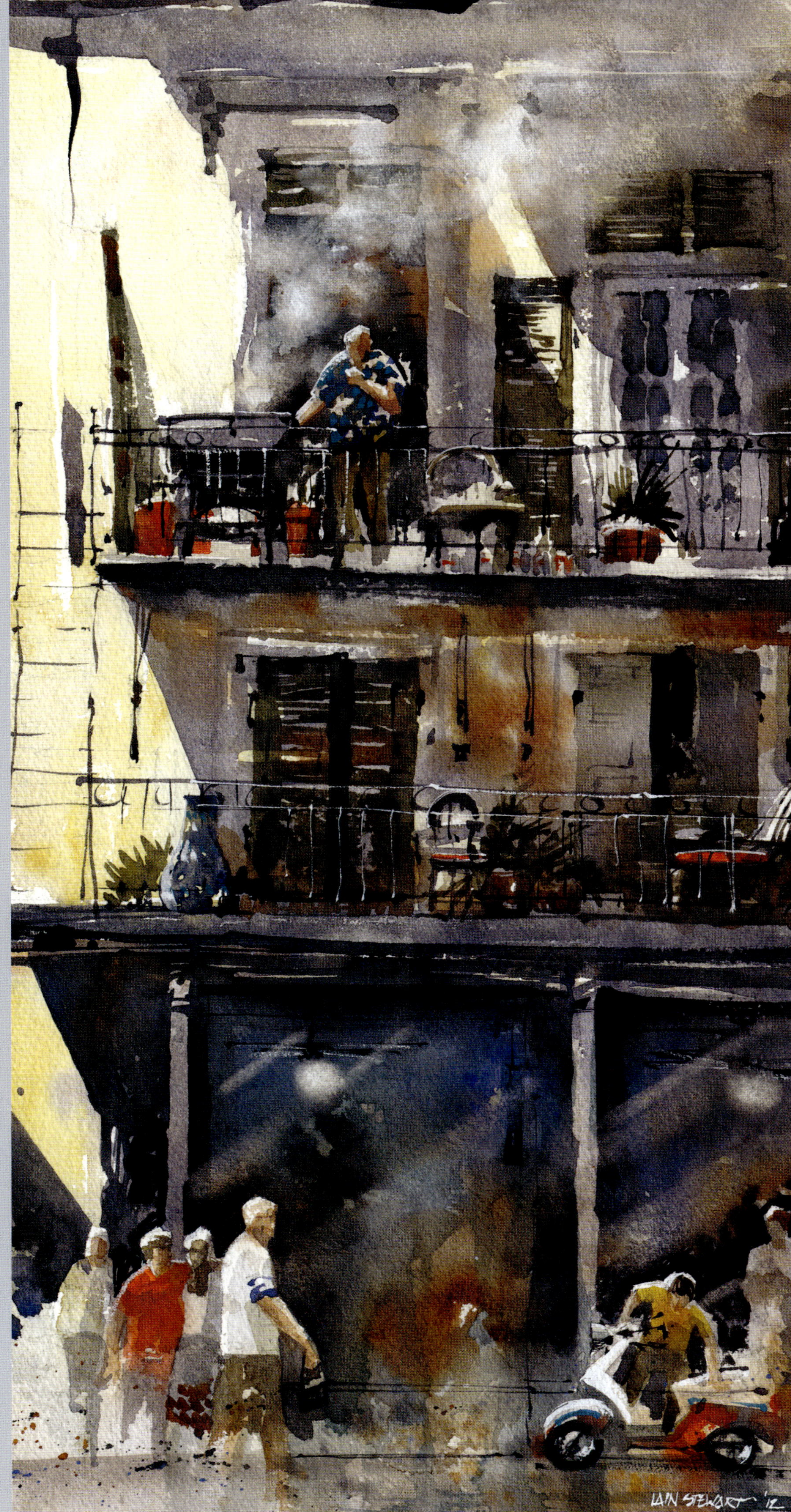

THURSDAY ON DECATUR – NEW ORLEANS | Iain Stewart
30" × 22" (76cm × 56cm) Transparent watercolor with gouache accents over graphite underdrawing on 140-lb. (300gsm) cold-pressed Arches

This is quite literally a "slice of life" in the French Quarter of New Orleans. On this busy public street we are able to see the private outdoor living space of the occupant who is contentedly cooking a bit of dinner. My goal was to show the overlap of private and public space in this dense urban setting without the image becoming fractured. My solution was to crop the drawing to focus on the people. I initially included the roofline of the building and used a lot of detail at the street level. But I decided that the real focus should be the grilling man on the third floor. I purposely left the second story balcony vacant to accentuate the transition from public to private, but, note: the doors at right on the second floor are slightly ajar as if someone has just left the seat with the red cushion.

Introduction

Here we are—*Splash 15*! It's hard to believe that it's been well over twenty years since I first started viewing slides on a light table in 1990 for the first edition of *Splash*, published in 1991. I had the opportunity, during the last stages of editing *Splash 15*, to attend the annual Florida Watercolor Society convention as a guest speaker. It was a wonderful experience and a delight to see a good number of *Splash* artists, some from many years ago, as well as many other artists. Watercolor painters are very dedicated and passionate about their craft—and it shows in the finished works! Watercolorists are masters of finding creative solutions, perhaps because watercolor can be so demanding and, at times, unforgiving. And, as usual, the artists in this volume have surpassed my expectations in giving inspired substance to our theme: creative solutions.

You, the artists represented in *Splash 15*, have proved that there are no limits on creative solutions—and that unless one has developed a formula, pretty much every single painting needs its own creative solutions! Many of you urged us not to rely too heavily on photo reference material, but to use it mainly for what it is called—a reference. Donald Patterson reminds us, "Your reference material is not sacred. It is what you do with it that counts."

Others remind us that for releasing creativity it is important to take risks. "The rewards of risk can include new confidence in your painting ability," David Savellano shares out of his experience. "Breakthroughs are the result of fearless exploration and problem solving!" says Jean Pederson. Sandrine Pelissier advises, "When becoming too controlling with a painting, take a risk, and let the paint find a life of its own."

"When your painting isn't working, give yourself permission to destroy and rebuild," counsels Yael Maimon. In the same vein Jani Freimann shares her secret: "Painting over the top of an already ruined watercolor painting eliminates the fear of making a mistake, turning the watercolor process into fun." In fact, Daniel K. Tennant offers this encouragement: "Don't ever give up on a painting. This still life took me over six years, on and off, and at one point I was ready to throw it out."

Likewise, Anne McCartney sums it up by saying, "Never get stuck thinking there is only one way to do something; there is always another way."

We will never reach the end of creative solutions. Watercolor artists will always find new ways to paint and express their vision.

Rachel

—Rachel Wolf

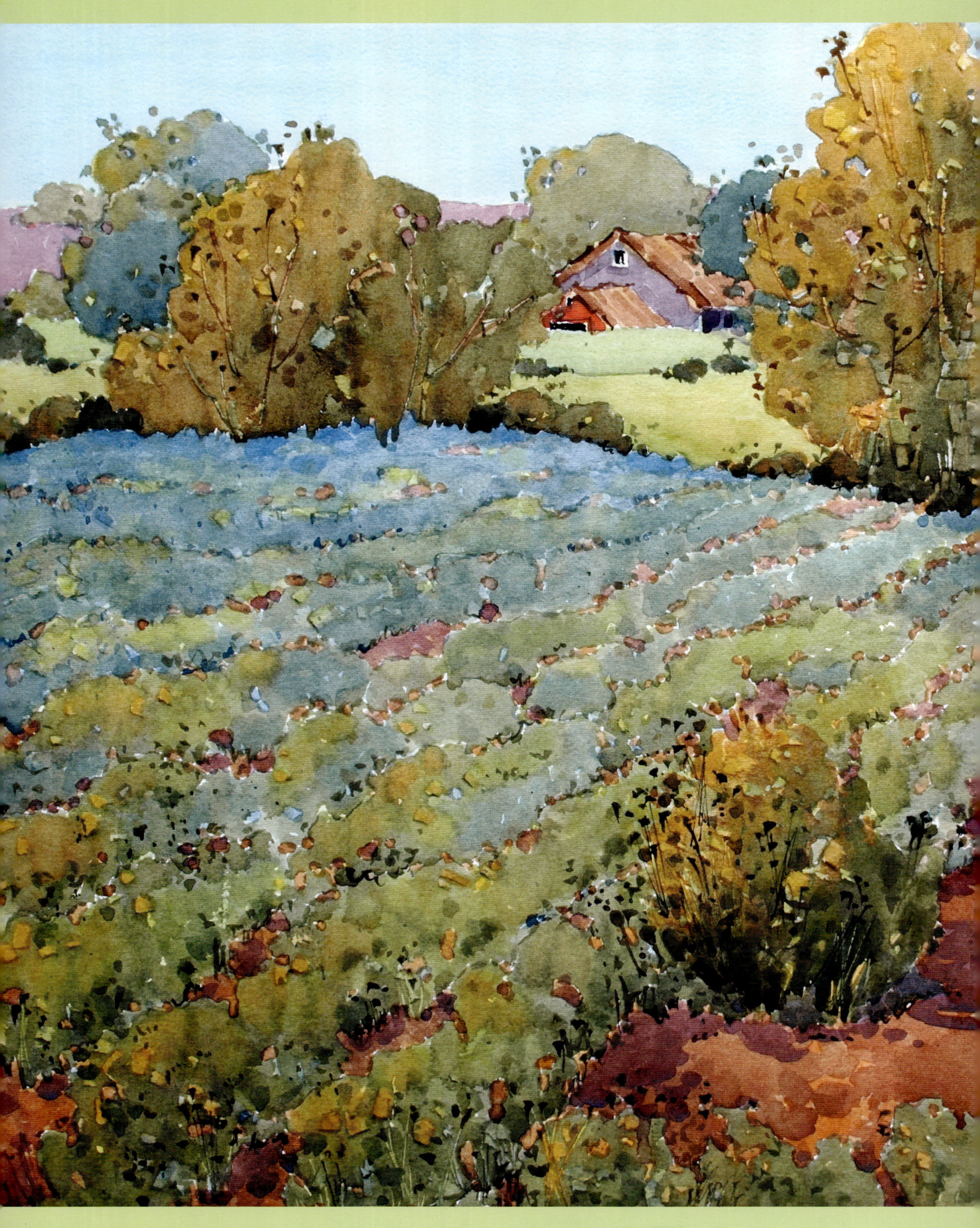

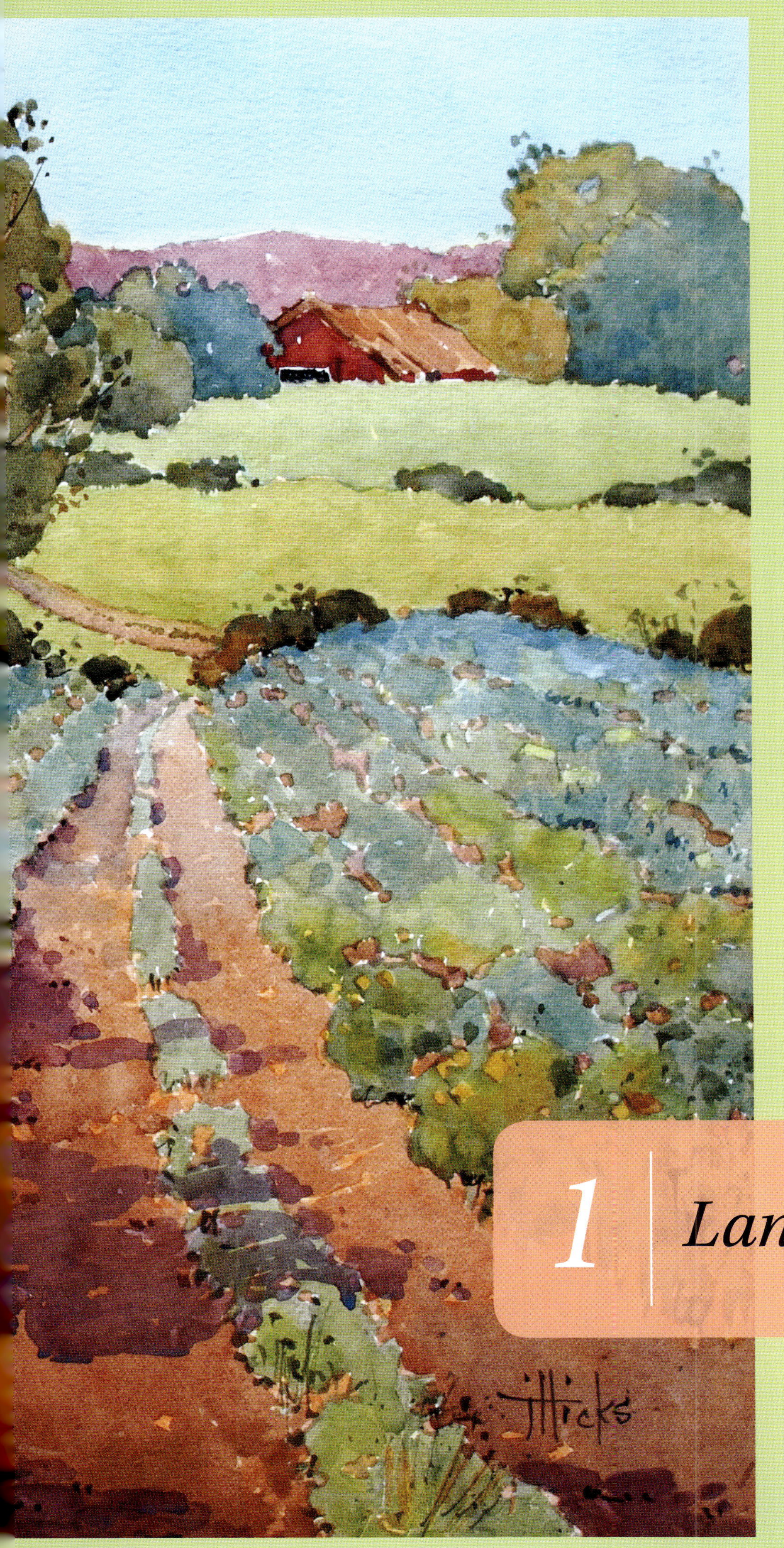

"Use artistic license and imagination as a creative solution!"

– JOYCE HICKS

◀ **PENNSYLVANIA IDYLL** | Joyce Hicks
18" × 24" (46cm × 61cm) Transparent watercolor on 140-lb. (300gsm) cold-pressed Arches

The lush Pennsylvania countryside is inspirational. However, I was disappointed that the field had already been harvested. Since I wanted crops there for textural interest, rhythm and depth, I simply painted the plants back into the scene. When you're out in the landscape, don't be a human camera. Delete, add or rearrange elements as seems best to you.

1 | *Landscape View*

"I search for the power of the forms and white of the paper."

– RICHARD H. DUTTON

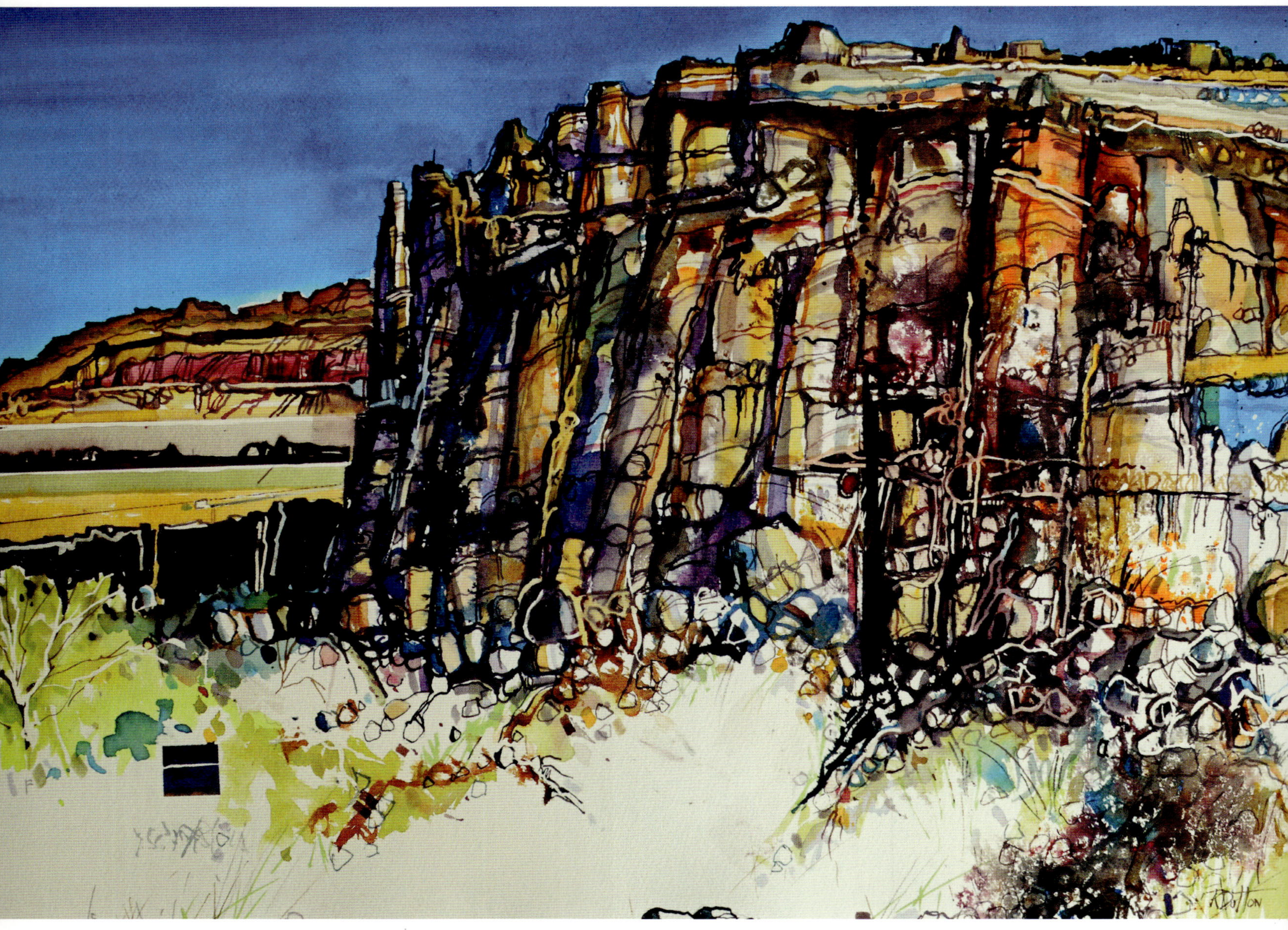

▲ **SACRED PLATEAU** | Richard H. Dutton
20" × 28" (51cm × 71cm) Transparent watercolor on 140-lb. (300gsm) cold-pressed paper

Sacred Plateau is a studio painting based on plein air watercolors, sketches and photographs done while traveling in the southwest part of the United States. I set out to experience the culture as well as the dramatic colors, forms and shapes associated with the area. I did not focus so much on the actual subject but rather on the unique abstract shapes that describe the subject. A big challenge was keeping the power of white paper, one technique that gives the viewer a pathway to the meaning embedded in the artwork.

▶ **HIGH TIDE: TORII GATE AT MIYAJIMA** | Laurel Covington-Vogl
20" × 14" (51cm × 36cm) Transparent watercolor on 140-lb. (300gsm) cold-pressed Arches

A torii marks the entrance to the sacred grounds of a Japanese temple, and the torii at Miyajima is at the entrance to the cove where Itsukushima Temple stands. At low tide the water recedes out past the massive gate and you can walk around its base. At high tide the water returns to a depth of about 7 or 8 feet (2–2½m) at the gate. When we visited we were able to see the gate at low tide on a beautiful sunny day and then at high tide at night. The next morning a light rain enveloped the area and the Vermilion Red of the torii literally glowed against the blue-gray of the surrounding mountains and the sea. Miyajima was once considered so sacred that ordinary people were forbidden to set foot on the island and worshippers approached by boat through the great torii out in the water.

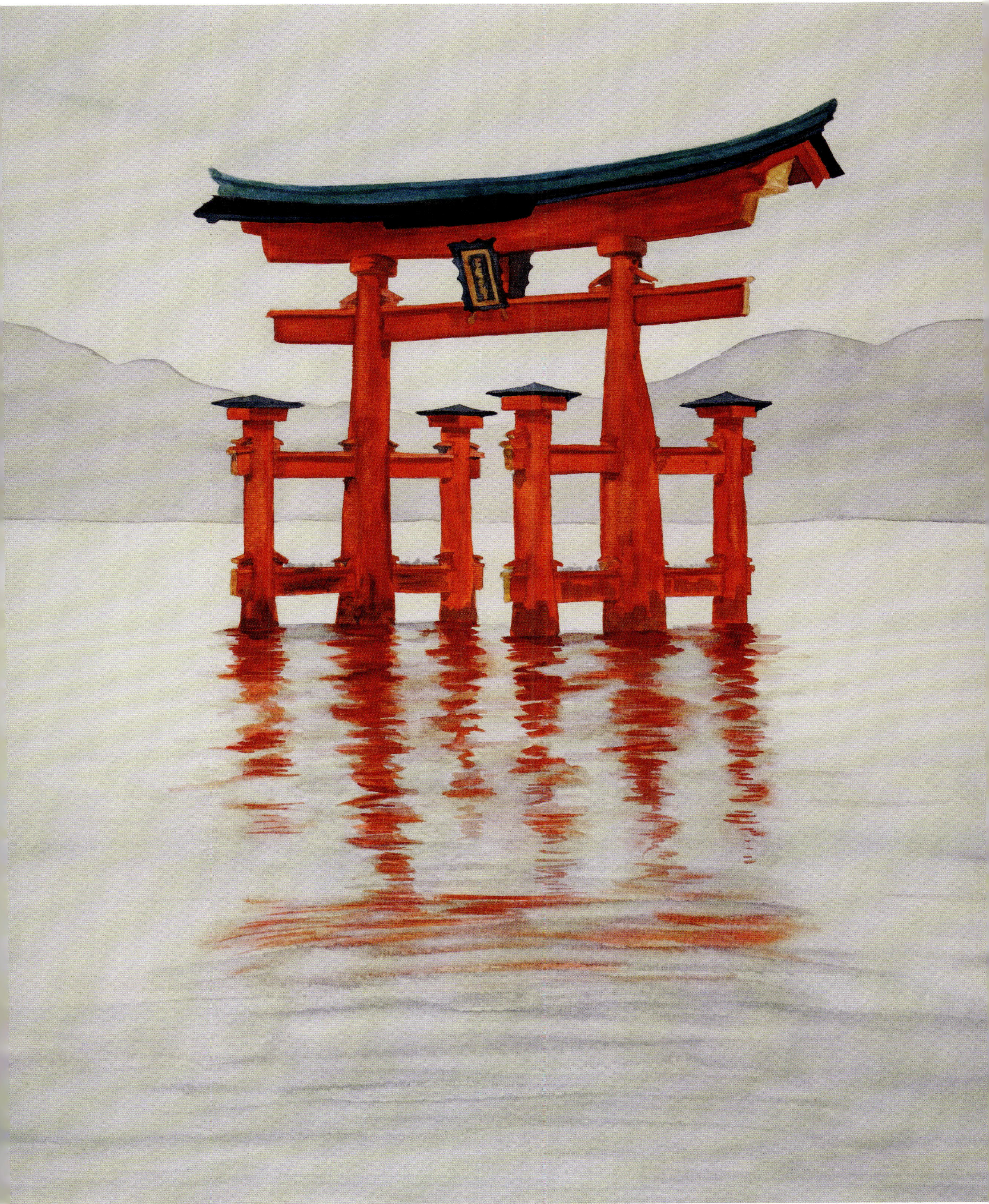

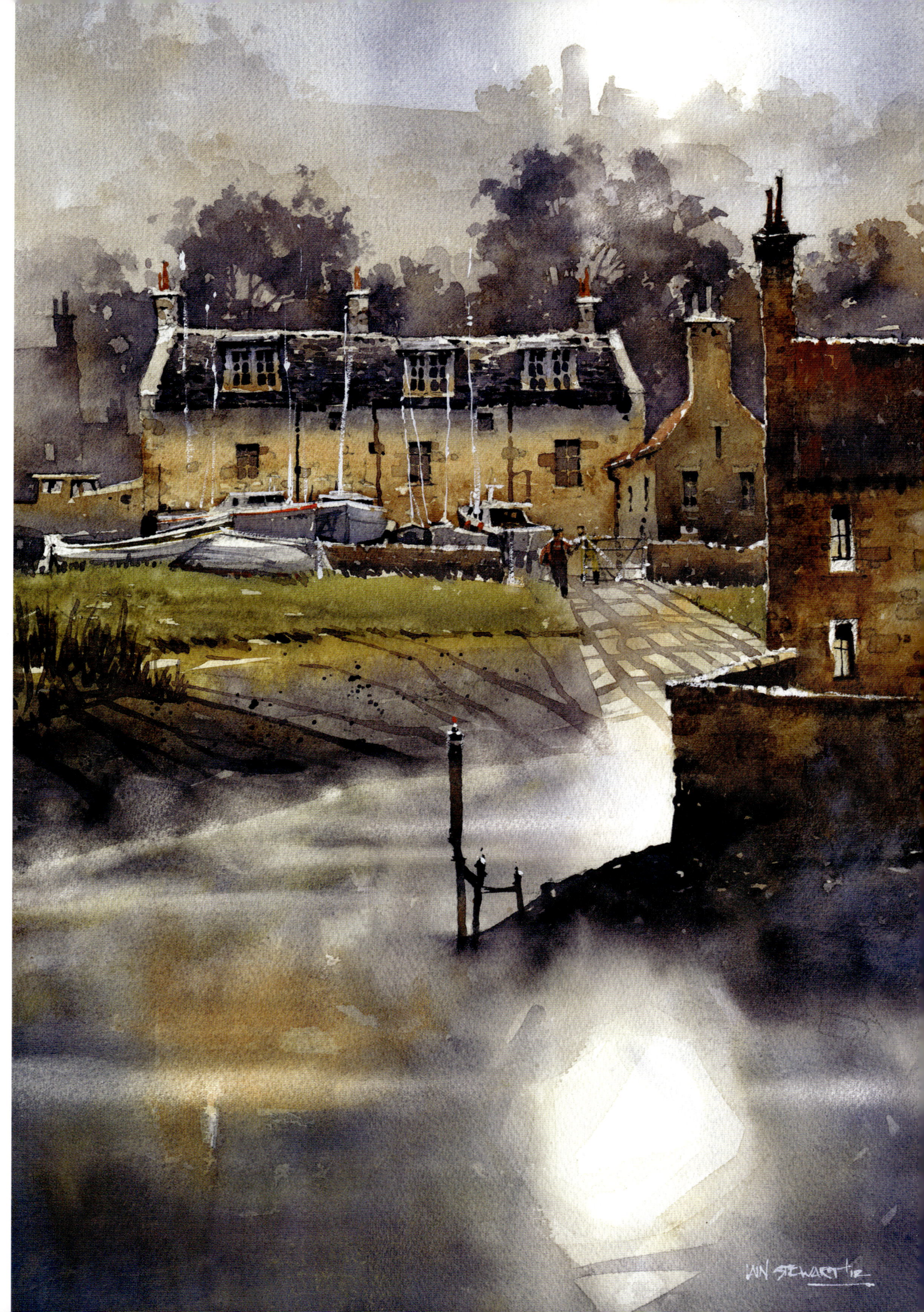

"Never get stuck thinking there is only one way to do something; there is always another way."

– ANNE MCCARTNEY

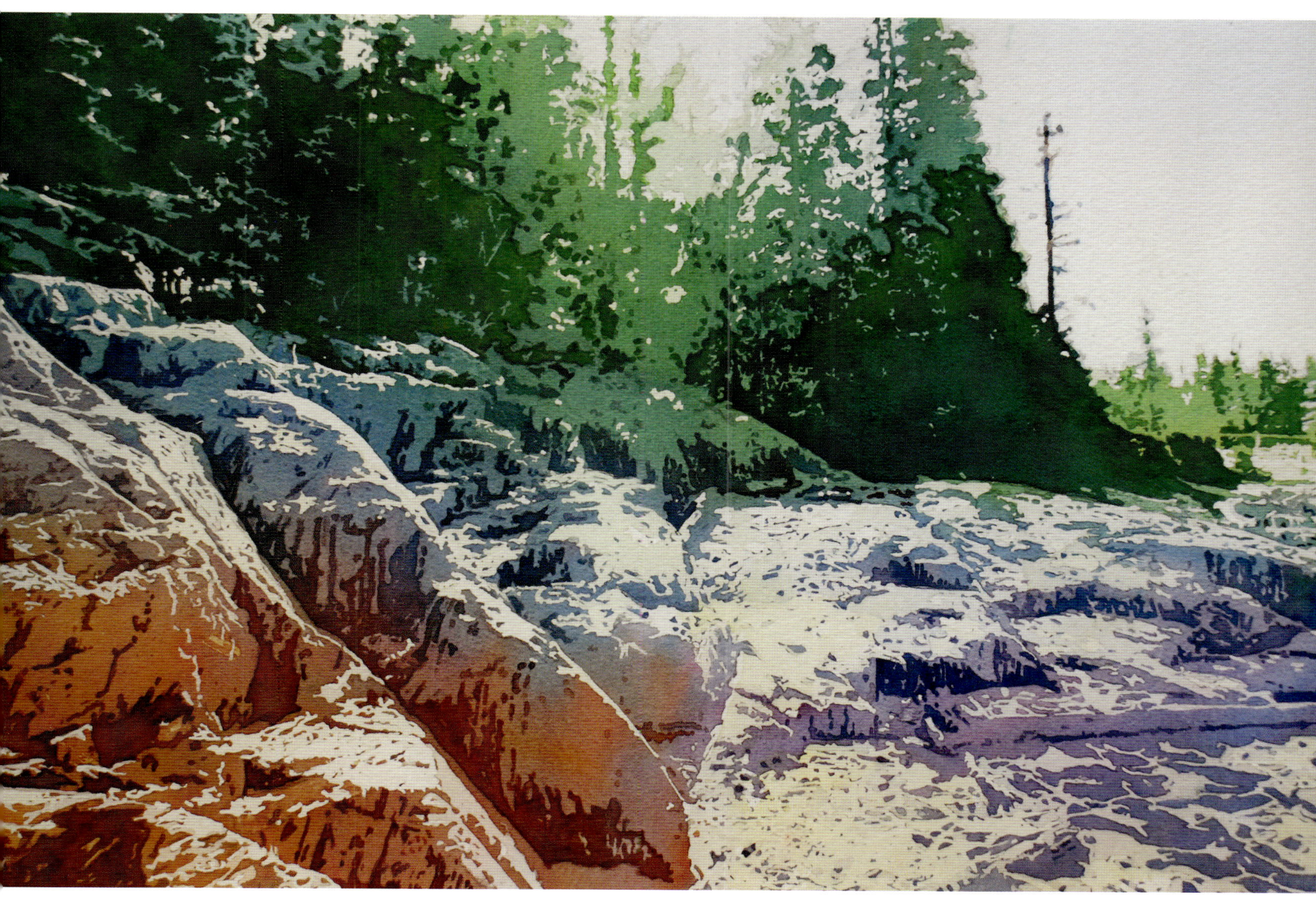

◀ **ST. ANDREWS BOATYARD – SCOTLAND** | Iain Stewart
22½" × 14" (57cm × 36cm) Transparent watercolor with gouache accents over graphite underdrawing on 140-lb. (300gsm) cold-pressed Saunders Waterford

Quite often my inspiration will come from multiple sources. The light in this painting is from a series of pictures I took after a winter rain in Alabama, and the setting is Scotland. I wanted to paint a blue morning with the sun starting to burn the clouds away as in the Alabama shots. I then searched my sketches and reference photos to find the right place with which to express my vision. In this instance the boatyards leading into St. Andrews harbor worked quite well.

▲ **SUPERIOR SHORELINE** | Anne McCartney
14" × 21" (36cm × 53cm) Transparent watercolor on 300-lb. (640gsm) cold-pressed Arches

Right from the start I regretted not delineating my planes better—usually there is a very definite break between my foreground, middle ground and background. Here, I thought I wouldn't start that way, and I ended up having to address the entire shape of trees and rocks all at the same time. The challenge became choosing the right colors and making sure they brought certain areas of that large shape forward and pushed others back. I put the rule "cool recedes and warm advances" to the test. This area, the north shore of Lake Superior in Canada, is one of my favorite places. It is easy to feel at peace there.

GLORIOUS DAY | Sy Ellens

19" × 13" (48cm × 33cm) Transparent watercolor on 300-lb. (640gsm) rough cold-pressed Arches

When I started doing aerial paintings, they all looked flat. In order to show height and depth and the curvature of the earth, I use several vanishing points. One point is on the horizon for the fields in the distance and another is above that for the fields in the middle, and still another point is higher for the fields closest to us. The fence lines are curved above and below the perspective lines to make it look hilly, while shading and shadows also help to create the illusion. I did this painting in my studio from memory.

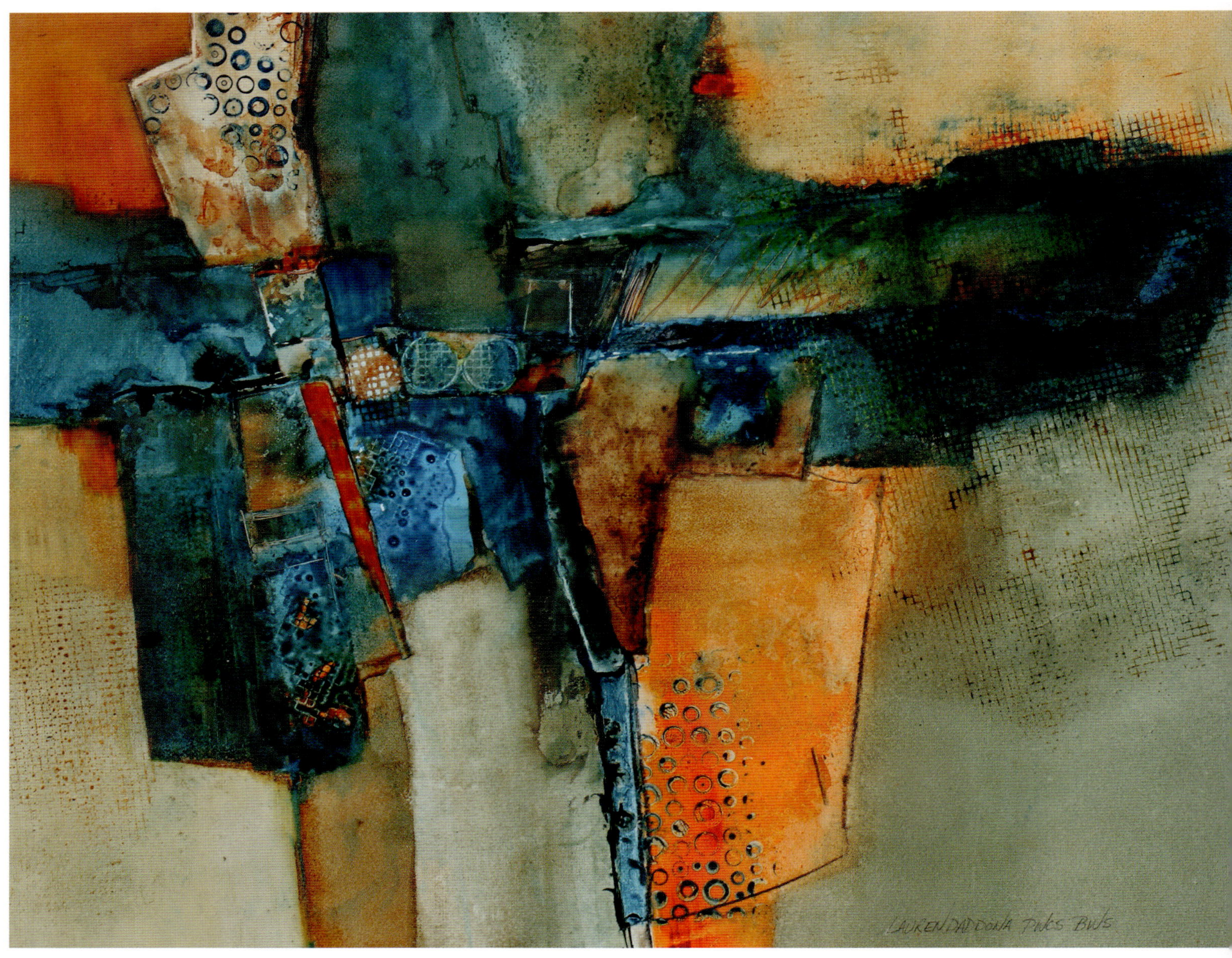

SOUTHWEST REVISITED | Lauren Keller Daddona

18½" × 23½" (47cm × 60cm) Transparent watercolor, watercolor inks and crayons on Yupo

My approach to watercolor is "Enjoy the process!" For *Southwest Revisited*, capturing the essence of a trip to Colorado Springs after I returned home was my objective. No photos were used. I wanted an emotional response to the beauty of the west.

On Yupo, a slick synthetic paper, I let the watercolors and watercolor inks flow. The pigments sit up on the surface allowing for exciting movement. Tools for texturing included screening, tubing and patterned paraphernalia. With watercolor crayons and pencils I added more controlled lines and then created restful areas by rolling the paint to solidify the cruciform composition. The complementary blues and oranges are indicative of the Southwest.

"For me, painting with my emotions is the beginning of creative solutions; I don't know exactly where I am headed and I let the painting take me on a journey."

– LAUREN KELLER DADDONA

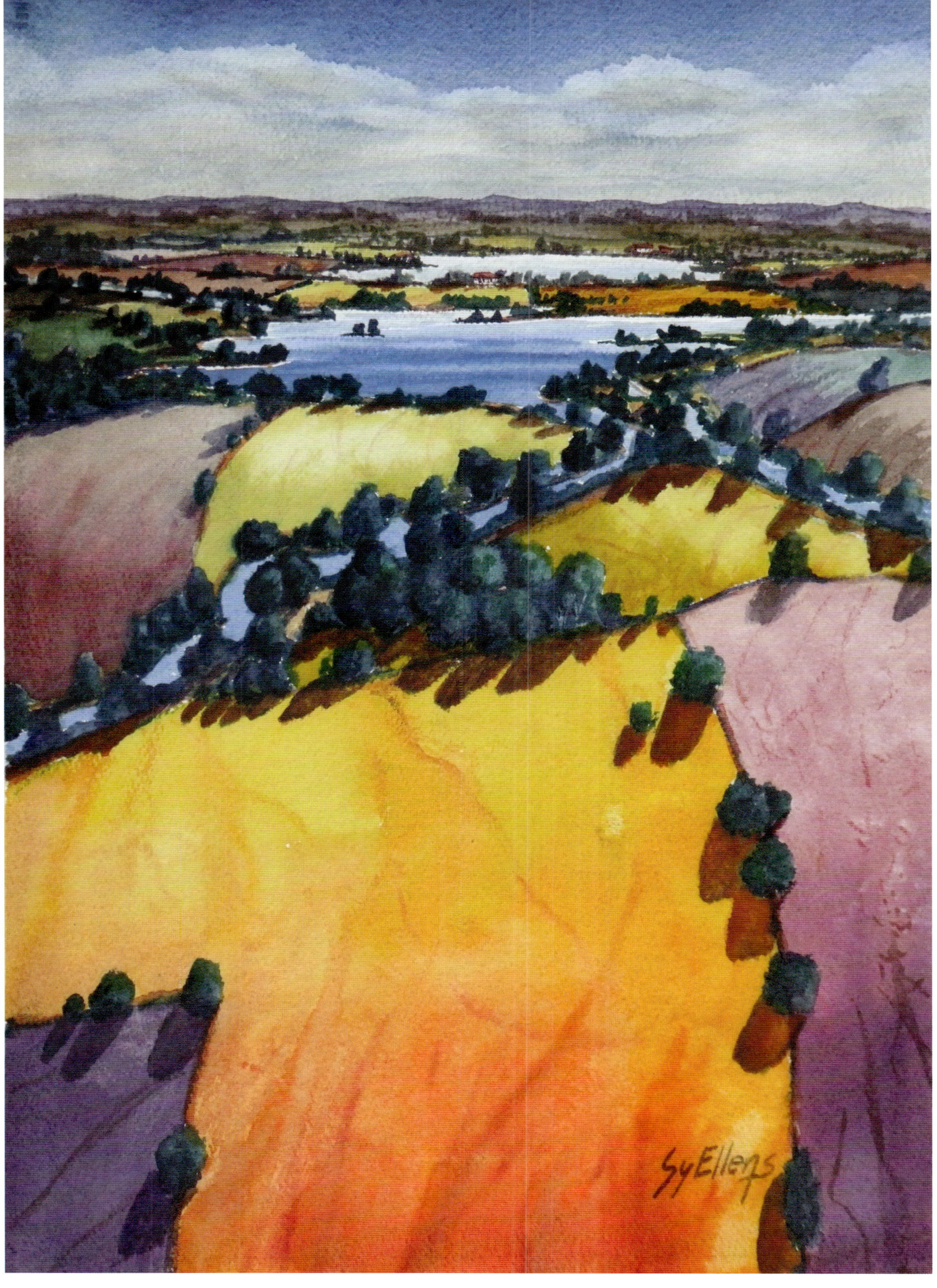
SyEllens

"Don't plan your clouds, let them happen."

– DEBBIE ABSHEAR

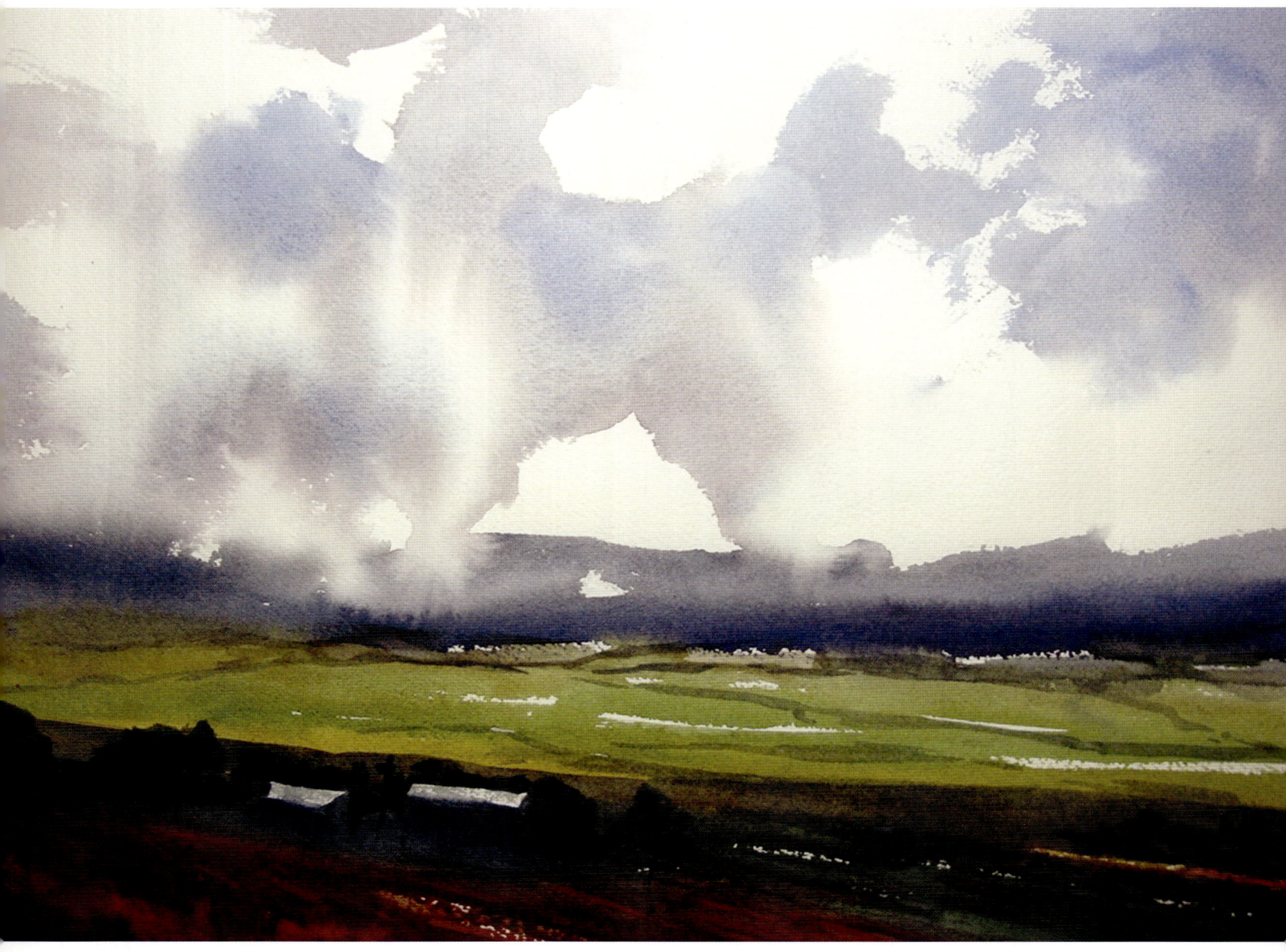

▲ **STORM CHASERS** | Debbie Abshear
11" × 15" (28cm × 38cm) Transparent watercolor on 140-lb. (300gsm) cold-pressed Arches

My goal in painting *Storm Chasers* was to portray a landscape filled with atmospheric perspective and to capture the spontaneity of a storm rolling across the plains. Using a squirrel mop brush, I randomly prewet the sky area with clear water. I then added pigment to the prewet areas and watched as the pigment began to paint the clouds. I elevated my board to allow the pigment to "rain" onto the mountains. I saved the random whites on the plains for interest and more purposefully for the roofs of the buildings. I learned from this painting to not fiddle—to let the painting paint itself. Water and pigments do amazing things!

▶ **READY TO FLY** | Fernand Thienpondt
29" × 22" (74cm × 56cm) Transparent watercolor on 300-lb. (640gsm) rough cotton Arches

The Belgian F-16s have to be on standby alert for a mission overseas. I wanted to express that threat and feeling of insecurity in my painting. That's why I put the plane right at the classic focal point along with yellow linear accents to further pinpoint the attention. To express the possibility of danger, I painted a stormy, threatening sky behind the fighter planes. On the foreground I took advantage of the rough structure of the paper to paint the tarmac of the airfield.

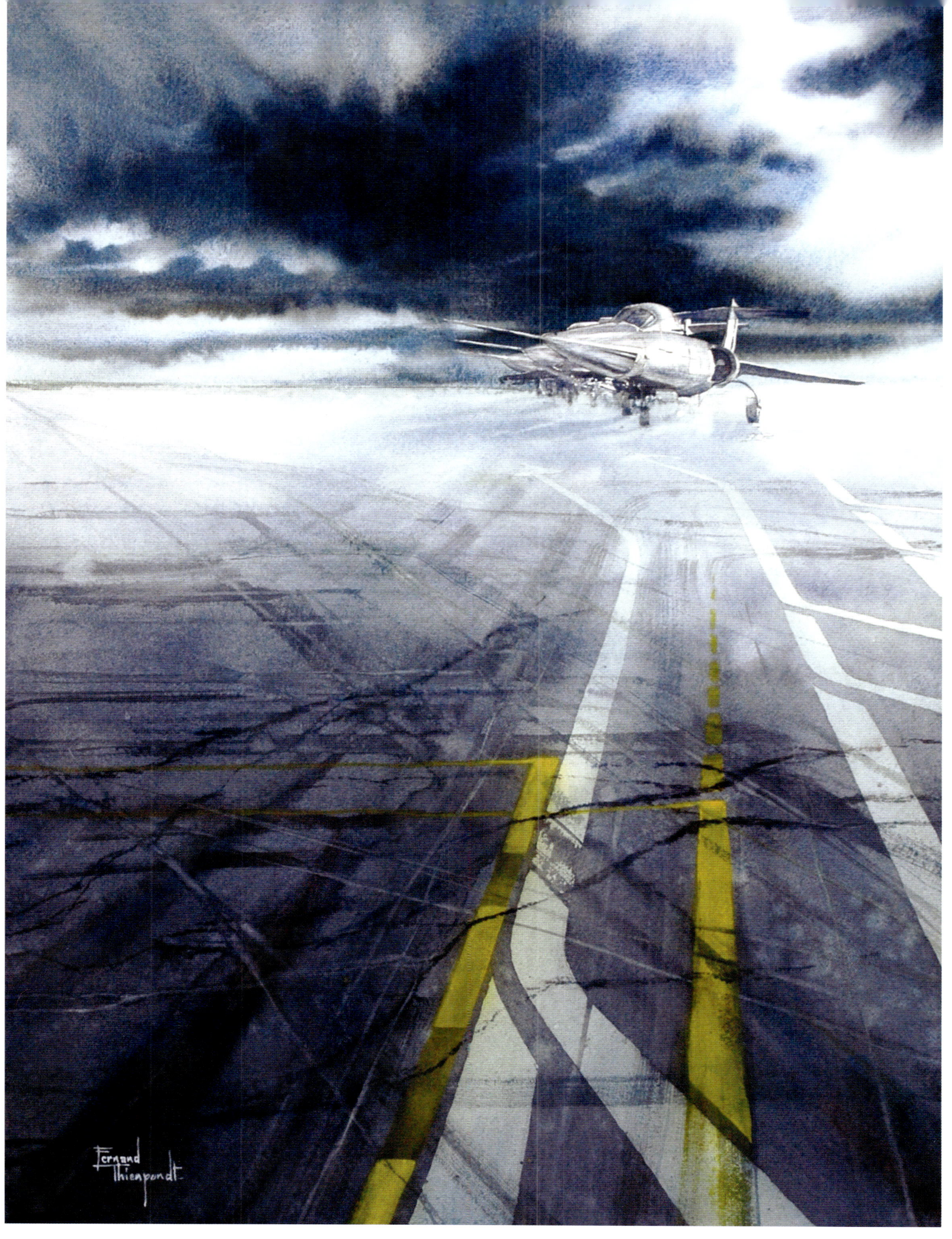

"Contrast in your painting produces excitement. You can achieve contrast through the use of values, edges, color temperature or color complements." – FERNAND THIENPONDT

FOUND IT IN WALDPORT | Joyce Hicks
18" × 24" (46cm × 61cm) Transparent watercolor on 140-lb. (300gsm) cold-pressed Arches

What did I find in Waldport? I found paradise along the Oregon coast in the form of a sun-drenched day. At every opportunity I follow old country roads in hopes of finding subjects that can be transformed into works of art. In reality, this particular subject was bland, and the cottages neglected, but the intensity of the sun gave it an inspirational feel. To allow the viewer to feel the same sunny warmth I felt that day as I walked along a dusty road that led to the edge of the sea, I exaggerated sunlight by placing my darkest value against the white of the watercolor paper and by laying down shadow patterns to imply its direction.

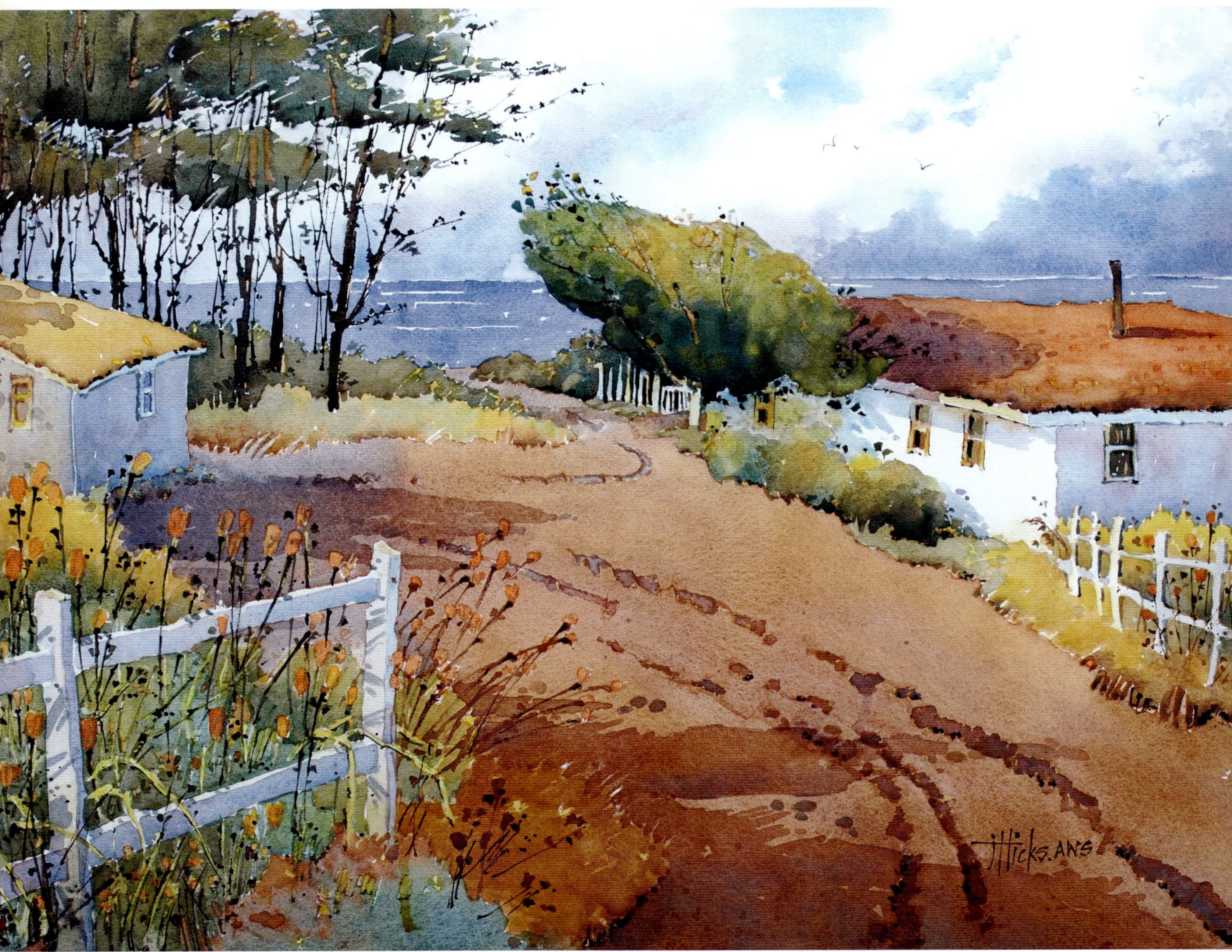

"Create the illusion of bright sunlight by using directional strokes, dramatic value shifts and strong contrast."

– JOYCE HICKS

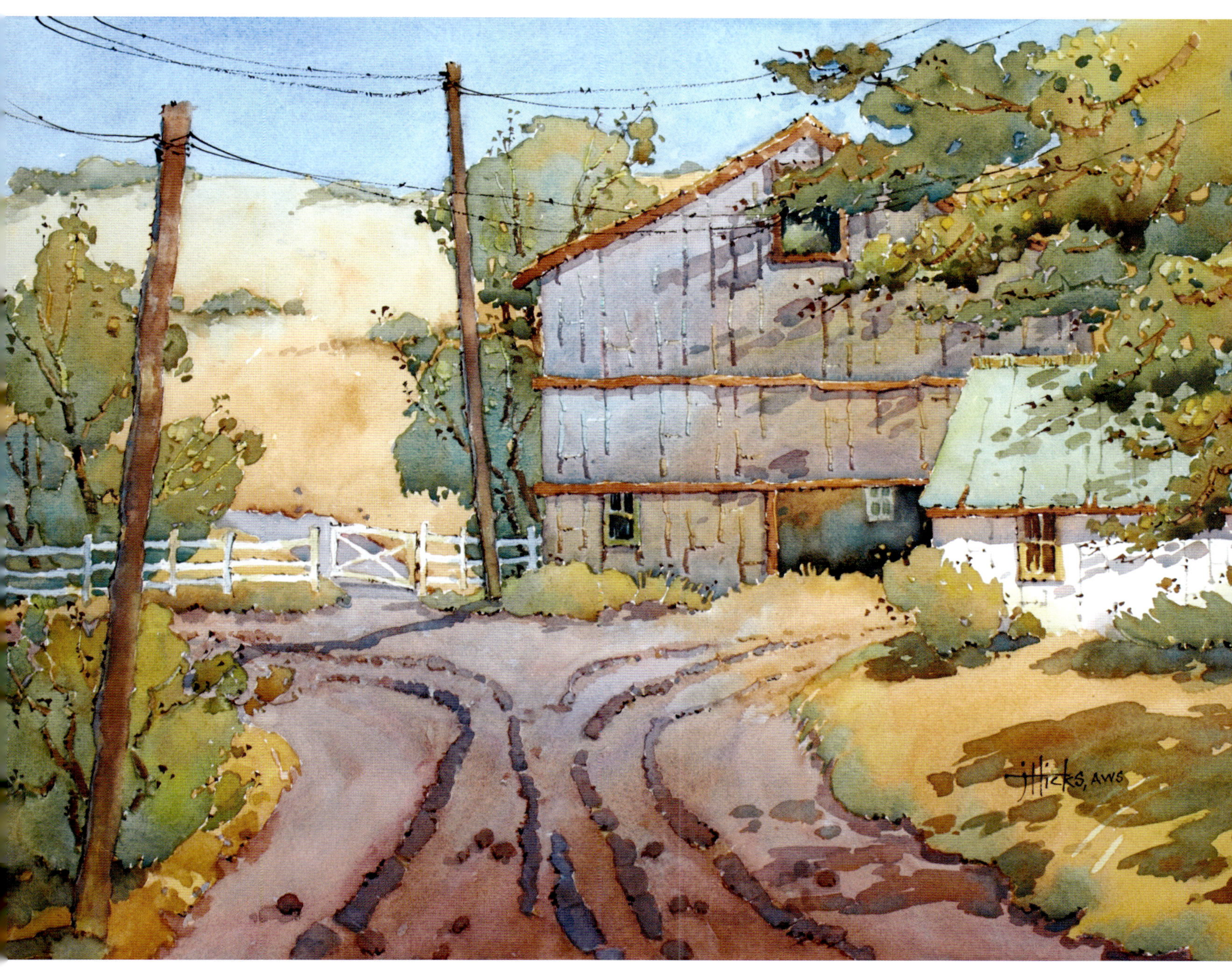

A BARN I SAW IN MOUNT PLEASANT | Joyce Hicks
18" × 24" (46cm × 61cm) Transparent watercolor on 140-lb. (300gsm) cold-pressed Arches

I spotted these old farm buildings as we explored the back roads of Laurel Highlands in Pennsylvania. I was initially struck by the contrast of strong architectural elements among the soft organic forms. I use a palette knife in virtually every painting. An oil painter uses a palette knife to apply paint, but a watercolorist uses it to take paint away. You can use the broad edge of the knife to scrape paint aside leaving marks of different shapes and sizes. It's a simple way to leave the impression of trunks, branches and leaves. It also makes thick and thin calligraphy-like lines with its point. I used it in this way for the planking on the front of the big barn. For the dark ruts in the road I waited until the paint was in a semiwet stage, then scraped in the design. Once the area was dry, I painted the marks with a dark mixture.

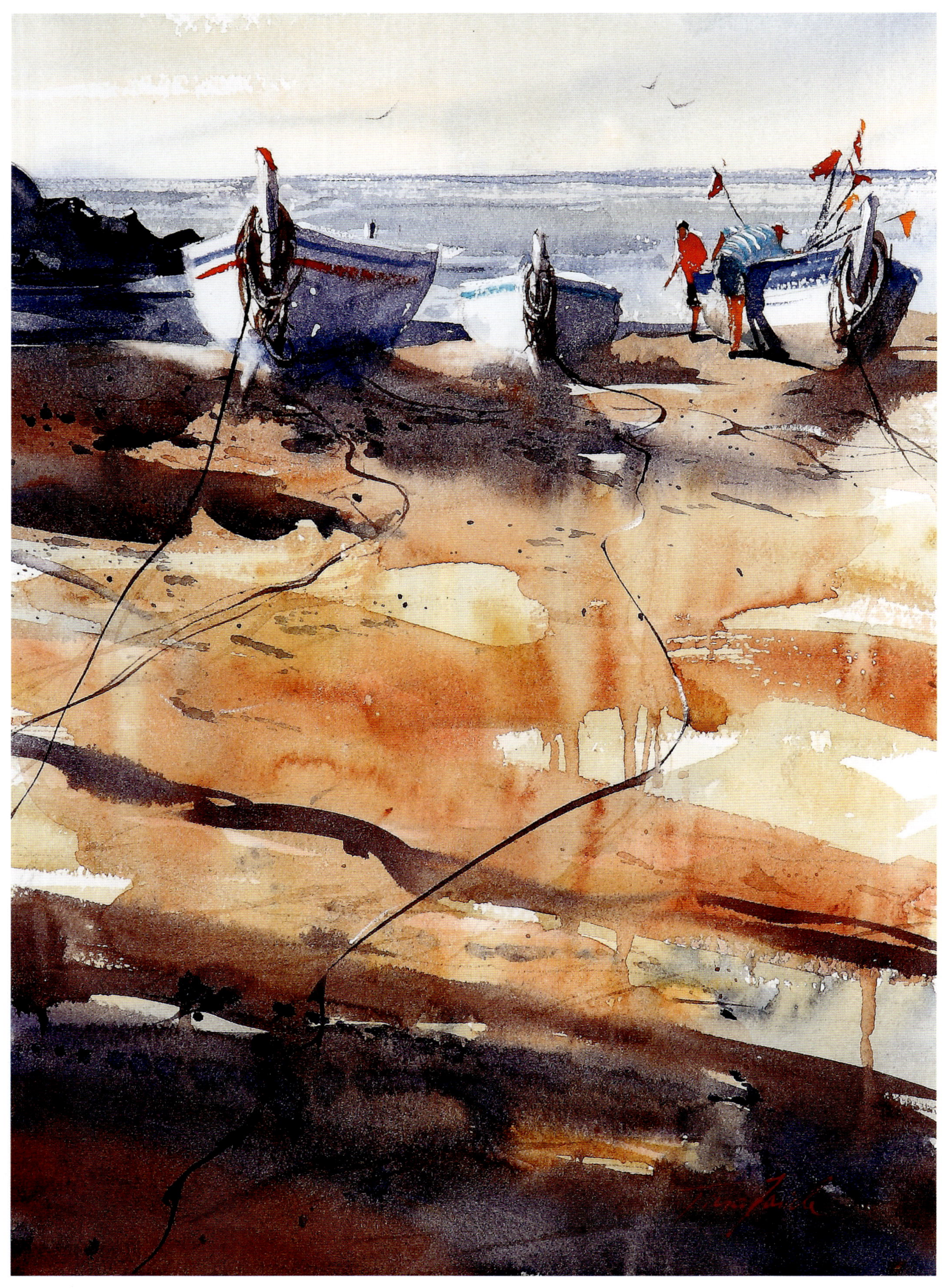

"Don't put too many things in the foreground or you just trip over them." – KRISTINA JURICK

VILASSAR DE MAR | Kristina Jurick
14" × 10" (36cm × 26cm) Transparent watercolor on 300-lb. (640gsm) fine grain Arches

The words of my teacher in the quotation come back to my mind whenever I deal with a large foreground area. For this painting of the Vilassar beach I invented the shadows, arranged the ropes in a pleasing way and let some splattering and splashing take care of the rest. Usually I use not more than three to five colors to achieve color harmony. For this one I used Raw Sienna, Burnt Sienna, Ultramarine, a touch of Cadmium Red and a bit of turquoise.

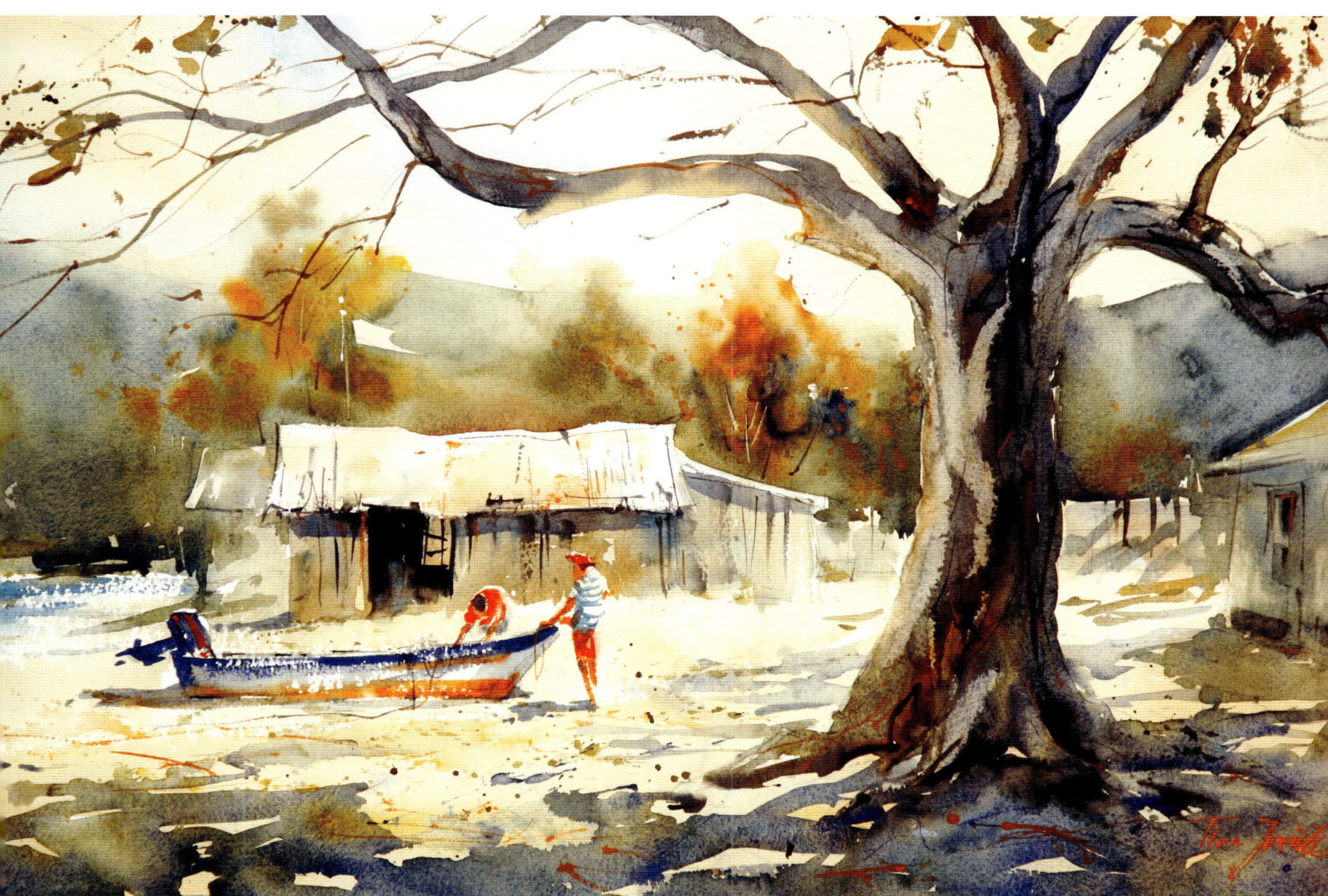

SONO BEACH, BRAZIL | Kristina Jurick
14" × 21" (36cm × 53cm) Transparent watercolor on 300-lb. (640gsm) Arches Torchon

I was invited to teach and exhibit at the Fourth International Watercolor Symposium in Paraty, Brazil. My friendly hosts toured me all around the area. Sono Beach is a real artist's dream. Several on-location sketches served as reference for this watercolor. The huge mass of green rainforest in the background was a challenge. I used my favorite mix of Quinacridone Gold and Ultramarine plus some Cadmium Orange. It is important to let the colors mingle on the paper and not to overmix them on the palette or the result will be mud, as blue and orange are complementary colors. The foreground shadow makes you step into the light toward the boat.

"Your reference material is not sacred. It is what you do with it that counts."

– DONALD W. PATTERSON

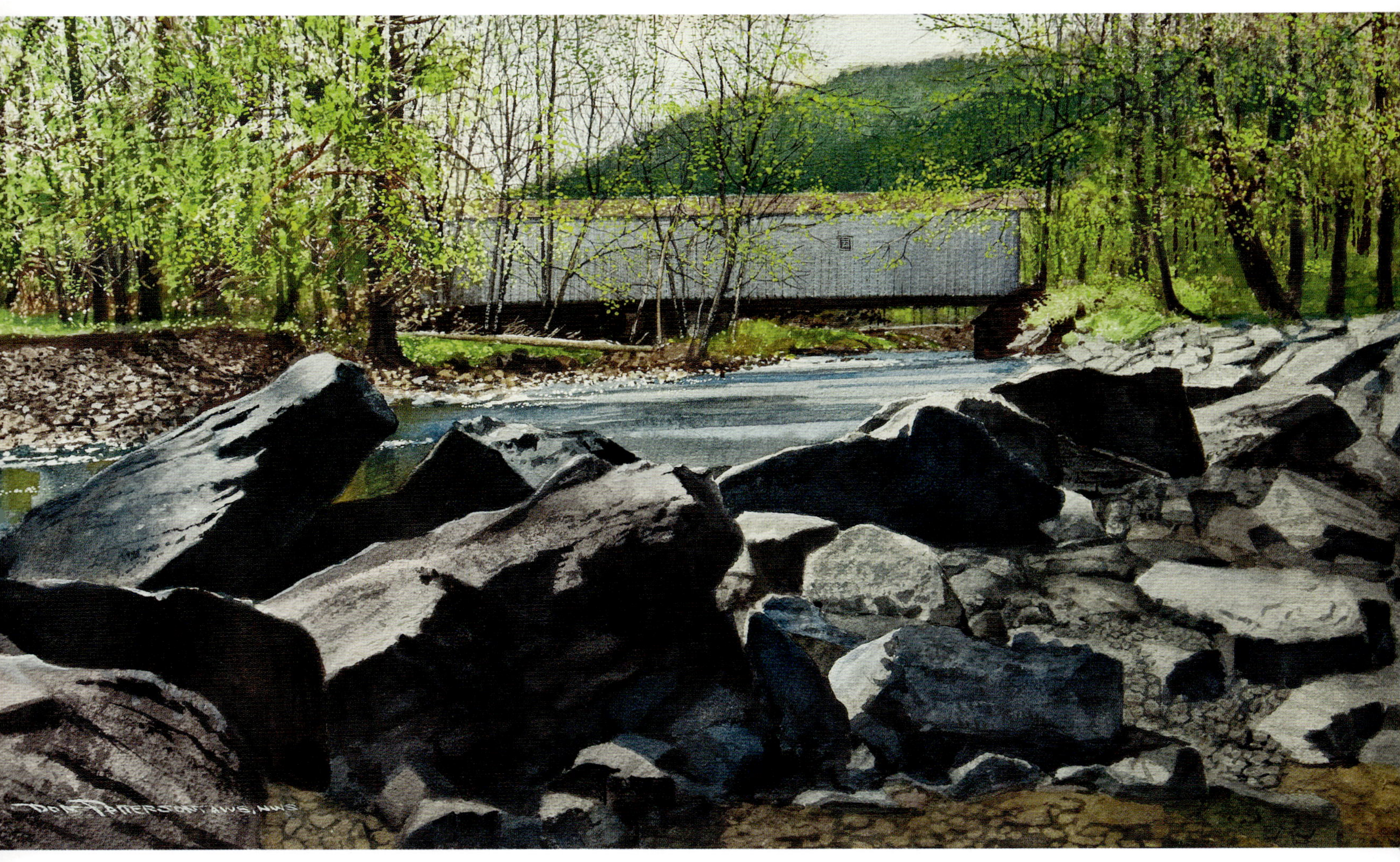

▲ **SPRING ROCKS** | Donald W. Patterson
12" × 20½" (30cm × 52cm) Transparent watercolor with gouache accents on 300-lb. (640gsm) cold-pressed Arches

I am a studio painter and use a camera to compose my compositions, but it is very rare to take a perfect picture. Inevitably there are always necessary adjustments, additions and subtractions. I was near completion of *Spring Rocks* and the result was disturbing. Something was not right—suddenly it hit me. The covered bridge was not holding its own with the foreground rocks. The solution was to add a hill behind the bridge so the viewer's eye stops at the bridge and hill then back to the rocks, rather than passing over it into the wide open sky. The reference photo for *Spring Rocks* was taken in early spring and looked a little bleak, so I also added the bright yellow green leaves.

▶ **ROCK MY WORLD** | Georgia Mansur
21" × 15" (53cm × 38cm) Golden OPEN acrylics on 140-lb. (300gsm) rough Saunders watercolor paper

Rock My World helped me pare back to abstract essentials, rather than try to paint every detail. Although it was created in the studio, plein air painting taught me how important it is to work quickly in the changing light. I liked the raw, truthful effects I was getting in my plein air studies and wanted to bring that freshness to my studio work. I stripped back my palette to focus on getting the values, big shapes and form. On larger pieces like this I often use scrunched-up plastic wrap in lieu of a brush to mass in the large shapes—it is impossible to be too precious using this technique. I like to keep the painting loose and flexible for as long as possible by using larger brushes or a credit card to apply paint. The challenge to myself was to communicate the raw emotion of the moment with an economy of strokes—more like poetry, less like a novel.

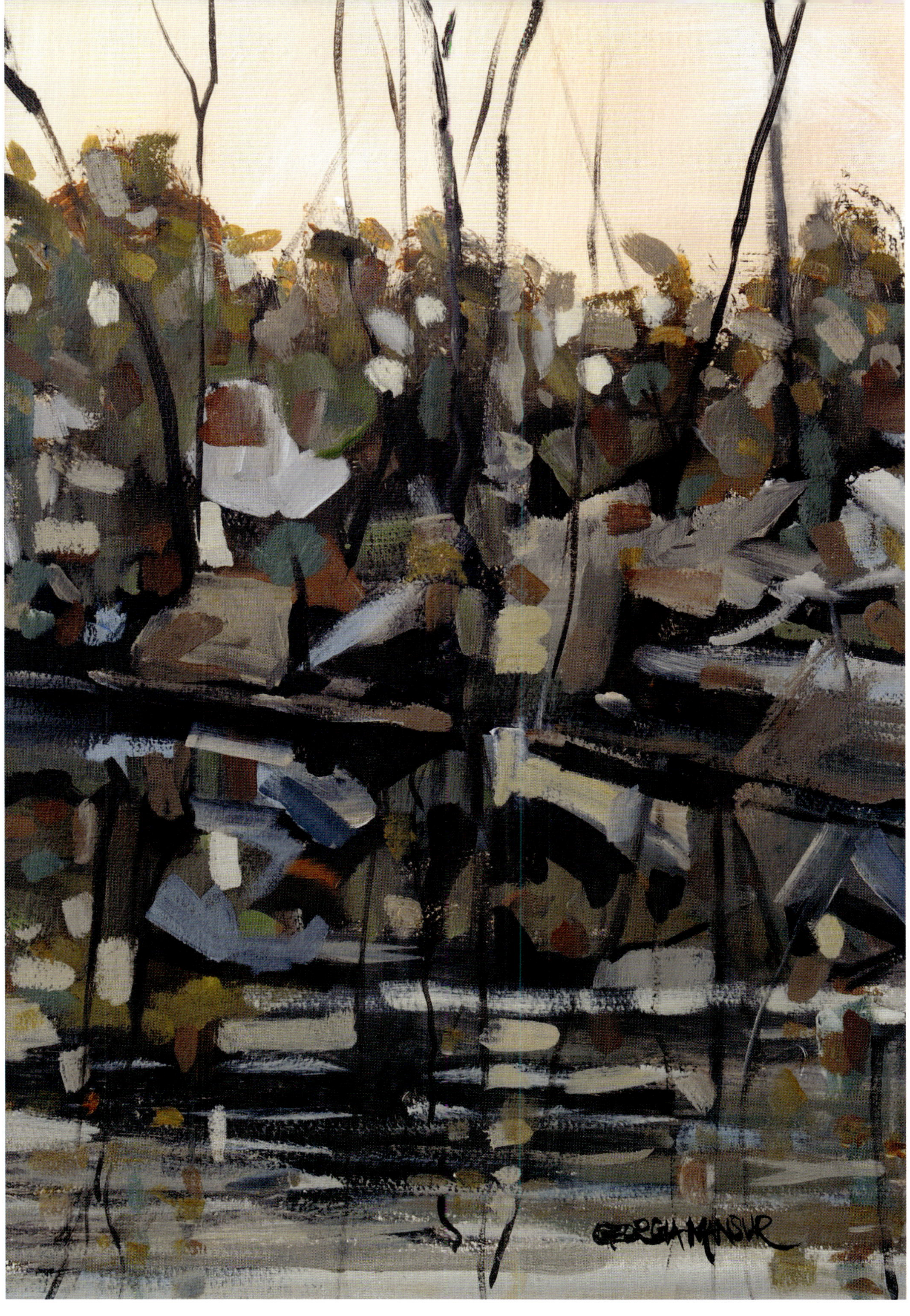

"Whenever my students are having color issues, it is almost always a value problem."

– GEORGIA MANSUR

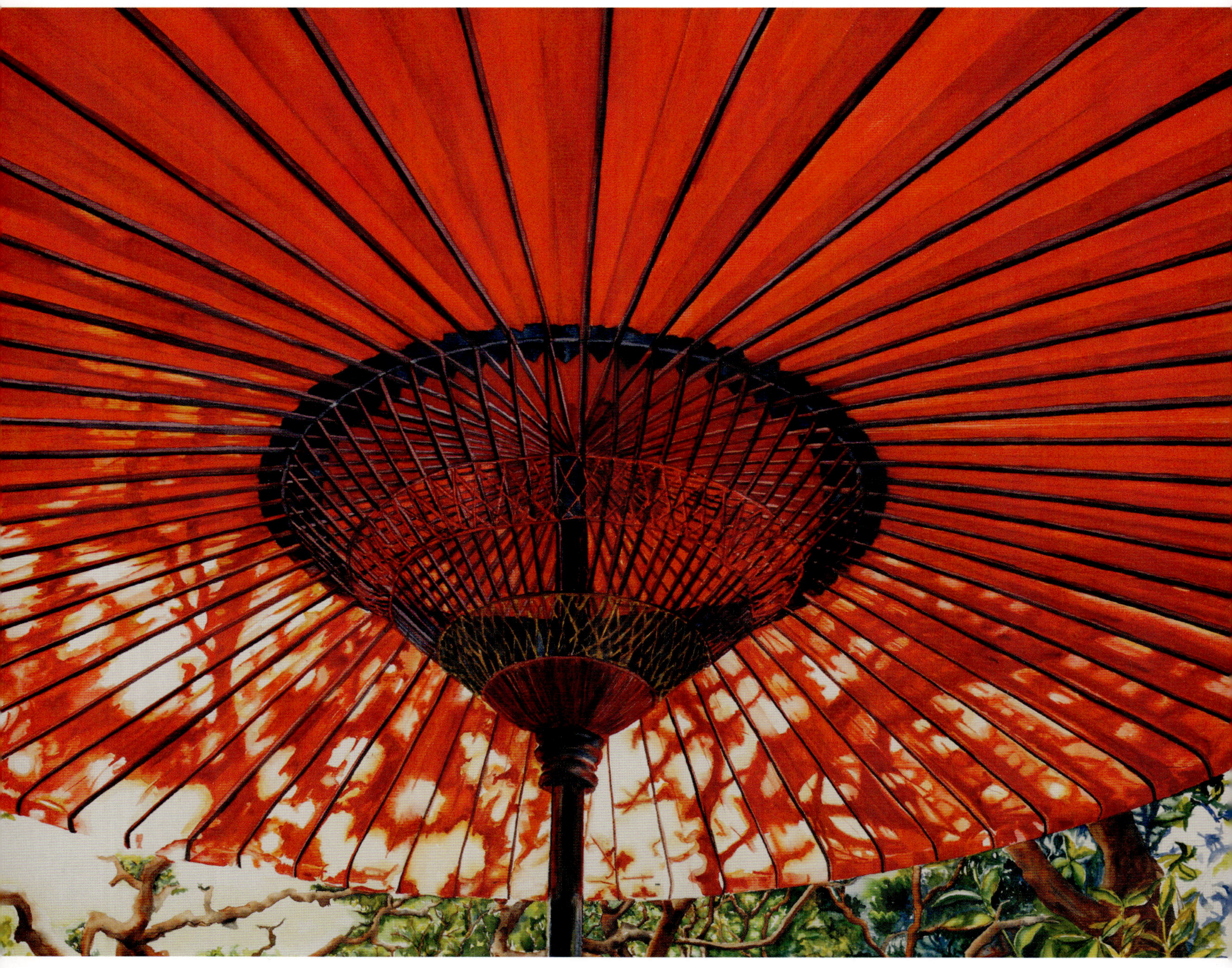

▲ **TEAHOUSE UMBRELLA** | Laurel Covington-Vogl
16" × 24" (41cm × 61cm) Transparent watercolor on 140-lb. (300gsm) cold-pressed Arches

There is no single formula for producing a good painting. I begin with the most challenging area and incorporate a dark value as soon as I can for reference. I use the margins of the paper to test colors and values, so by the time I am finished there is a mosaic of color swatches along the border. *Teahouse Umbrella* was developed from my photos of a red umbrella that I saw in the garden of a teahouse I visited in Uji, Japan. I was drawn to the light and shadow patterns that could be seen through the umbrella. The rich red color was difficult to develop, and I experimented with several colors of red as well as mixtures of red and yellow until I found the right vibrancy.

"Connecting shapes in a painting is most important. After that comes tonal value, and color is last."

– PRAFULL B. SAWANT

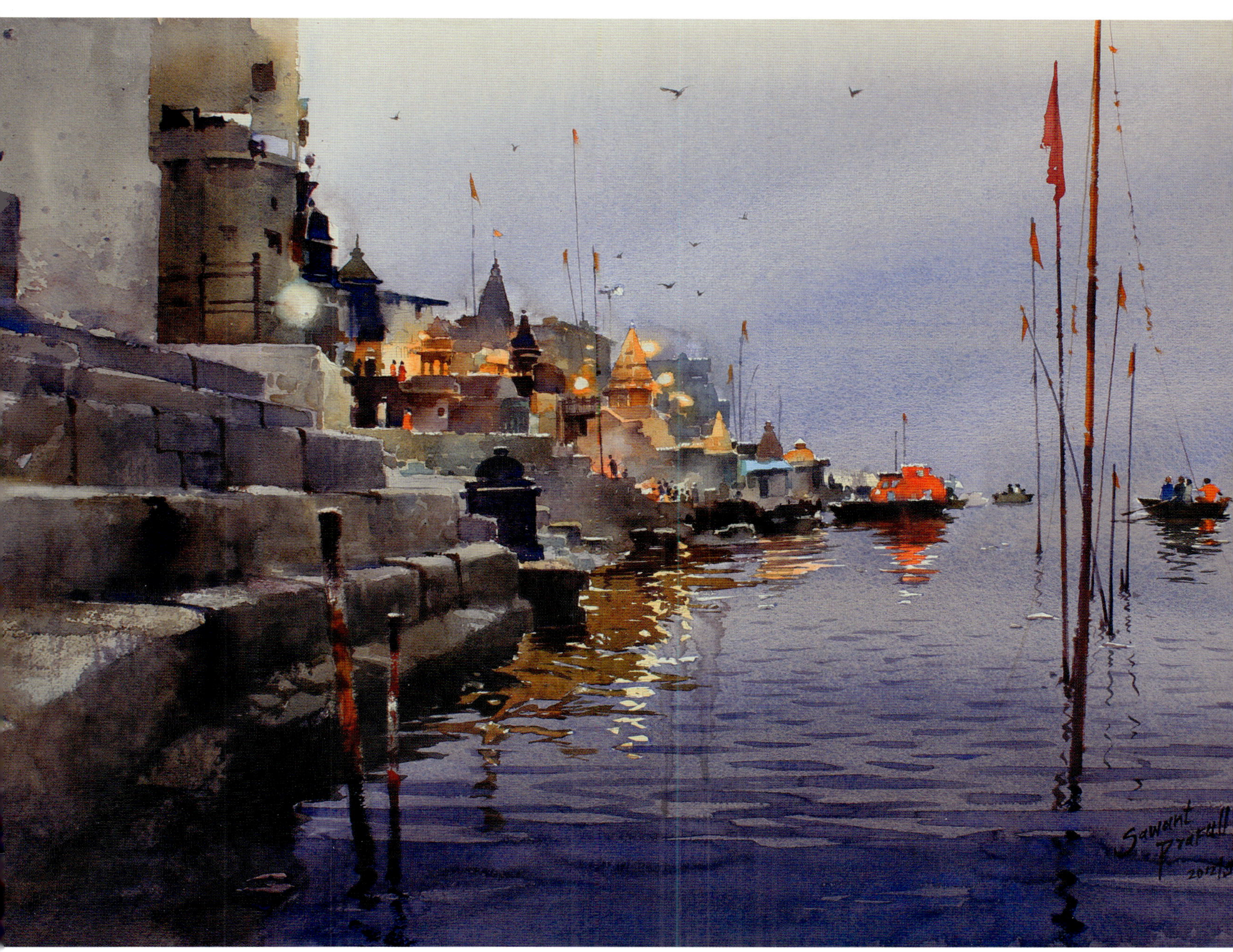

EVENING AT BANARAS GHAT | Prafull B. Sawant
22" × 30" (56cm × 76cm) Transparent watercolor on 140-lb. (300gsm) cold-pressed Arches

This was painted on-site one evening, sitting on the bank of the River Ganga, which flows through Banaras, a world-famous tourist destination. I study values. Where is the white, where is the light, where are the dark values? How does it all relate to the background? Initially I used Scarlet Red with Ultramarine Blue with a gray tint for the sky and water. I never underestimate the power of a single brushstroke. I try to pick up the right amount of pigment on the right brush at the right time for the right place in order to capture the mystical mood of evening on the water. Tone is king; color is a mere assistant.

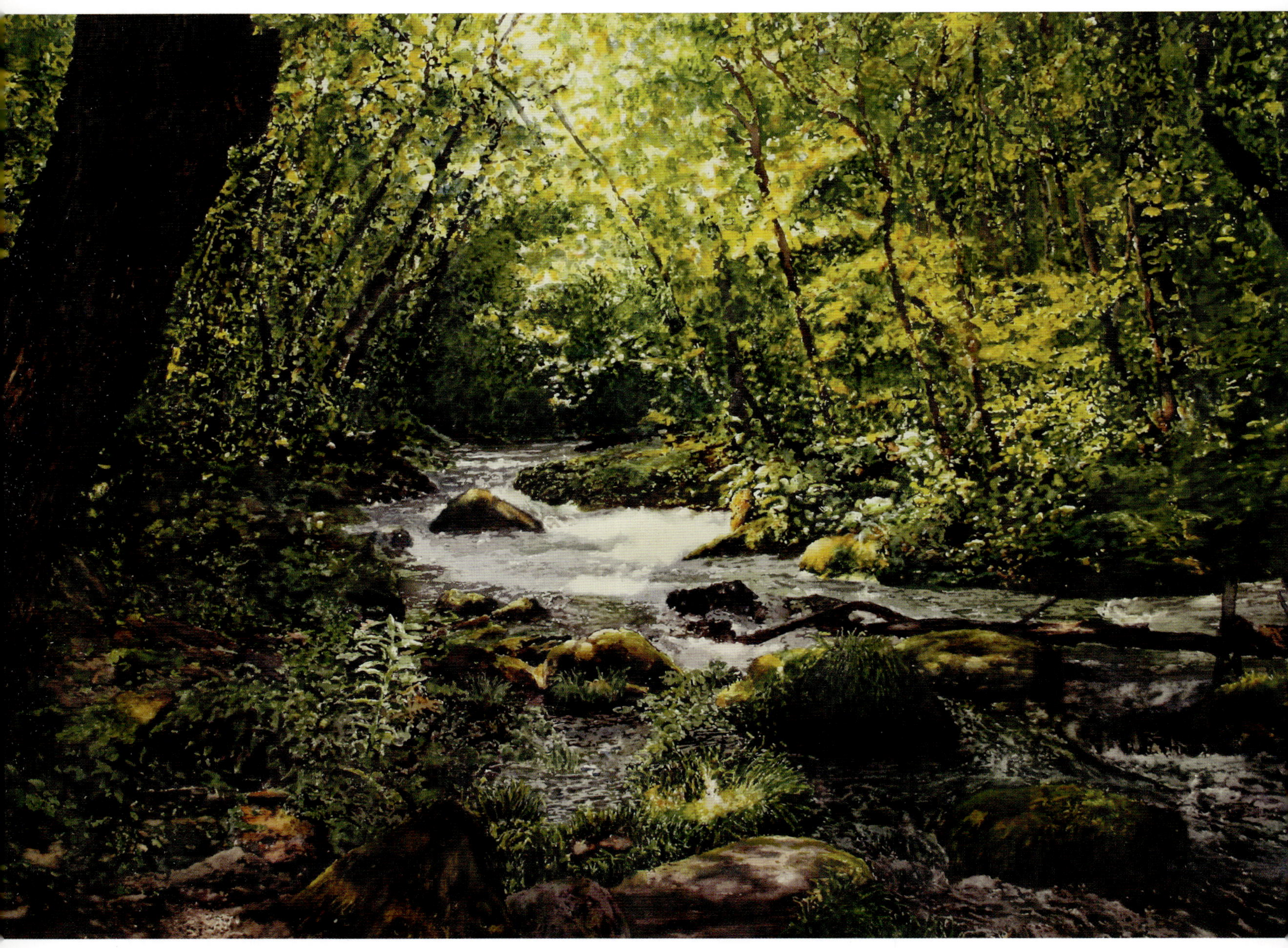

▲ **DESTINATION FOR PEACE OF MIND** | Duncan Simmons
7½" × 19½" (19cm × 50cm) Transparent watercolor on 300-lb. (640gsm) cold-pressed Arches

I love painting landscapes. *Destination for Peace of Mind* was painted in my studio from a photograph. I paint realistic paintings that are full of detail. The objective is to keep the colors from bleeding together. I used a limited palette of Cadmium Red Deep, New Gamboge and French Ultramarine Blue, plus the compatible colors of Hooker's Green, Sap Green and Mars Violet. This helps with harmony and a large range of values. I painted from the foreground to the distance, from light to dark, and then from dark to light. Most of the dark areas in the tree trunks were painted first and masked to help me keep track of the details and create a peaceful landscape.

HOVERING SEMBLANCE | Parag D. Borse
15" × 21" (38cm × 53cm) Watercolor on Arches

I did this painting with the help of a photograph. I first make a pencil sketch on the paper. Then I select a color of a high key and apply a wash on the paper. Beginning my work on the focal point, I move from light to dark and complete the work. To me, the state of creativity is the absence of *I*. And the experience of beauty makes me without self. In that experience, everything seems to be abstract and unknown, and so I paint it on the paper as an unknown. Therefore, I think bringing our consciousness into the area of unknown is the real solution to creativity.

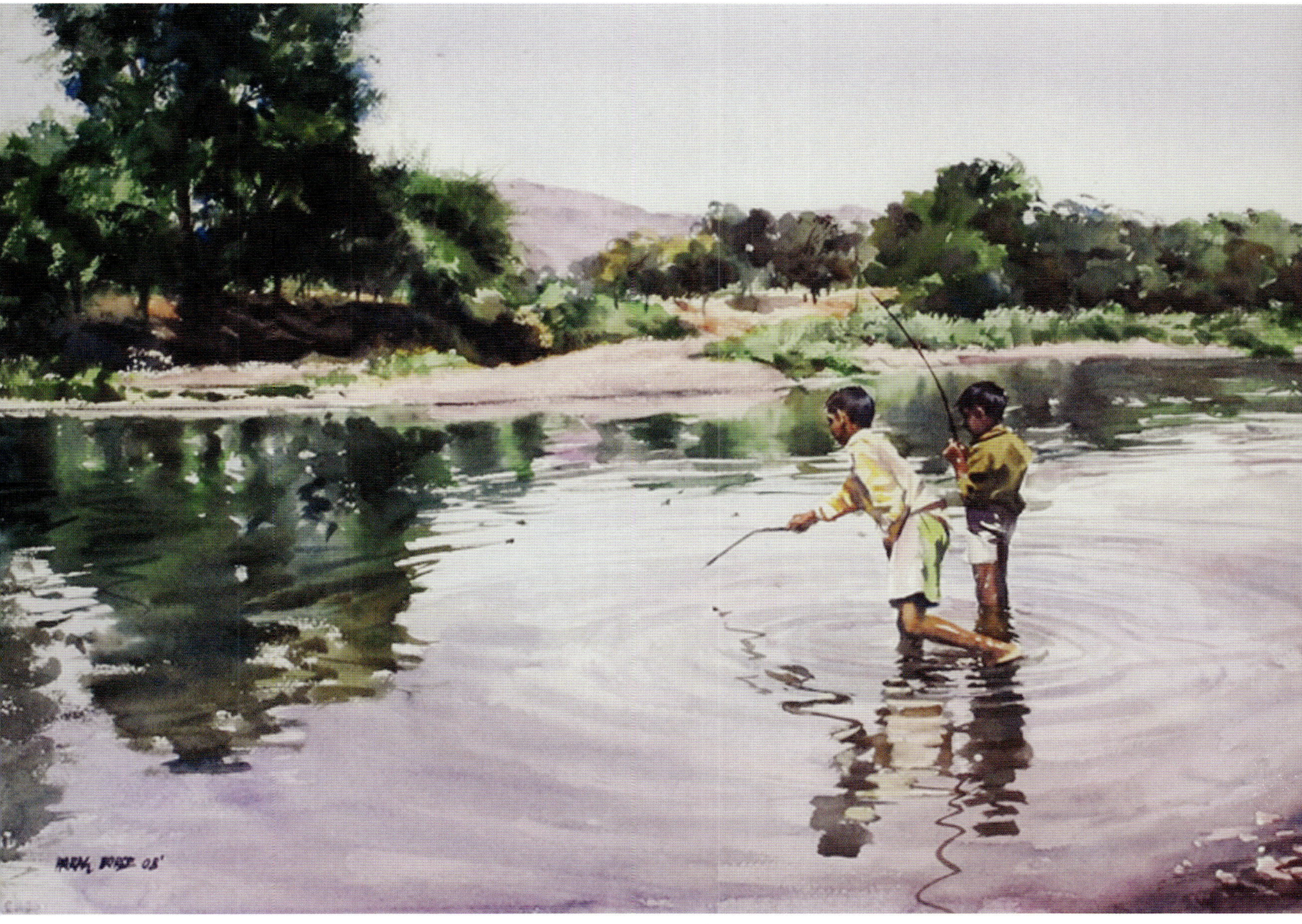

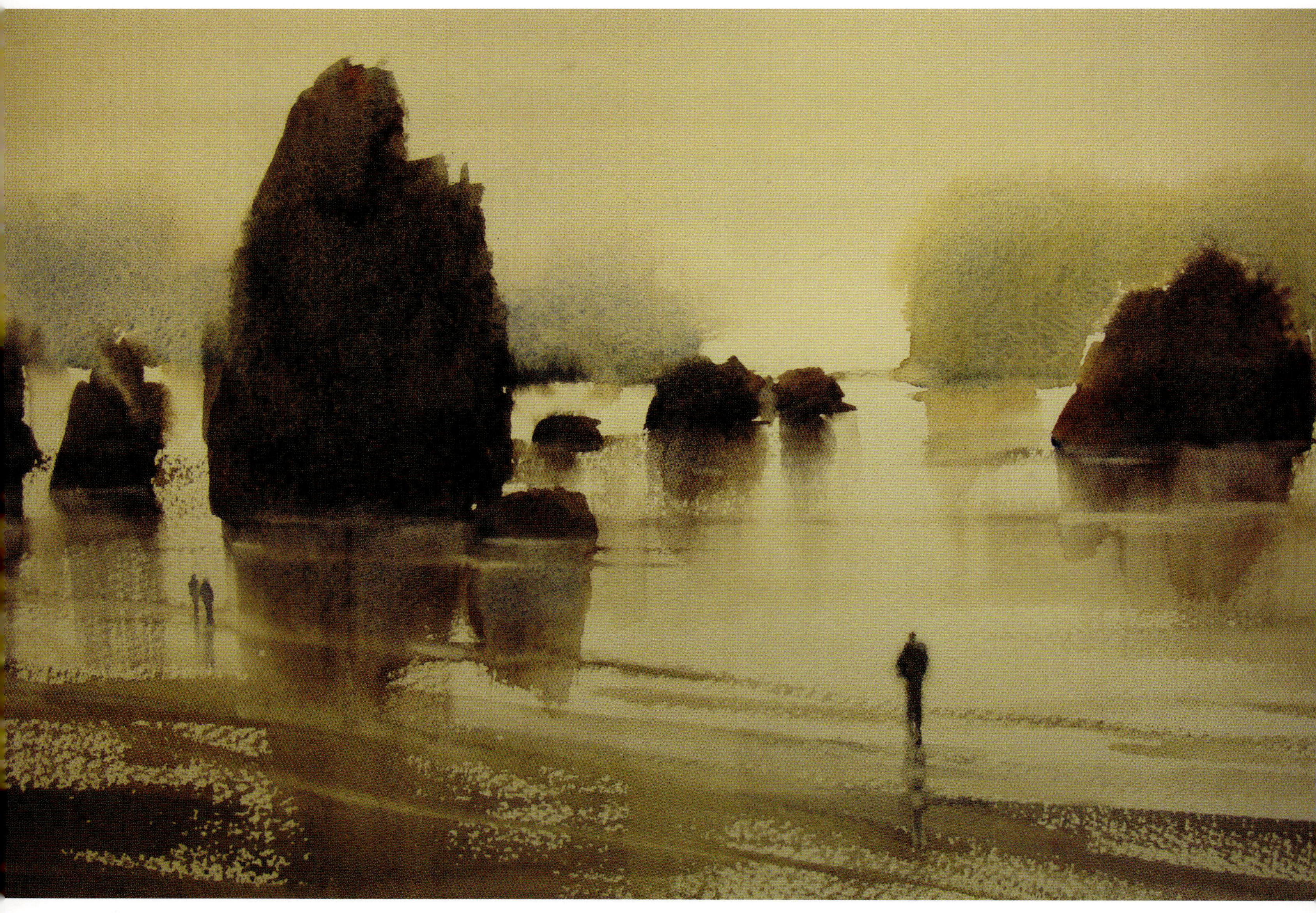

▲ RAINY DAY, BANDON | Kathy Collins
11" × 15" (28cm × 38cm) Transparent watercolor on 140-lb. (300gsm) cold-pressed Fabriano Artistico

Over one spring weekend, I accompanied my husband to Bandon, Oregon, where a world-famous golf course hugs the coastline. Not being a golfer, I was along for the ride and the possibility of beach sketching even though the weather forecast was mixed. As it turned out, gray clouds soon moved in, and the golfers ended up disappointed by two days of steady drizzle. But I stayed warm and dry in the car while sketching the dramatic rock formations, immersing myself in the hazy look of a wet day. The trip inspired a whole new series of rainy day paintings in which I tried to achieve a soothing flow of mist with muted values and a limited palette.

"Composition is created by eye paths; some dominate by value contrast and others serve as secondary helpers."

– HAROLD DEAN SMITH

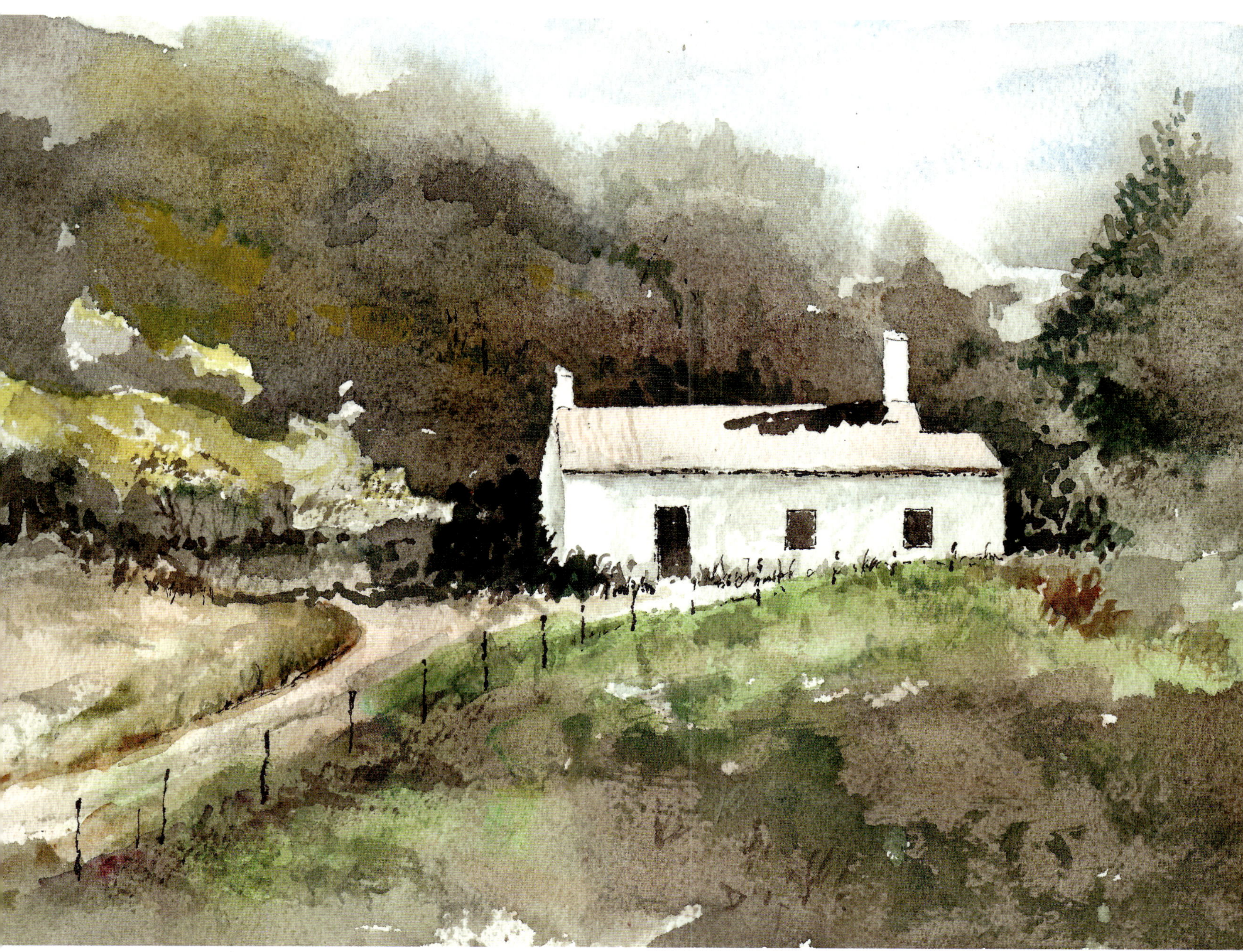

▲ **OLD FARM BUILDING, PORTUGAL** | Harold Dean Smith
7" × 9½" (18cm × 24cm) Transparent watercolor on 140-lb. (300gsm) cold-pressed cotton paper

This painting was based on a digital snapshot taken from a moving tour bus. I wanted to bring back images of what the country looked like, not just monuments. Normally I paint detailed realistic images, but on this occasion I wanted to enjoy the mingling of colors and the power of suggestion, letting each viewer's mind add from their memory. I realized after studying the photo that the trees behind the building were in fact the reflection from the window of trees on the other side of the road. But they serendipitously provided a good background for the building and the driveway, adding to the composition.

DARK SANDS BEACH | Juan Peña

19" × 25" (48cm × 64cm) Watercolor on 260-lb. (550gsm) double elephant paper

Dark Sands Beach is a wet-into-wet painting about the California coastal fog. That fog is sometimes called "the June Gloom." Many visitors come to California in the summer months and are quite disappointed to see the cold, wet foggy weather. The best time to visit the West Coast without the fog is in the spring or fall. Wet-into-wet watercolor painting is a technique of painting in which the artist wets the surface of his paper, then paints on that wet paper surface. I began painting on location in watercolor in the 1960s when it was not popular to paint en plein air or in a representational style.

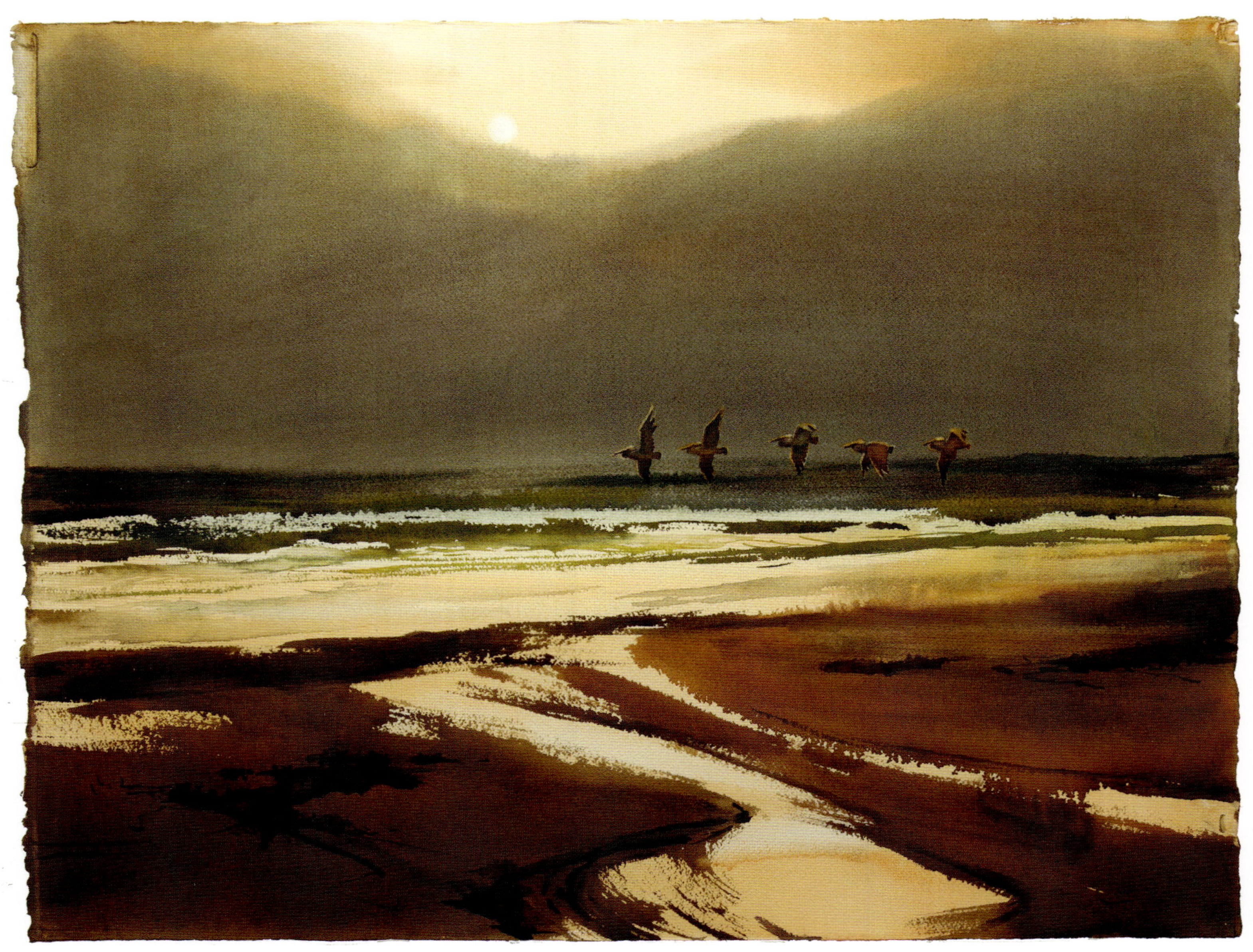

NO. 3 SHAFT HOUSE STAIRS | Peter V. Jablokow

30" × 22" (76cm × 56cm) Transparent watercolor on 300-lb. (640gsm) hot-pressed Arches

This painting captures the moment I panicked while climbing the stairs of an abandoned copper mine in Calumet, Michigan, teaching me the power of being surrounded by my subject. My painting process is a similar adventure. To feel my life is in control, I start by defining every line and detail in pencil, using a ruler to line up perspective angles and vanishing points. Next, chaos ensues when I start splashing on what feels like arbitrary layers of colors. While feeling lost, I go back and forth, adding and deleting pigment until the painting eventually comes back into focus. I hate the chaos but love the control and feel gratified when I end up with a combination of both.

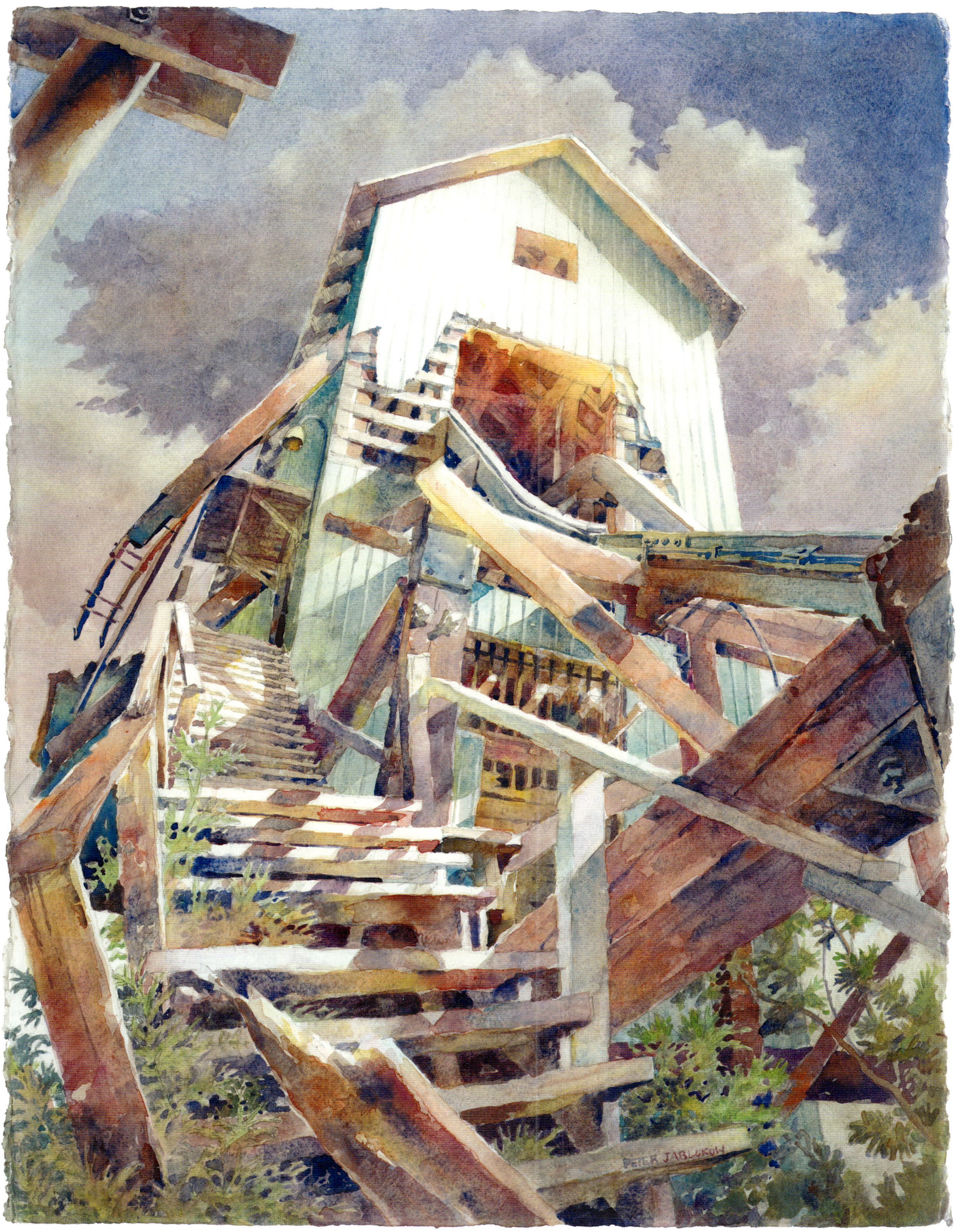
PETER JABLOKOW

WESTMORELAND FAIR | Frederic S. Briggs
15" × 20" (38cm × 51cm) Transparent watercolor on 140-lb. (300gsm) Canson Montval

Having returned from the English Lake District, I was anxious to paint this scene with a spectacular sky I encountered. I painted this as a demonstration for my students at the Schuler School of Fine Arts, so I had only one opportunity to get it right. Designing my composition so as to allow the sky to be the dominant feature was my creative solution. The placement of the huge oak tree and the figures for scale in relation to the sky quickly fell into place. Having the sky quite wet enabled me to model it boldly, painting directly across the pencil drawing of the tree. When pleased with the outcome of the sky, I did my foreground and carefully filled in the tree with a medium flat brush.

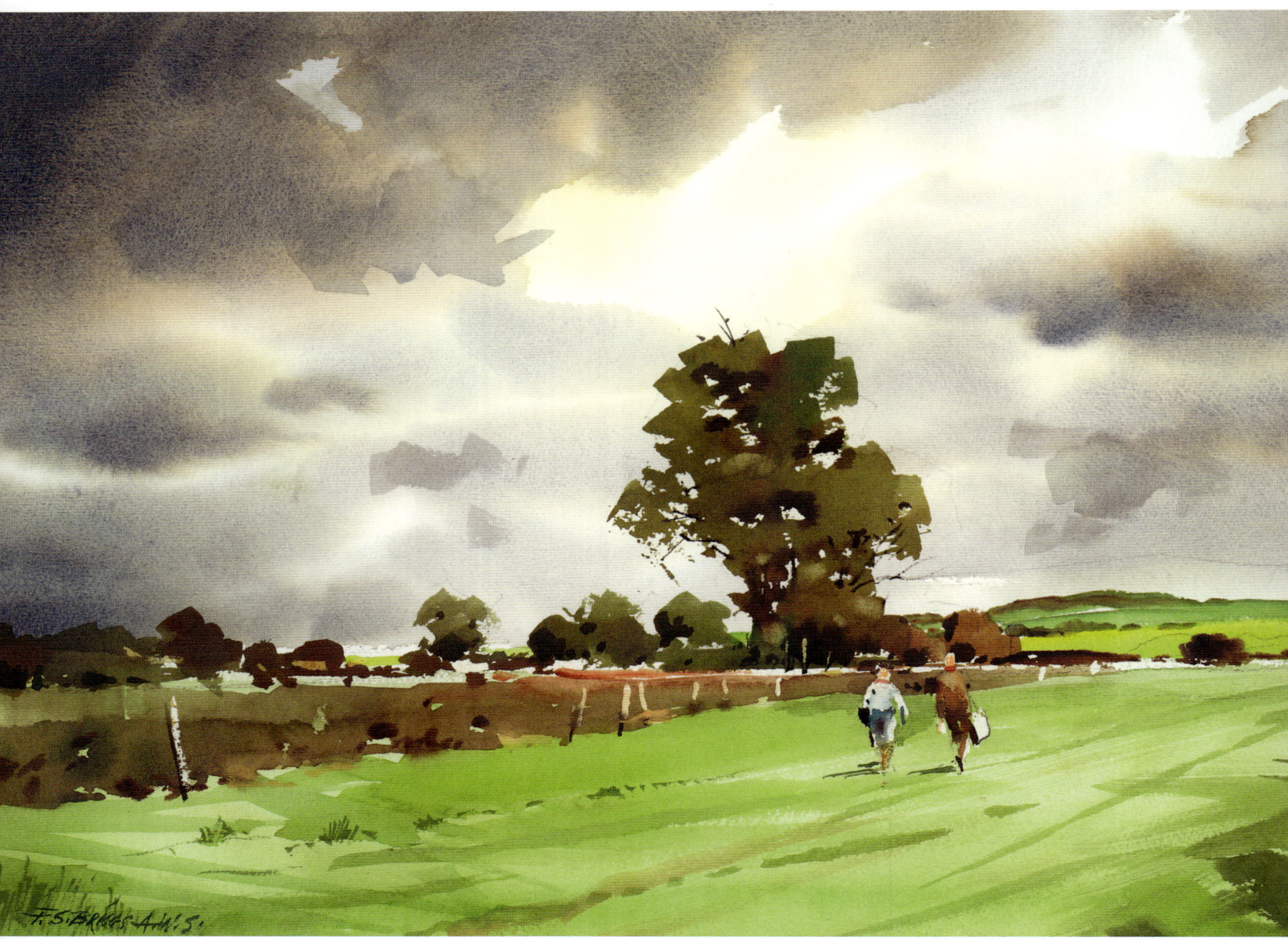

FAIRMOUNT ROAD – OHIO | Thomas W. Schaller
24" × 18" (61cm × 46cm) Watercolor on 140-lb. (300gsm) rough Saunders

In my teaching I always stress the importance of identifying the story that you wish your paintings to tell. This rural scene is of the road that leads to the farm where I grew up. So the unusual composition—the road disappearing in the distance is placed directly in the center on the image—had a purpose. I was hoping to evoke in the viewer a rather nostalgic sense of both time and distance passing—the past, present and future are divided—but also literally melting together by employing techniques from wet-into-wet to near dry-brush applications.

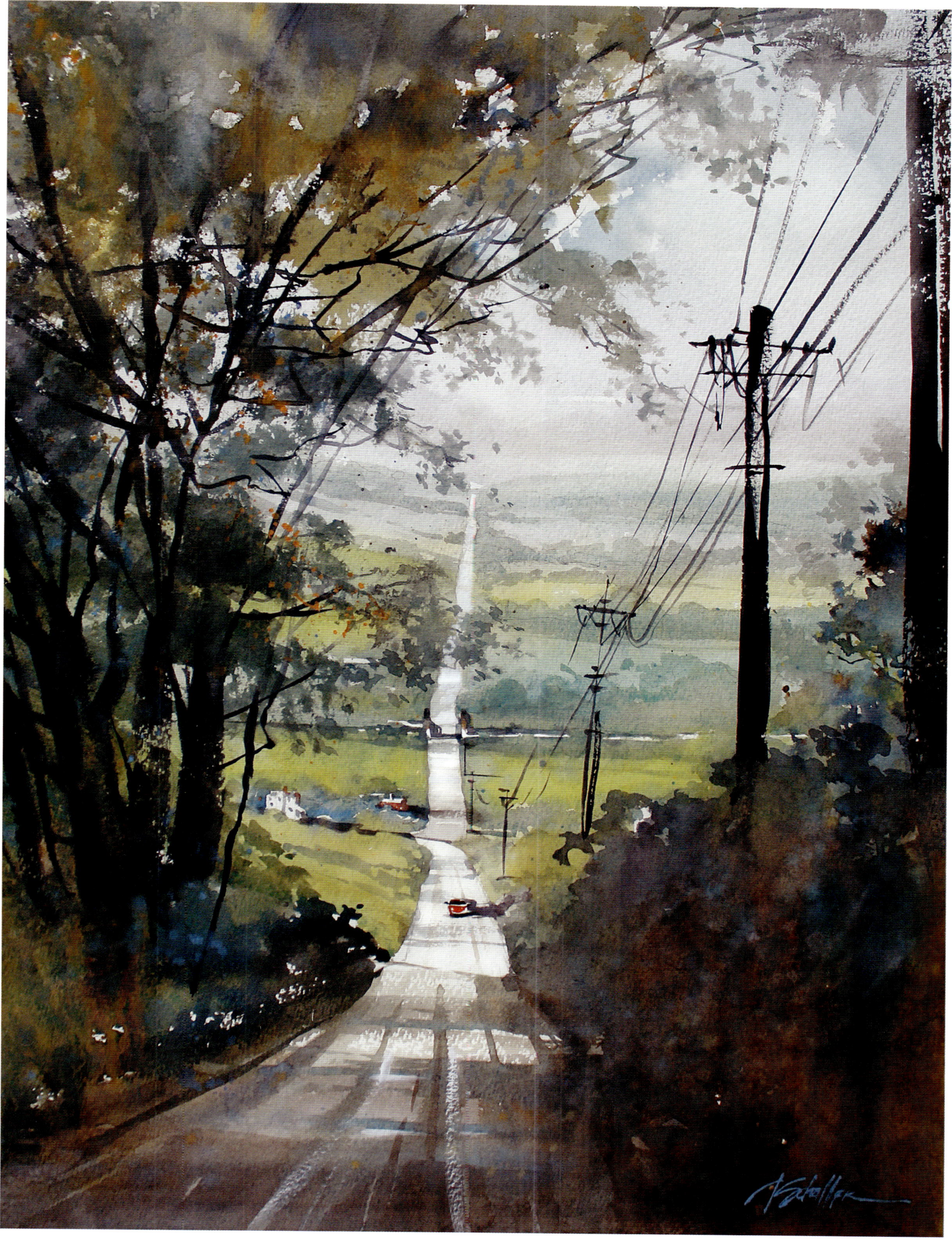

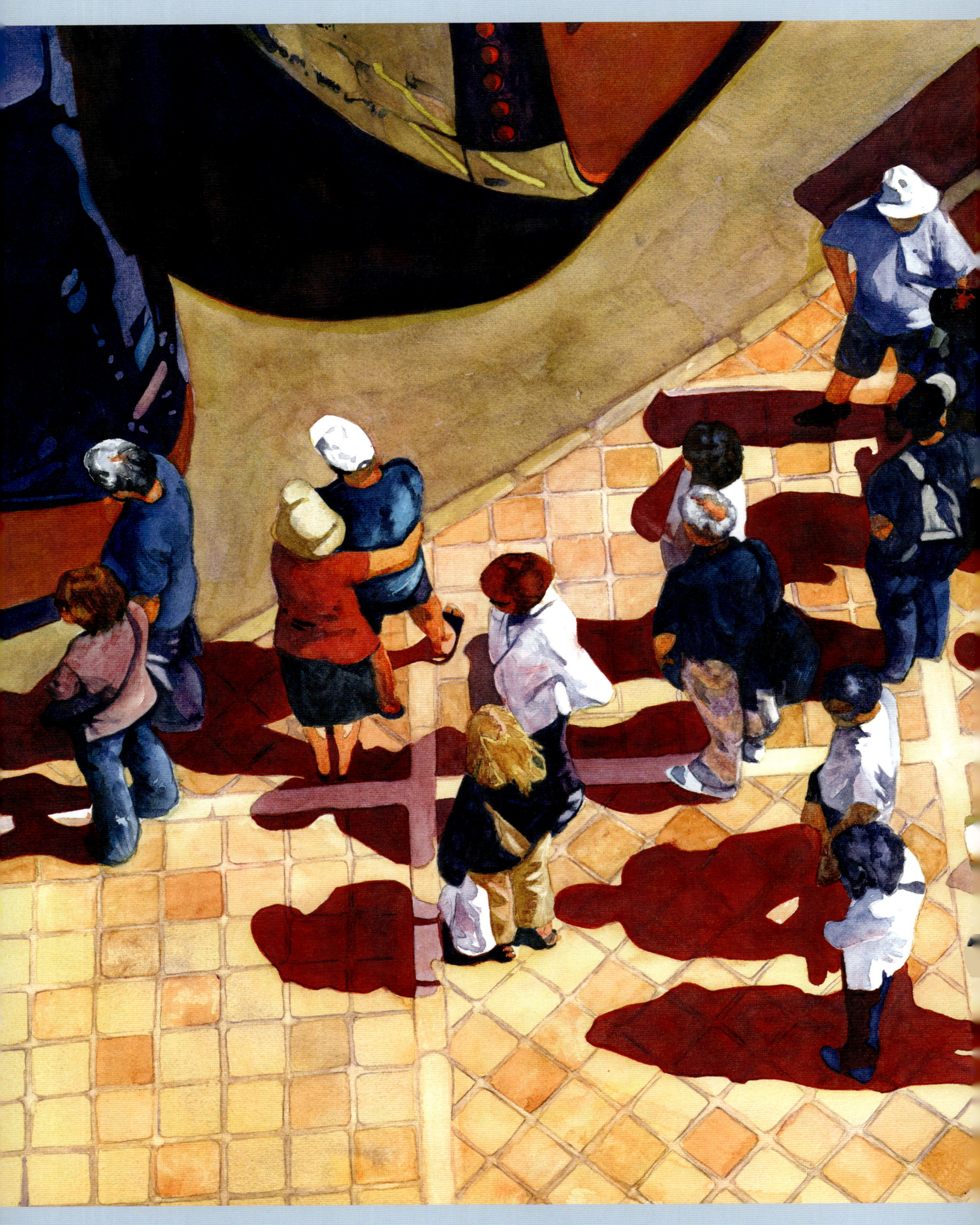

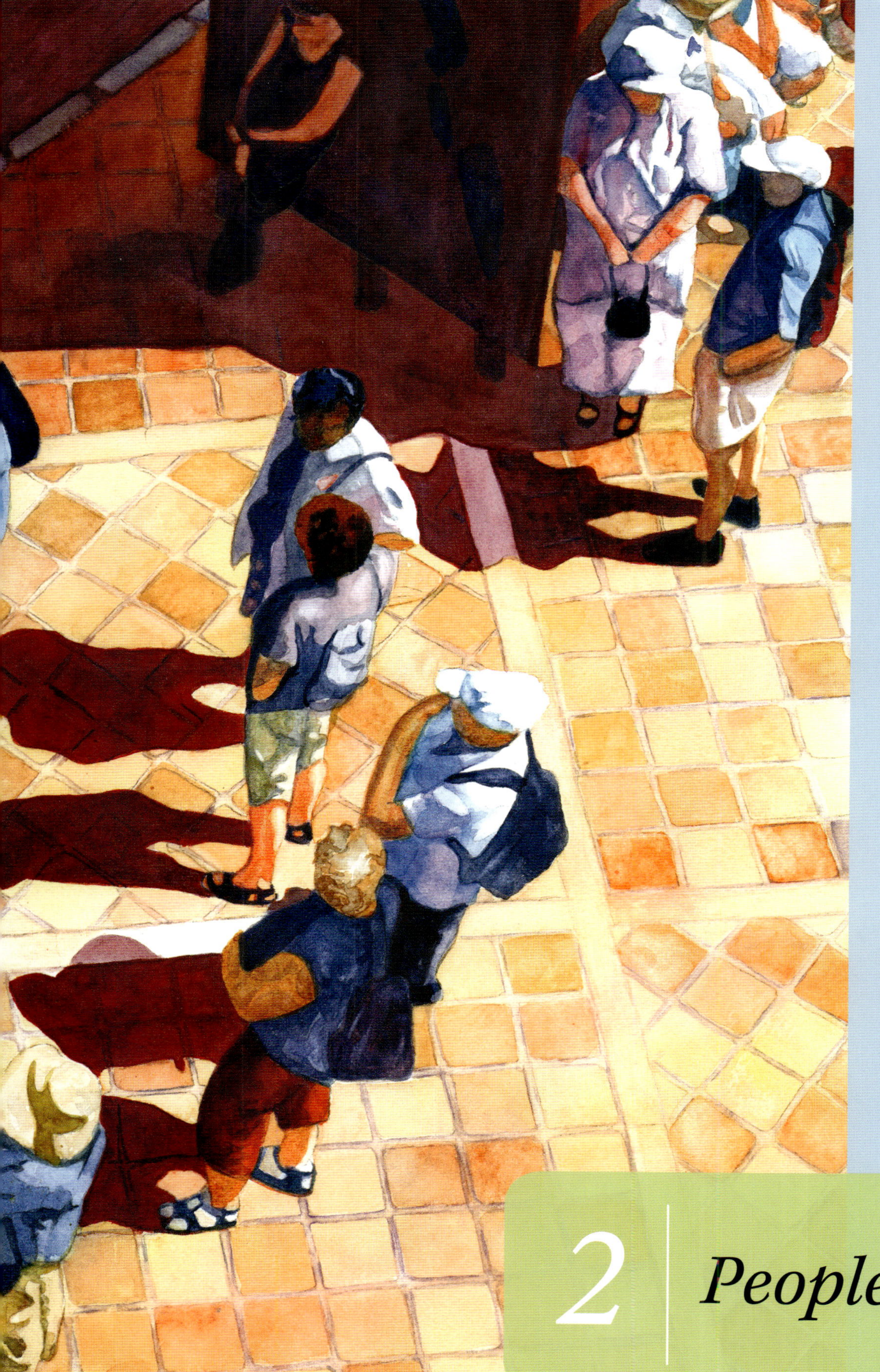

◀ NEXT BUS TO TORREMOLINOS
Lynn Hosegood
21" × 28" (53cm × 71cm)
Transparent watercolor on
cold-pressed Arches

The light in southern Spain illuminates the exciting Spanish colors, especially in contrast to the vivid white buildings and the sienna/orange tiling. My intention was to capture the busyness of the place, the light, and take advantage of the aerial views offered by the tiered streets. To this end I used complementary colors and placed the curved- shaped people in a formation that echoed the rectangular shapes of the tiling. But it needed something more to express the bright light. My solution was to brighten the colors of the shadows with warm orange and red glazes and use them to connect the figures. More warm outlining added to the glow of the scene.

2 | *People in Motion*

SAT ON THE WALL | Graham Berry
11" × 20" (28cm × 51cm) Watercolor on Saunders watercolor board

My camera proved invaluable when I was painting the boats in the harbor of Puerto de la Cruz, Tenerife. I looked behind me and noticed all the people sitting on the wall just passing time. I took numerous photos and could immediately visualize the painting. It's the kind of subject where painting from life isn't practical. I tried to treat the figures as abstract shapes and colors. Lots of pure color was used on the figures and street signs. I painted the dark background with Burnt Sienna, Alizarin and French Ultramarine and took care to leave the white of the paper for highlights.

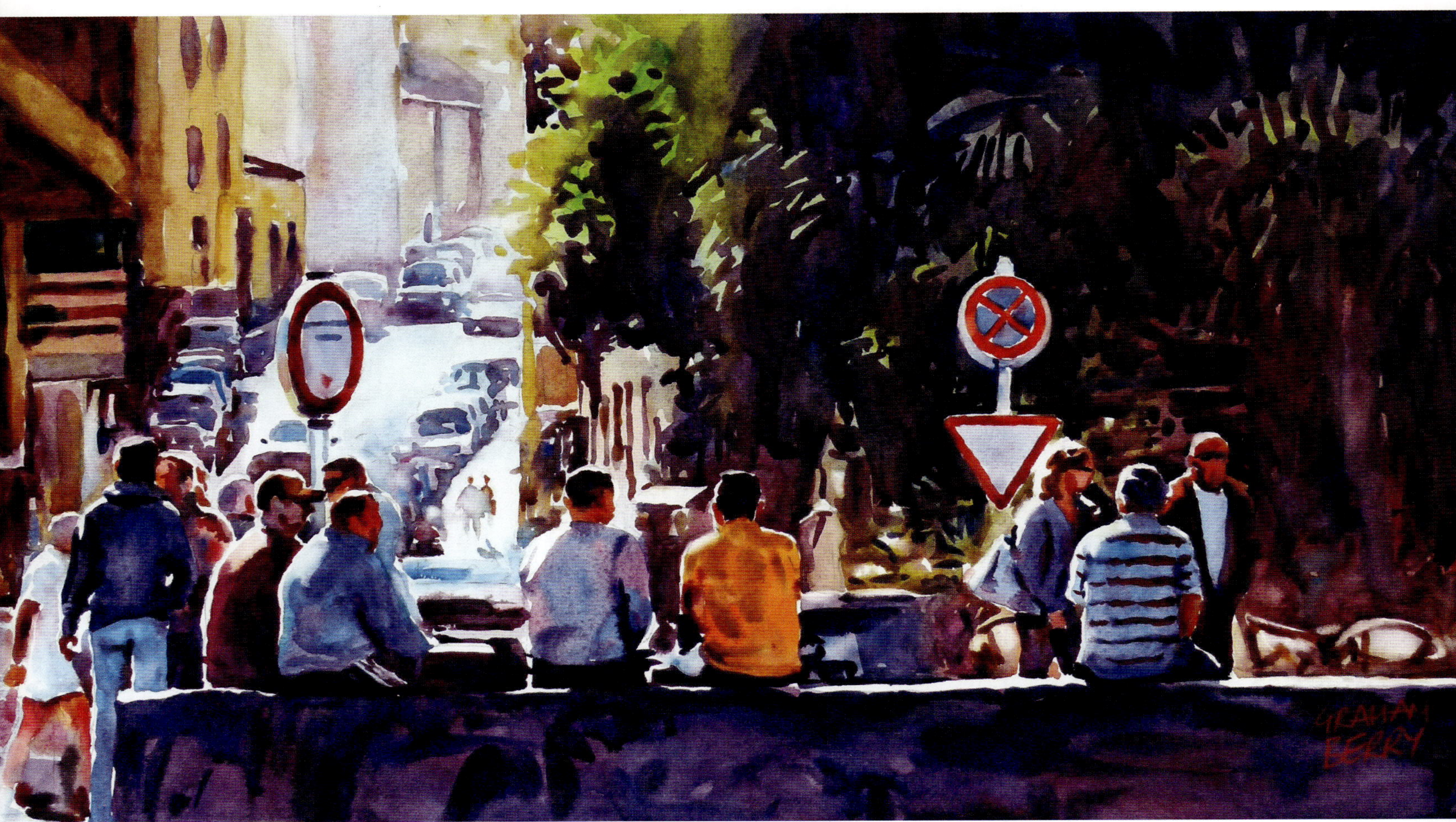

"The search for creative solutions starts as soon as I select a subject to photograph and continues in the viewfinder. My feeling for the subject at the time will be put into the painting."

– GRAHAM BERRY

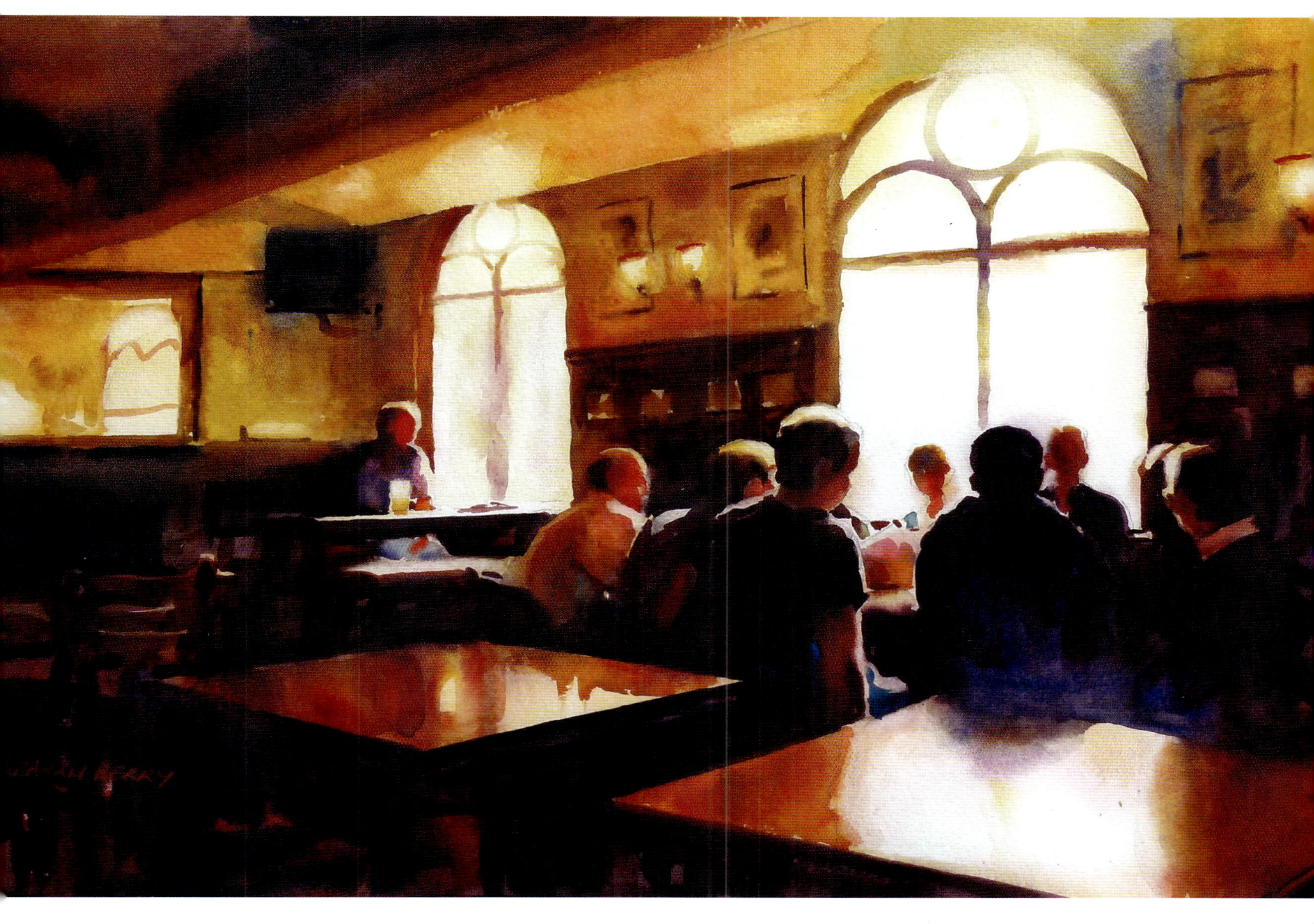

MEETING IN THE PUB | Graham Berry
18" × 27" (46cm × 69cm) Watercolor on 300-lb. (640gsm) rough Saunders Waterford

After some editing and cropping on my computer I printed out a couple of photos to work from in my studio. After sketching the image onto the paper with a soft pencil, I began my first pale wash. While the wash was still wet, I softened some of the edges with a damp brush and paper towel. After allowing the paper to completely dry with the help of a hair dryer, I began my second wash with a lot more pigment. I began to define the shapes with the stronger washes, allowing colors to mix on the paper. The darks are mainly French Ultramarine and Burnt Sienna; the reflected light off the polished table is almost all Ultramarine Blue. Hardly any detail was required for the figures as they are just abstract shapes created by the light from the window.

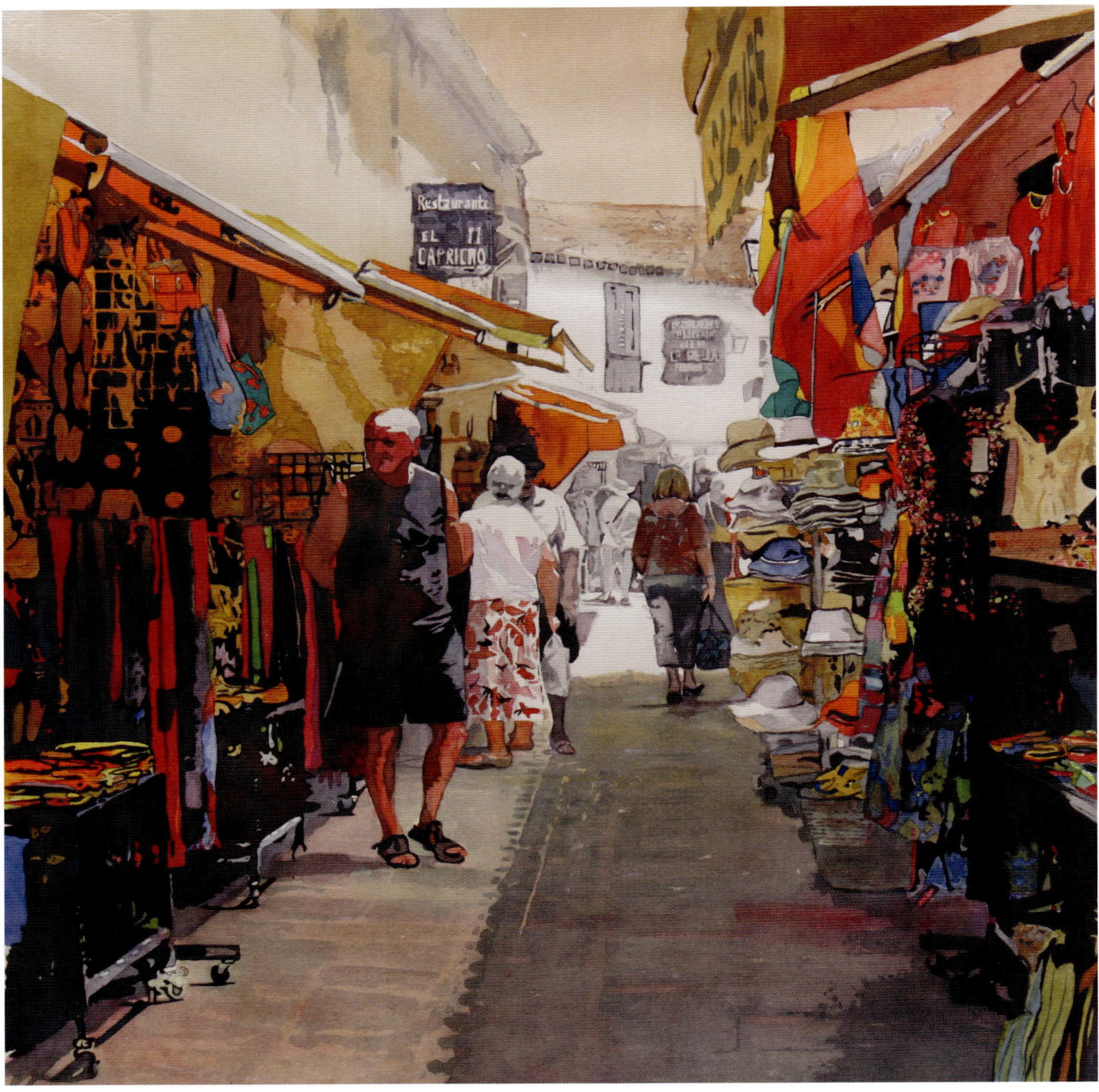

▲ MIJAS MARKET, SPAIN | Lynn Hosegood
20" × 20" (51cm × 51cm) Transparent watercolor on cold-pressed Arches

I approach every painting with a set of questions that present themselves to reach particular goals. Here the major problem was how to design an image of a very busy, brightly lit market scene without creating confusion. I paid attention to the values that created larger shapes to unify the items that vied for attention. I rendered the individual items as small, flat, colorful shapes in predominantly warm colors with a few cool accents. I made the foreground man blend in well with the environment by using similar coloring and value. I left the upper background area light with some details in warm tones of gray as contrast to the overall dark foreground, and used the lady with a colorful skirt as linkage.

▶ AGAINST THE LIGHT | Kris Parins
29" × 21" (74cm × 53cm) Transparent watercolor on 140-lb. (300gsm) cold-pressed Arches

A chilly March day in Times Square, New York, provided the atmosphere and design inspiration for a collection of reference photos. I knew right away that I wanted to make several paintings of the constantly shifting scene. Some unifying elements in the series are the hourglass shape of the lightest values and the minimal level of detail of the backlit figures. The color palette is also consistent for all the paintings, using only four Winsor & Newton transparent watercolors: Aureolin Yellow, Rose Madder Genuine, Cobalt Blue and French Ultramarine Blue.

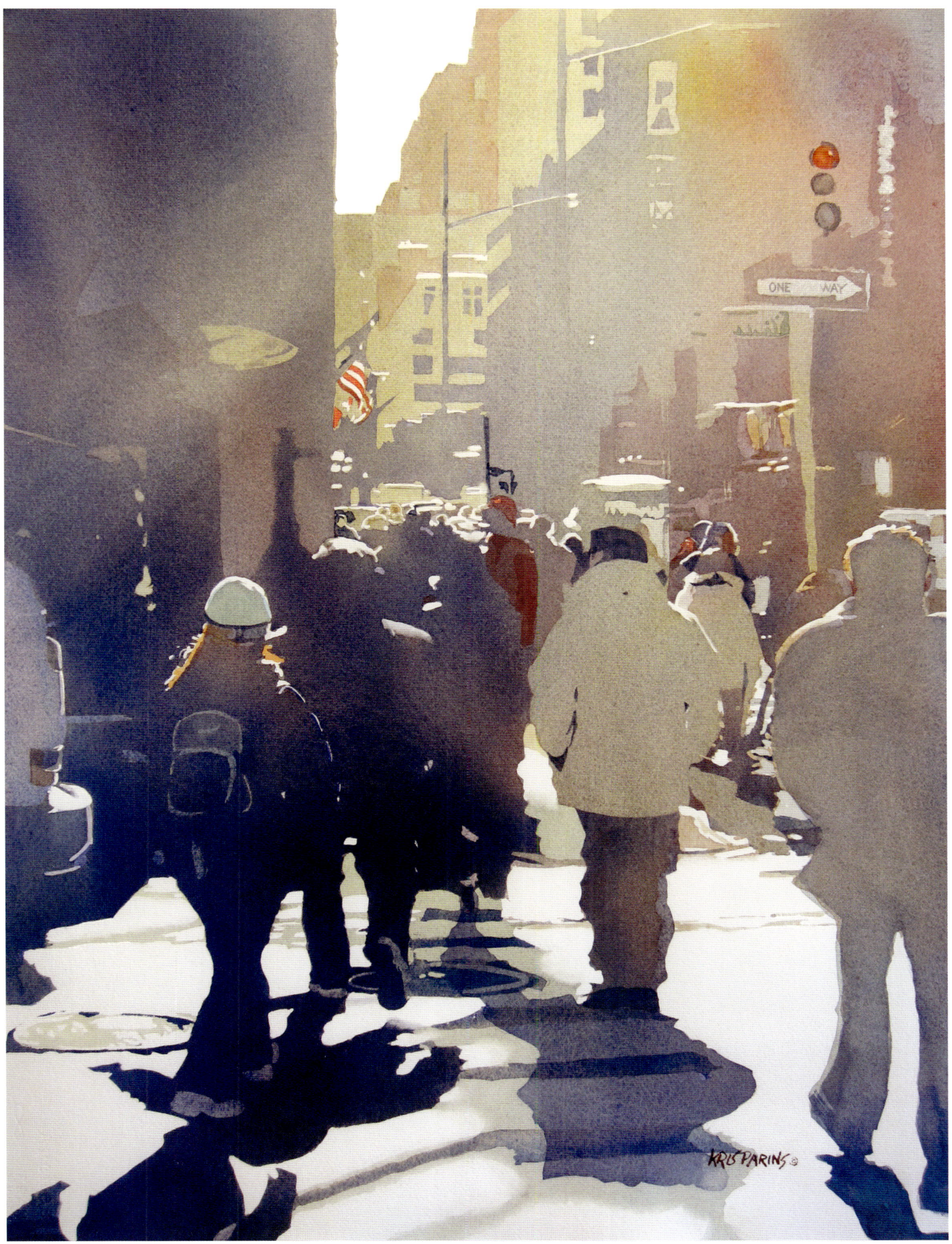
ONE WAY
KRIS PARINS

MORNING MIGRATION | Wen-Cong Wang
20" × 28" (51cm × 71cm) Transparent watercolor on 300-lb. (640gsm) cold-pressed Arches

On the way to the Kanas Lake in Xinjiang, I was overwhelmed by the serenity and dynamism of this herd in the soft light that penetrated the chilly air. Even without a photo, I was strongly inspired to compose this view. To capture the dreamlike atmosphere, I decided to create different textures for the trees and the ground. I painted wet-into-wet in the background. When dry, I used a toothbrush and splattered, first masking fluid to reserve lights, then paint from warm to cool, light to dark. Finally, a bit of gouache was applied to highlight the focal area. To enhance the mysterious quality of the work, I deliberately lightened the values of the shadows to create a sense of floating.

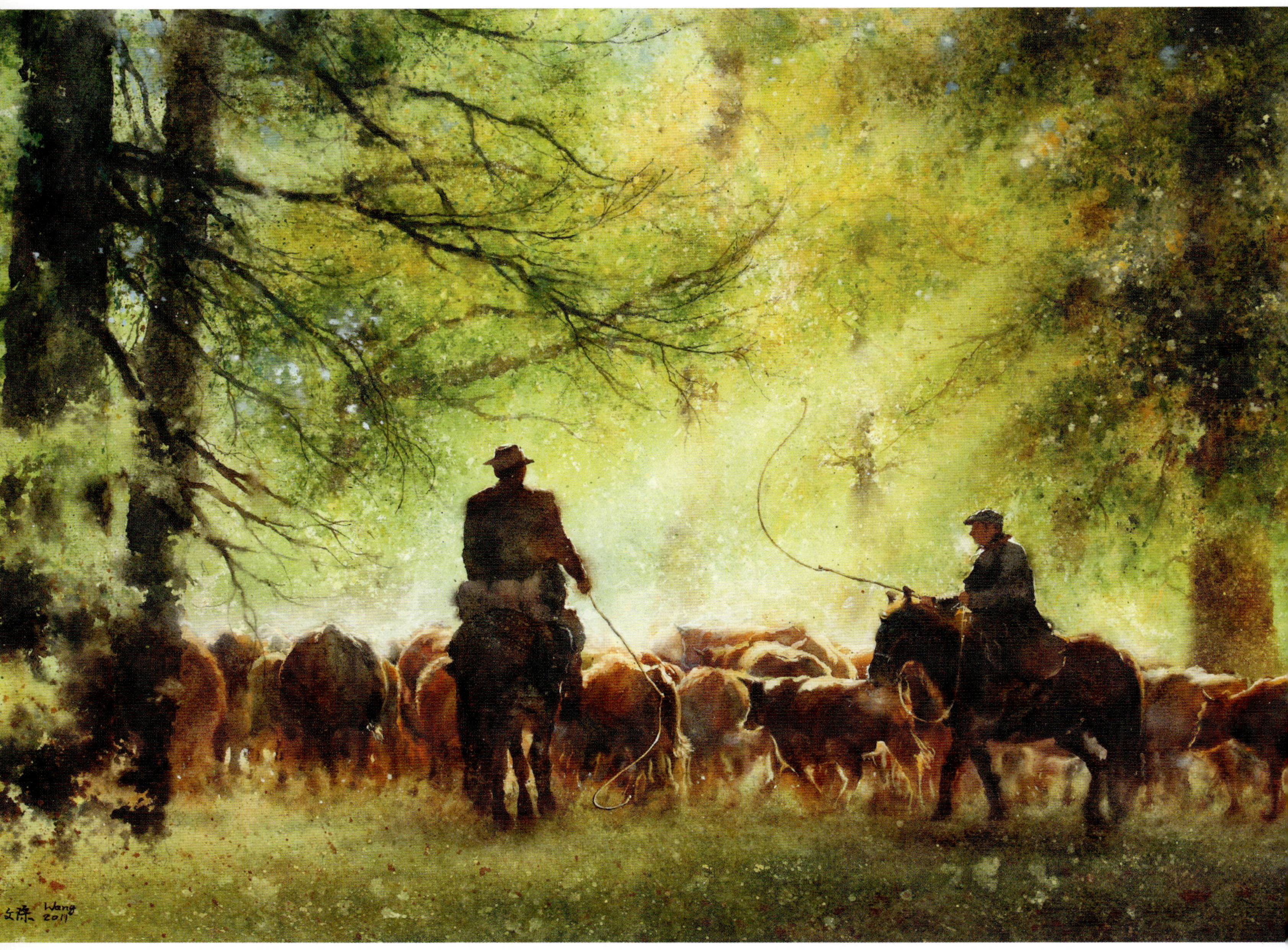

RAVELLO | Rose Edin
28" × 19½" (71cm × 50cm) Transparent watercolor on 300-lb. (640gsm) cold-pressed Arches

The horizontal and vertical shadows from the grape trellis were a perfect background for the figures strolling below from where I took the photograph in Ravello, Italy. My problem was to get the soft edges behind the figures. Liquid mask was applied to the carefully drawn figures. Then the background and the pathway were painted on a very wet surface with the warmer colors closer to the figures. I then experimented by using a misting spray bottle, spritzing each area before applying the shadows. The cool colors of the shadows helped to pop out the figures.

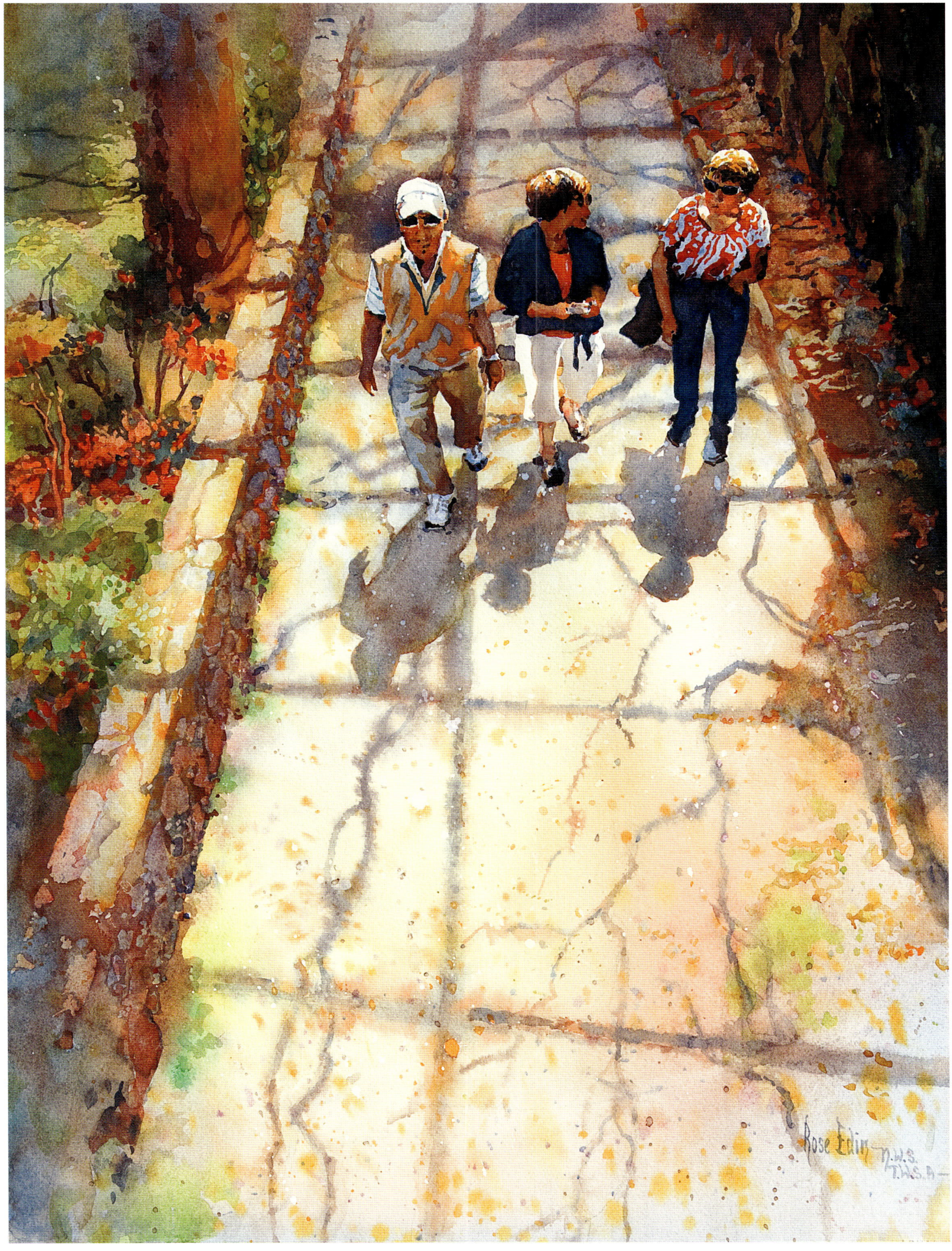
Rose Edin N.W.S.
T.W.S.A.

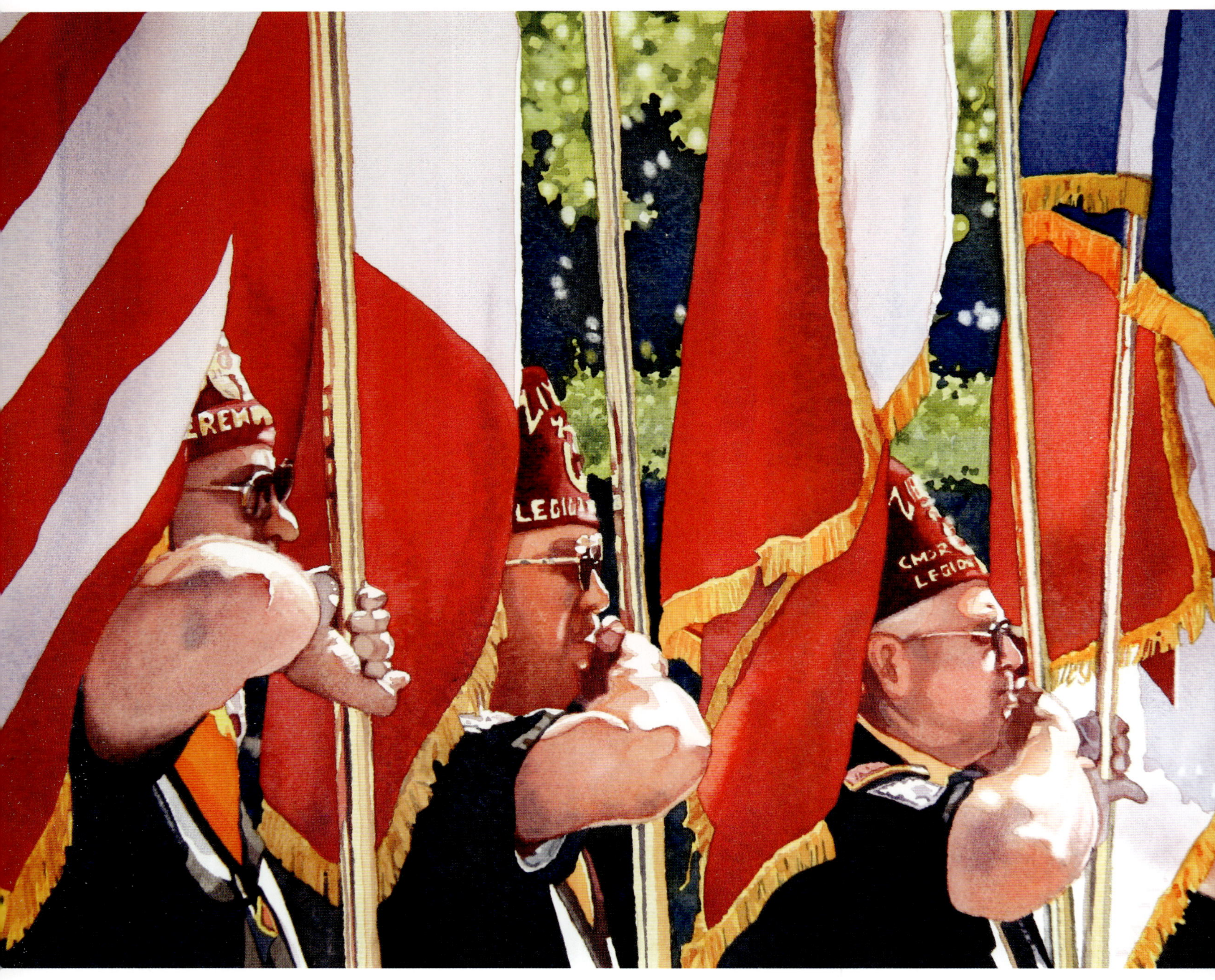

▲ **HONOR AMERICA** | Catherine P. O'Neill
11" × 14" (28cm × 36cm) Transparent watercolor on 300-lb. (640gsm) Arches

My family and I enjoy taking in all the sights and sounds during the annual summer parade in my hometown. My challenge in capturing that experience is to design a painting that suitably portrays the lively atmosphere. This composition's focus on the bright colors and proud demeanor of the flag bearers captures the mixture of nostalgia, tradition and patriotism I feel as we gather each year for the big event.

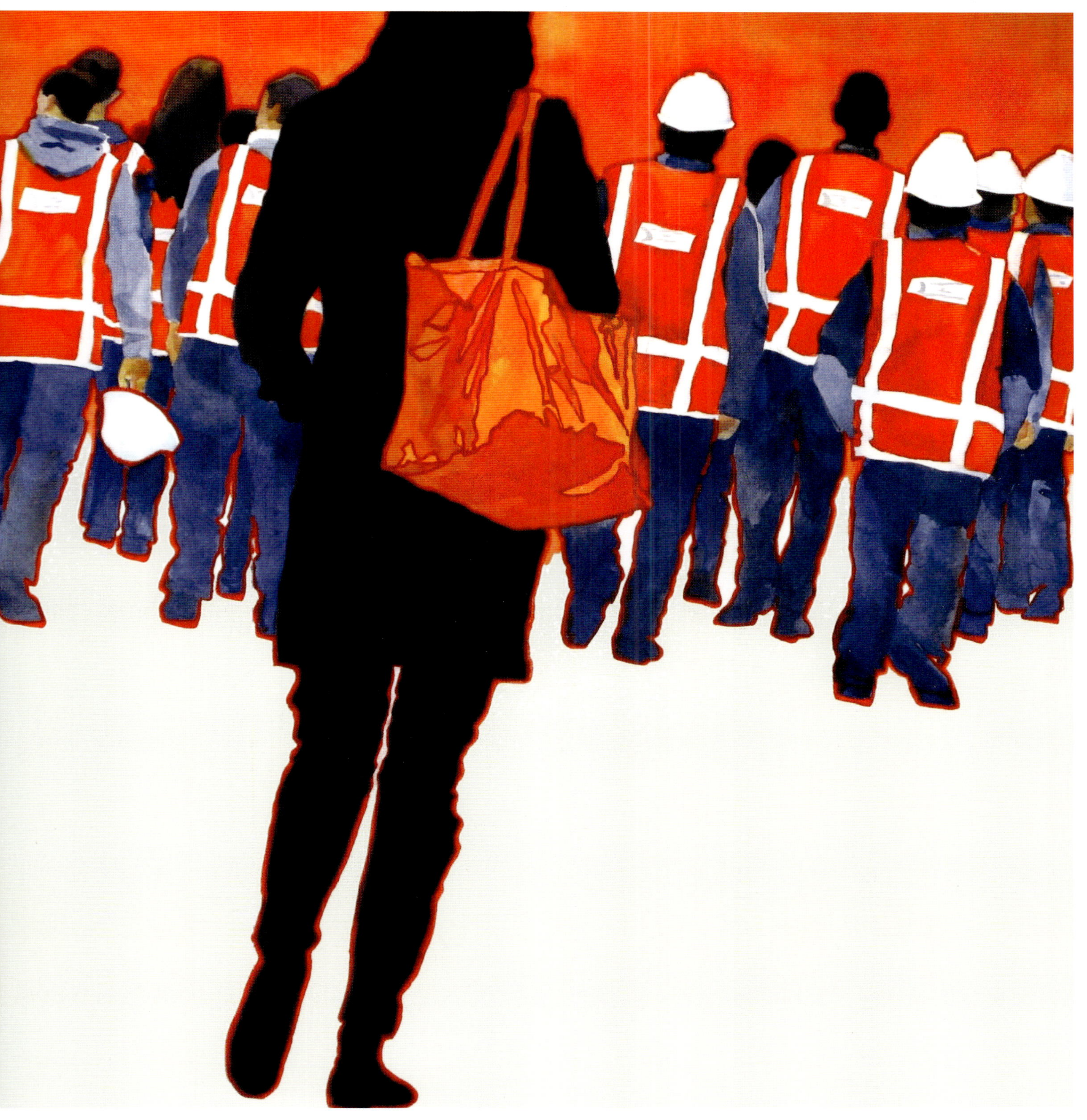

▲ **MONDAY PEOPLE** | Susan Webb Tregay
20" × 20" (51cm × 51cm) Watercolor on 140-lb. (300gsm) cold-pressed Arches

I was captivated by this blaze of orange in the midst of New York City. After taking several photos of the workers, in my viewfinder I caught the woman carrying something black. I immediately envisioned her with an orange bag. Security in New York became my theme. I stuck to the simplest color strategy of all—complementary colors, in this case orange and blue. Then I created a straightforward design, which unfortunately seemed static. After testing several angles on my computer's photo program, I tipped the painting down on the right, choosing a very subtle angle. This made the painting come alive.

NEW LIFE FOR OLD THINGS | Lisa Ambrose
14" × 28" (36cm × 71cm) Transparent watercolor on 400-lb. (850gsm) cold-pressed Arches

I completed this work using nearly a dozen separate photographs taken while on a recent trip to Pasadena. Normally I am a perfectionist when it comes to accuracy, but with this piece I felt the compositional structure of the work was paramount. As a result, inaccuracies in perspective were overlooked in some areas to favor compositional interest. Although the result is believable at first glance, I think the visual disorientation is more interesting to me than if the perspective had been completely accurate.

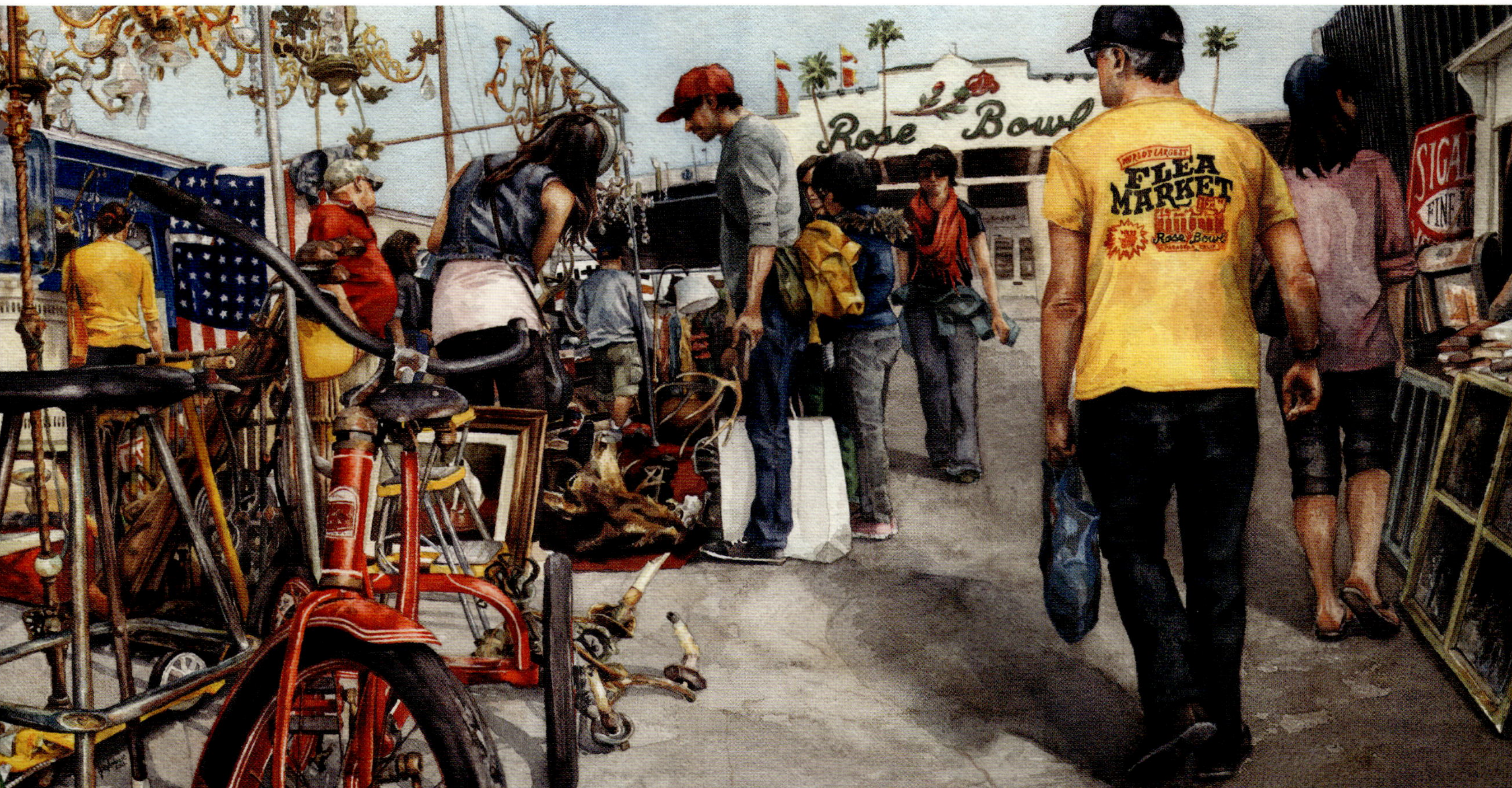

"Never set a wash tray uphill from a painting."

– LISA AMBROSE

FORTY-TWO HATS | Lisa Ambrose
21½" × 15½" (55cm × 39cm) Transparent watercolor on 400-lb. (850gsm) cold-pressed Arches

This was an exercise in laying down shadow areas with lighter layers overtop to create softer shadow edges. I used both photos and video shot during the Fort Worth Stockyards Rodeo to develop the design. With the painting nearly complete, I mixed a thin dark wash to lay over the crowd. However, in an instant I managed to overturn the contents of the wash tray over the entire painting. The painting could not be salvaged and had to be restarted. The second wash attempt was successful, but I learned a valuable lesson.

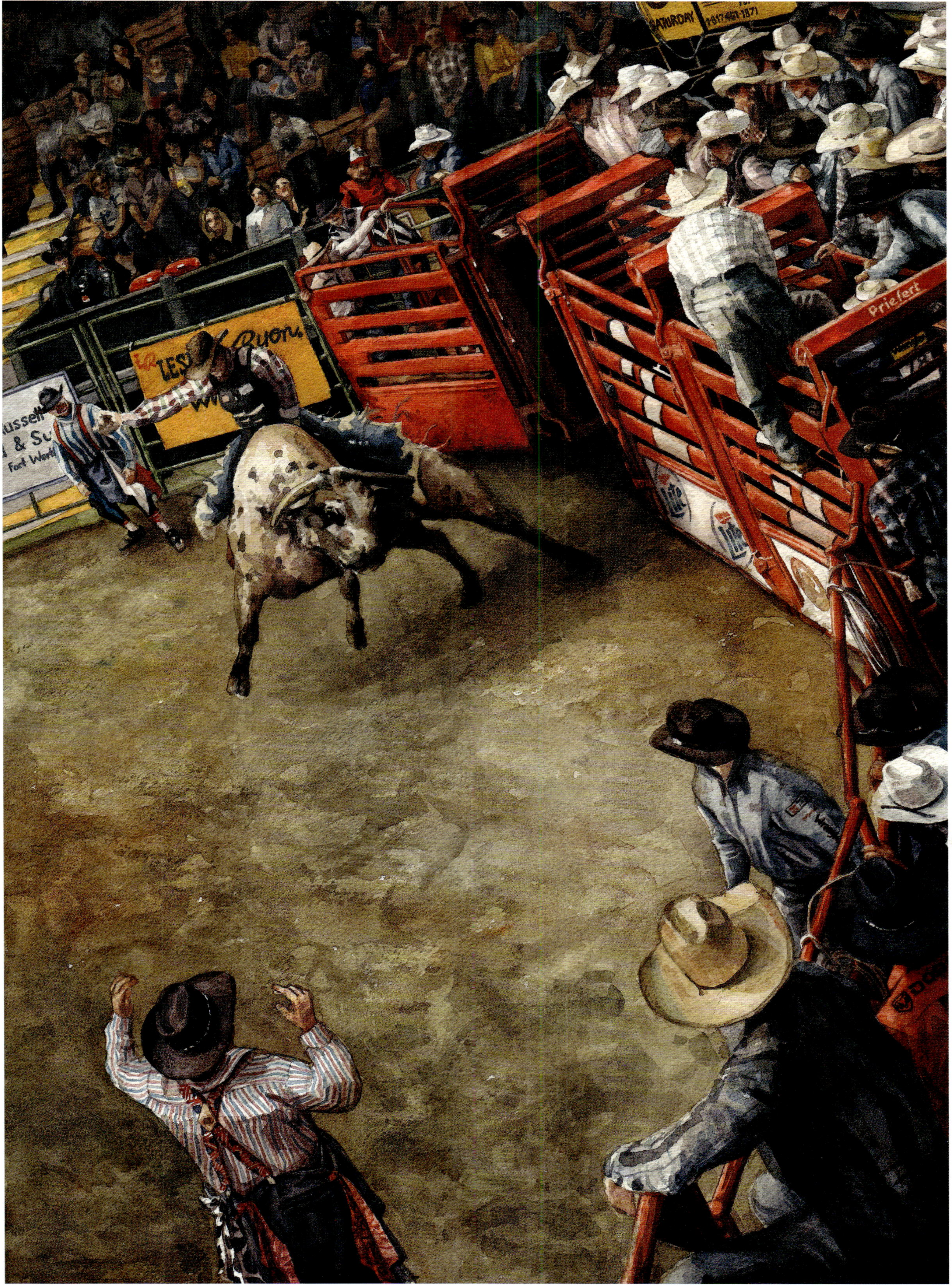
SATURDAY
Priefert
Lite

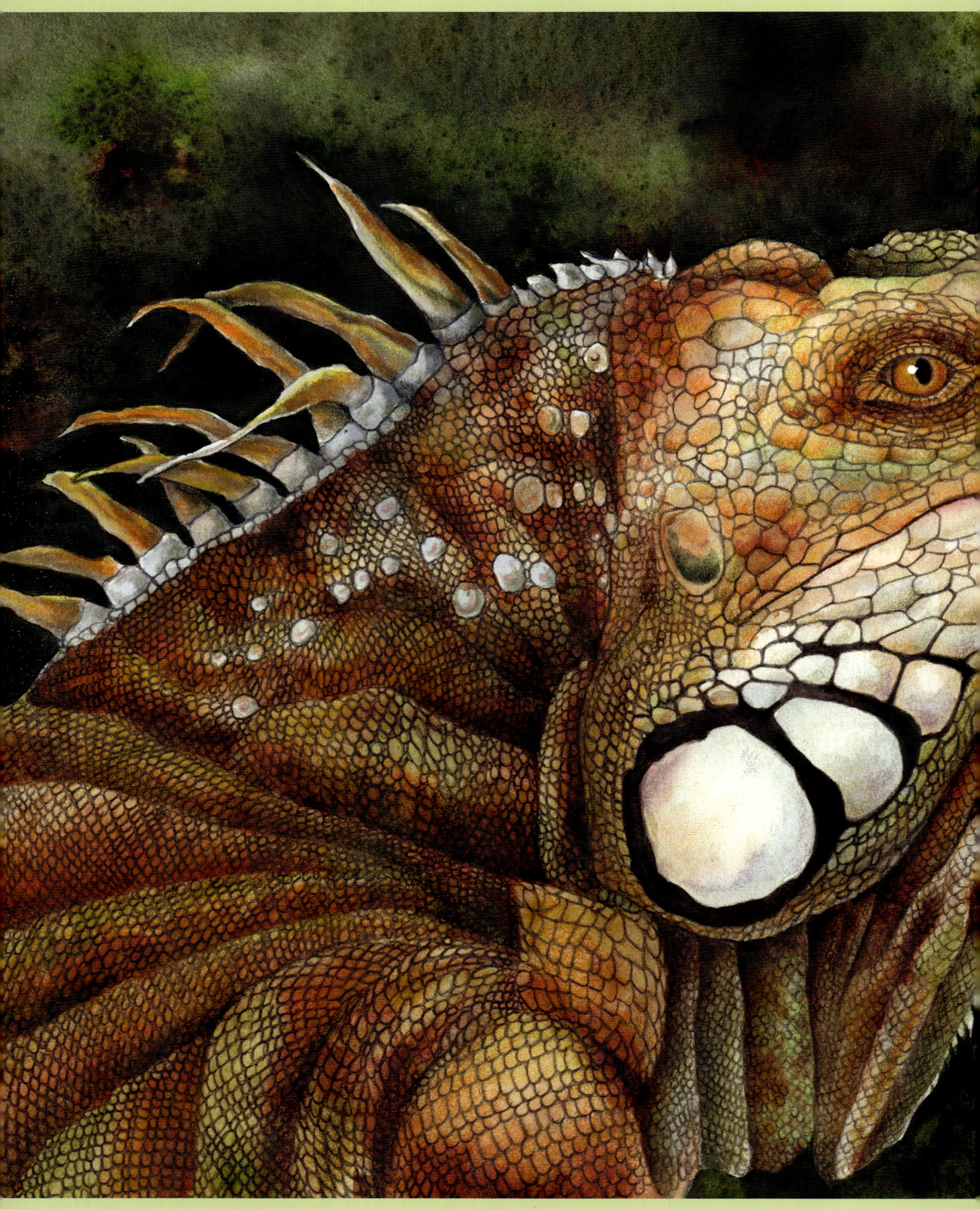

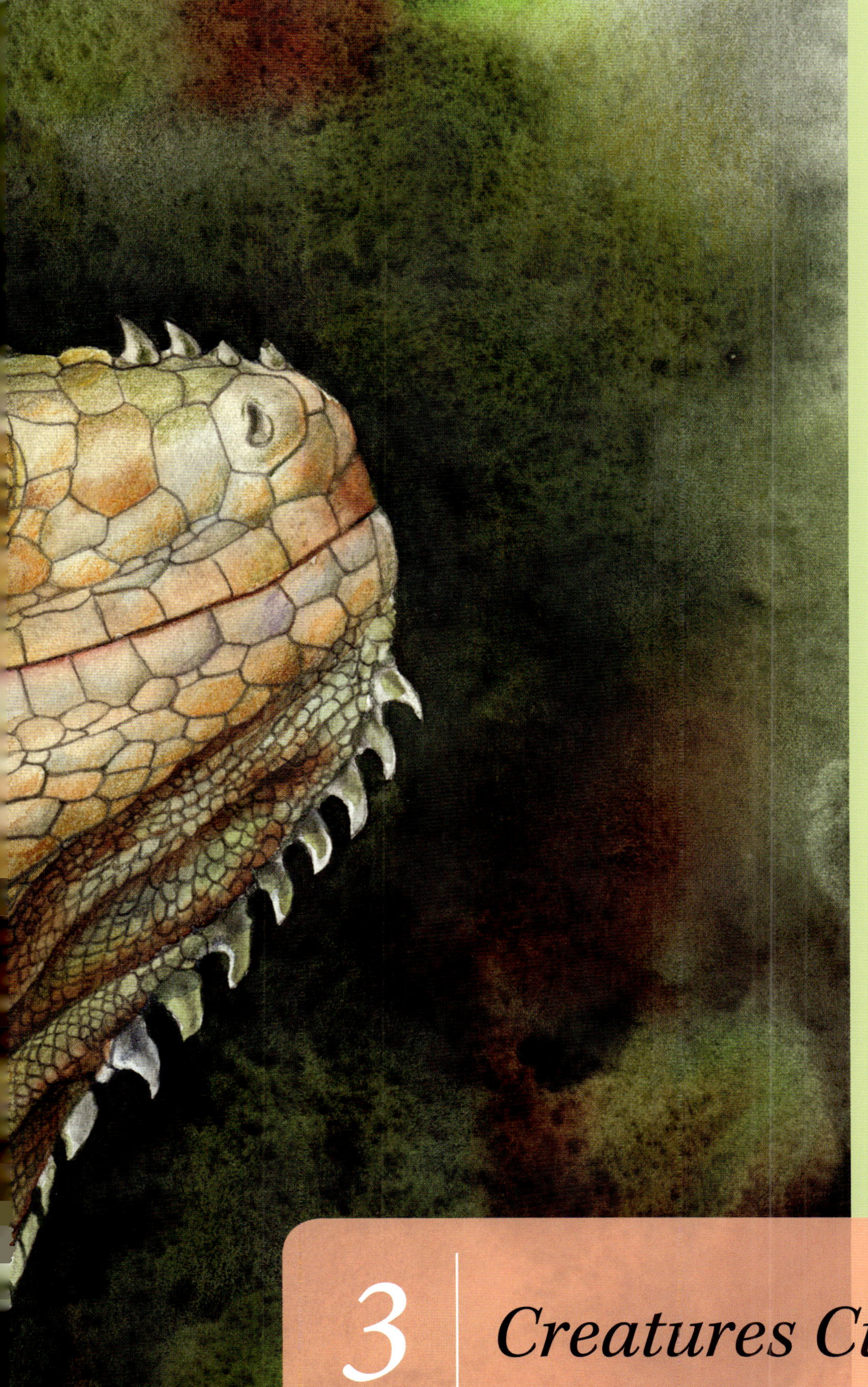

"When in doubt, do a small sample before you take the leap in order to avoid disappointments."

– MINDY LIGHTHIPE

◀ **SEÑOR IGUANA** | Mindy Lighthipe
9" × 12" (23cm × 30cm) Watercolor and Prismacolor colored pencils on 300-lb. (640gsm) hot-pressed Fabriano watercolor paper

I had a personal encounter of the reptilian kind when I adopted a rescue iguana and had him pose for me in my studio. I painstakingly captured the fine details of his scales in graphite on my watercolor paper. After doing a test with paint over graphite, I realized I was going to lose most of the detail. My solution was simple. With a black Prismacolor Verithin colored pencil, I redrew the detail. The wax resist from the colored pencil kept the detail intact while I painted with transparent watercolor.

3 | *Creatures Cute & Curious*

"Don't avoid grays; they enhance the other colors in your painting."

– GRACE F. HAVERTY

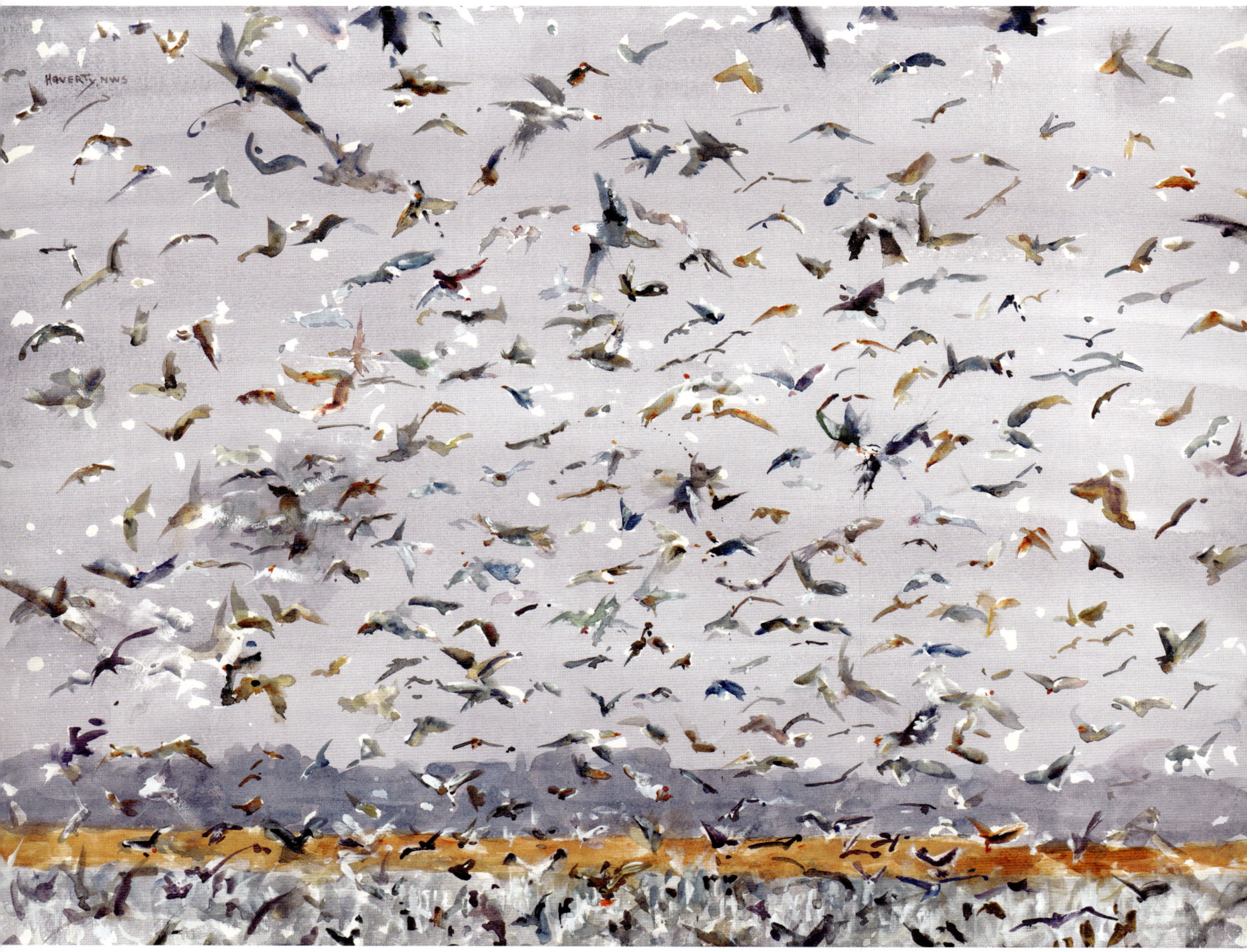

▲ **SNOW GEESE** | Grace F. Haverty
22" × 30" (56cm × 76cm) Watercolor on 140-lb. (300gsm) cold-pressed Arches

How to depict thousands of birds in flight! I was overwhelmed. My love for the subject ruled, and I decided that if I used masking fluid at random, I might be able to suggest movement, light and the glorious soaring of those geese. Over the dry fluid, I painted a gray sky, typical of North Dakota's winters, and then I brushed on suggestive strokes to imitate wings, feathers and motion. After I completed *Snow Geese*, I could almost hear the flapping of wings as the geese flew away from the winter toward the south through the icy gray sky.

▶ **KOI POND – YELLOW LEAVES** | Soon Y. Warren
22" × 15" (56cm × 38cm) Transparent watercolor on 300-lb. (640gsm) cold-pressed paper

Choosing subject matter is the first part of my creative process. Nature provides endless inspiration with versatile settings—from dawn to dusk and rainy days to foggy ones or sunny days across all four seasons. Observing this koi pond, I was concerned that painting flawless reflections in the water (my interest in this painting) would be difficult. However, studying the light value of the water and the shapes of the reflections made the process seem simple—almost effortless. I layered several washes to complete the water. Then I started to create the details of the reflections by adding clean curved lines.

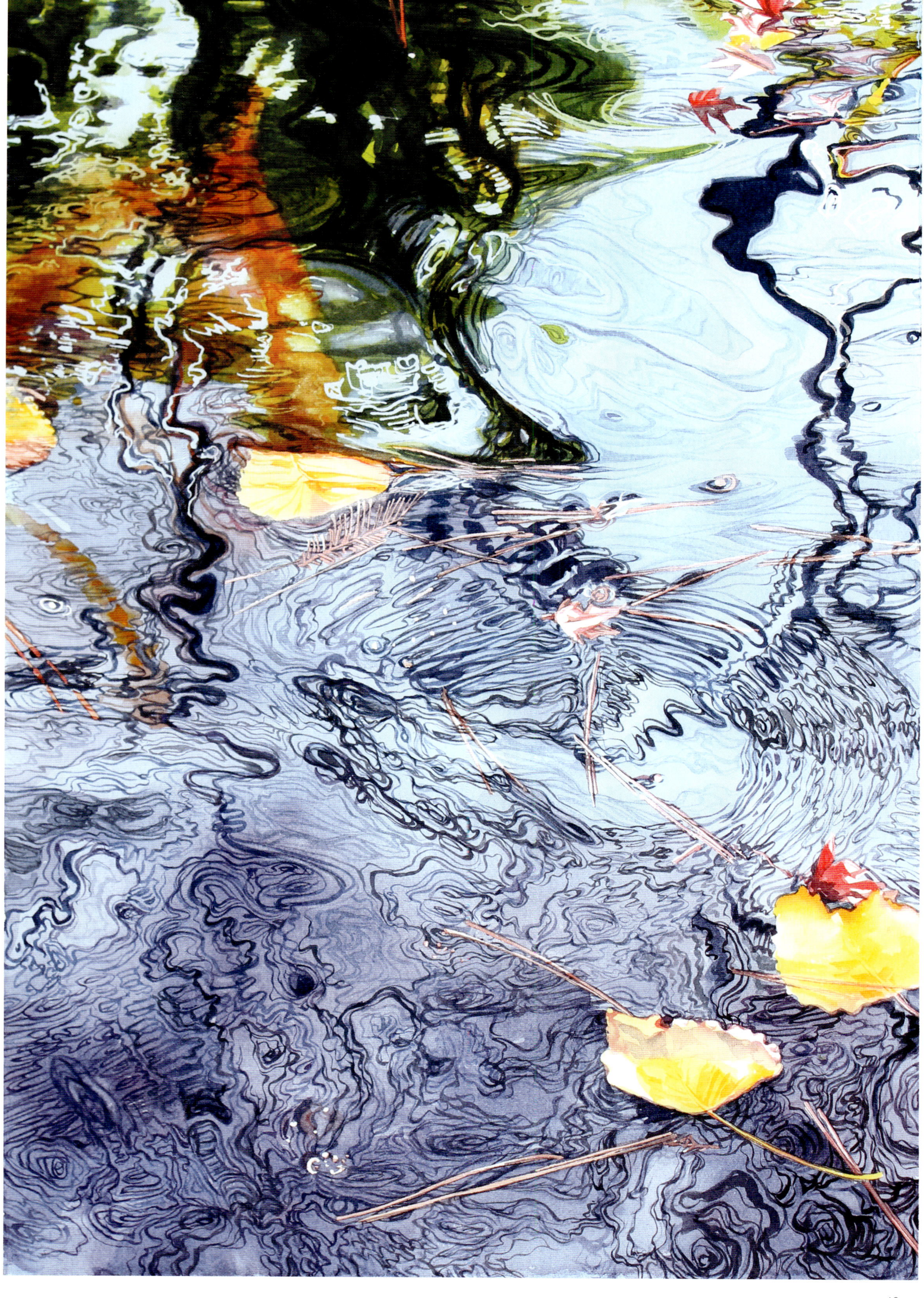

▼ **LEAVING AGAIN?** | Robin Sevester Avery
17" × 23" (43cm × 58cm) Transparent watercolor and acrylic on hot-pressed Fabriano Artistico

This is my Labradoodle, Sophie. I had to solve the problem: How do I create an exciting painting from a cream- and neutral-hued subject? OK! I will be like the Fauvist and use bright colors. For this painting I wanted to play warm against cool. I chose purples, blues and magenta against white, yellows and golds. Some whites of the paper were saved, but I also mixed up acrylic white in a ketchup squirt bottle and painted the furry curls with the tip. This gave a different dimension to the texture. Sophie not only feels blue when I leave but *is* blue—in my painting!

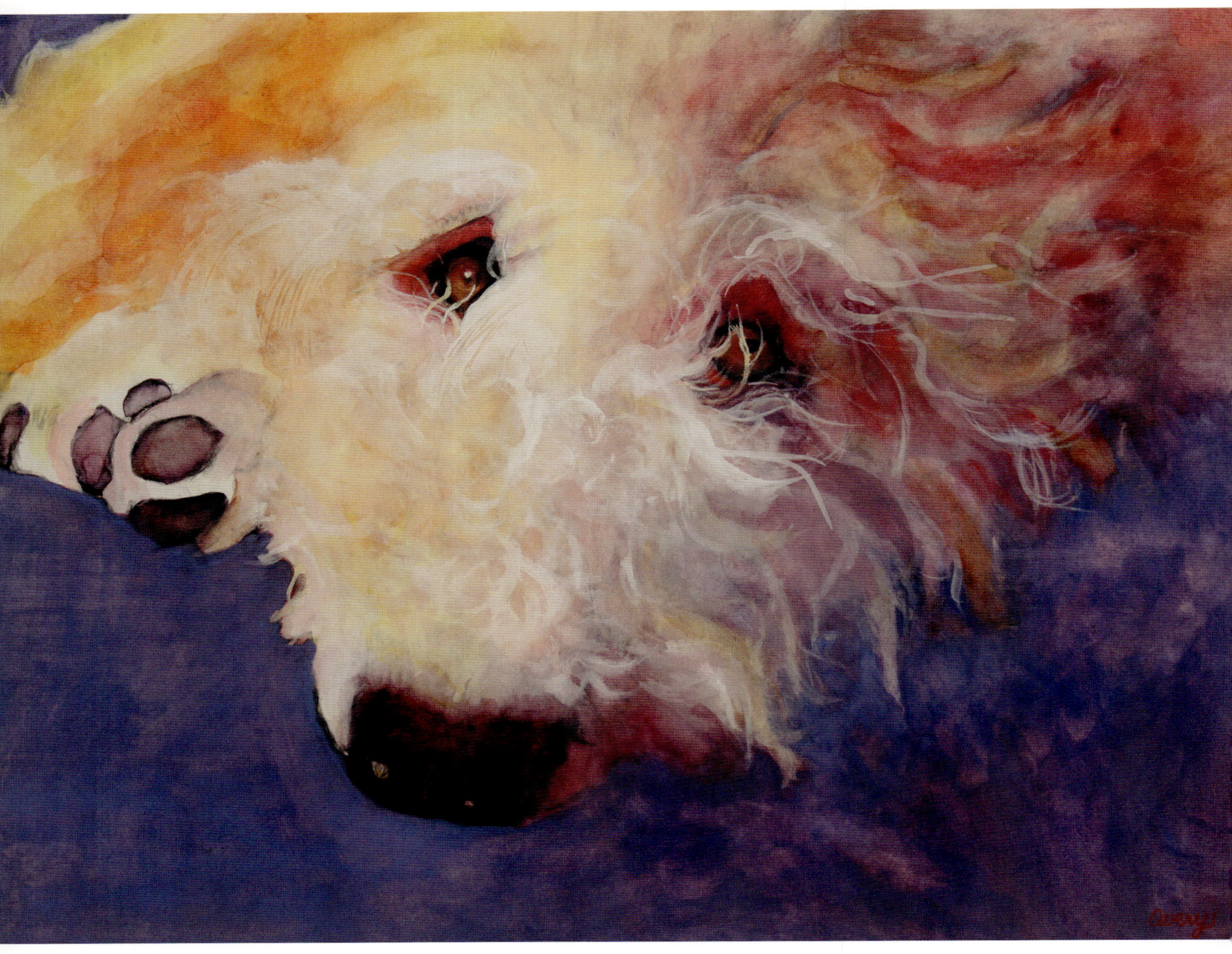

▶ **YAWNING** | Yael Maimon
58" × 44" (147cm × 112cm) Transparent watercolor on 140-lb. (300gsm) Fabriano Artistico

For *Yawning* I used two of my reference photos for composition and general direction. Painting the wide-open jaw was the greatest challenge. I worked and worked on that jaw and wasn't happy with the result. It just didn't look natural. I realized that some serious risks must be taken. I decided to destroy and rebuild. I also got bolder with my blues and reds. I played with the colors, creating overlapping warms and cools. Finally I got the effect I was after—capturing my subject's spirit, not only its appearance.

"When your painting isn't working, give yourself permission to destroy and rebuild." – YAEL MAIMON

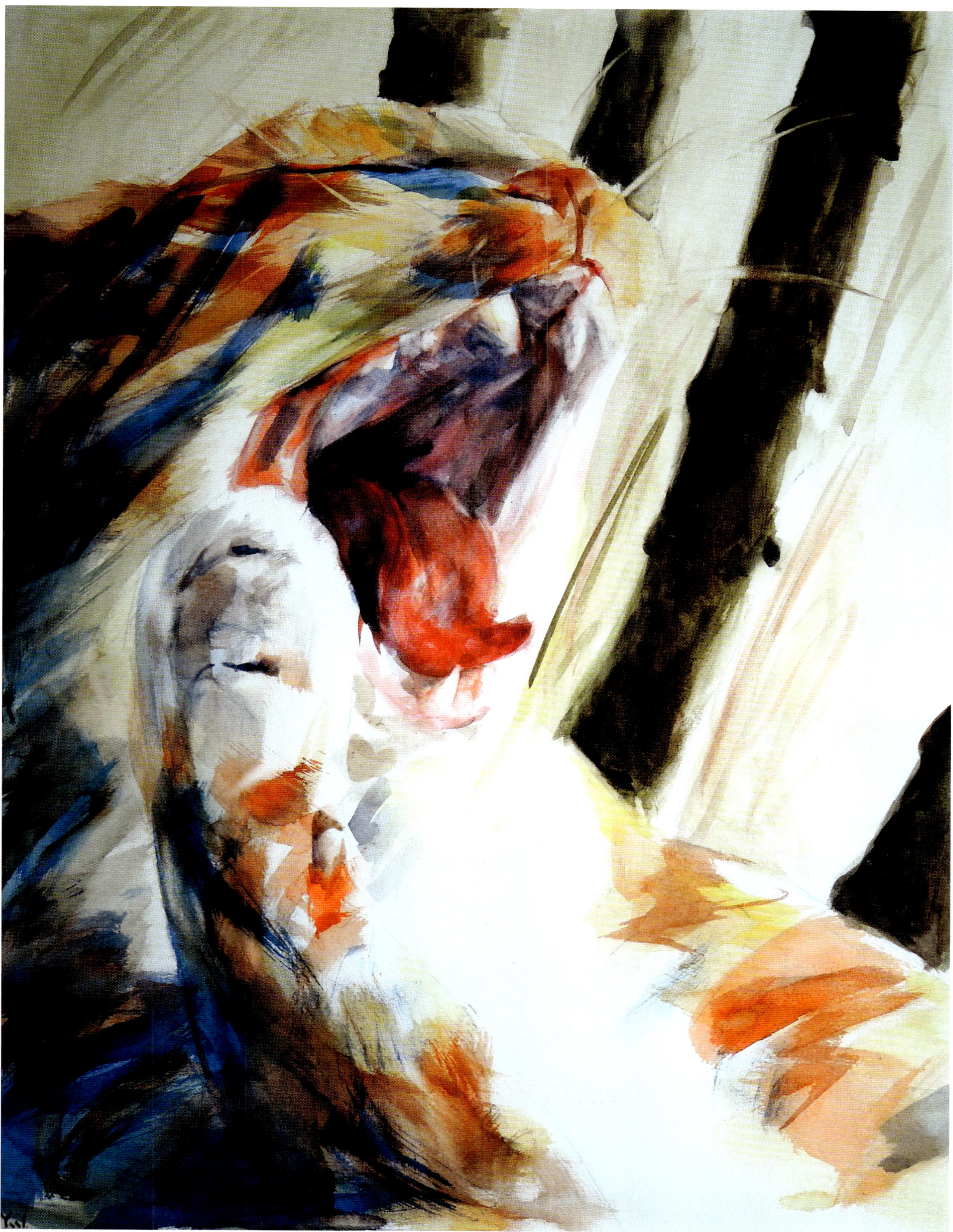

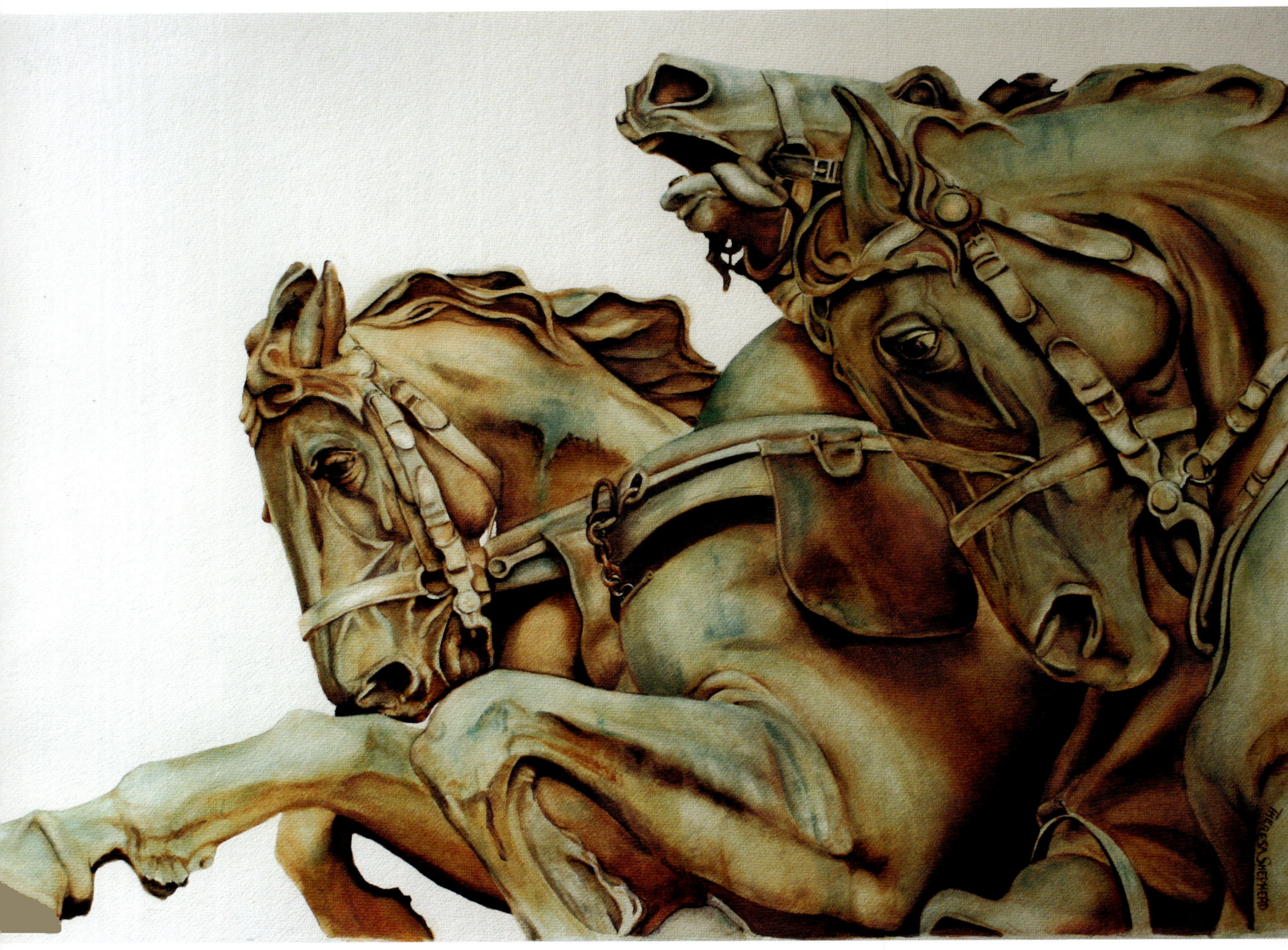

▲ **UNFURLED DEVOTION** | Theresa T. Shepherd
21" × 30" (53cm × 76cm) Transparent watercolor on 300-lb. (640gsm) cold-pressed Arches

On a visit to Washington, D.C., I was captured by the statues near the Capitol building. The fallen horses and riders in these statues created a stirring scene. I had to paint the overwhelming feeling of devotion I saw in these horses' images. I sat down on the step and drew contour drawings against the bright summer sky. I also took photos so I could finish my drawing in my studio to begin this painting. To save the whites, my creative solution was in the application of the masking fluid to the background. A white background gives the subject matter the intense focus I wanted. I painted the entire painting in Raw Umber. I gradually went from light to dark values and finished with a patina color.

▶ **HEY GORGEOUS** | Darlene Kaplan
38" × 30" (97cm × 76cm) Chinese watercolors on rice paper

Painting with Chinese watercolors can be a real challenge when painting something as colorful as a peacock. The mineral colors soak into the rice paper, producing a soft look. For the stronger colors I needed, my solution was to add purple to the Indigo Blue on the tail feathers and stone green over the blue on the back of the peacock. I wanted to keep the tail expressive without making it too dense. The original sketch was done from life in the Florida Everglades. Oriental art is all about beautiful brushstrokes and showing the energy (chi) in the painting. It is also about what you don't see so that the mind will fill in the blanks.

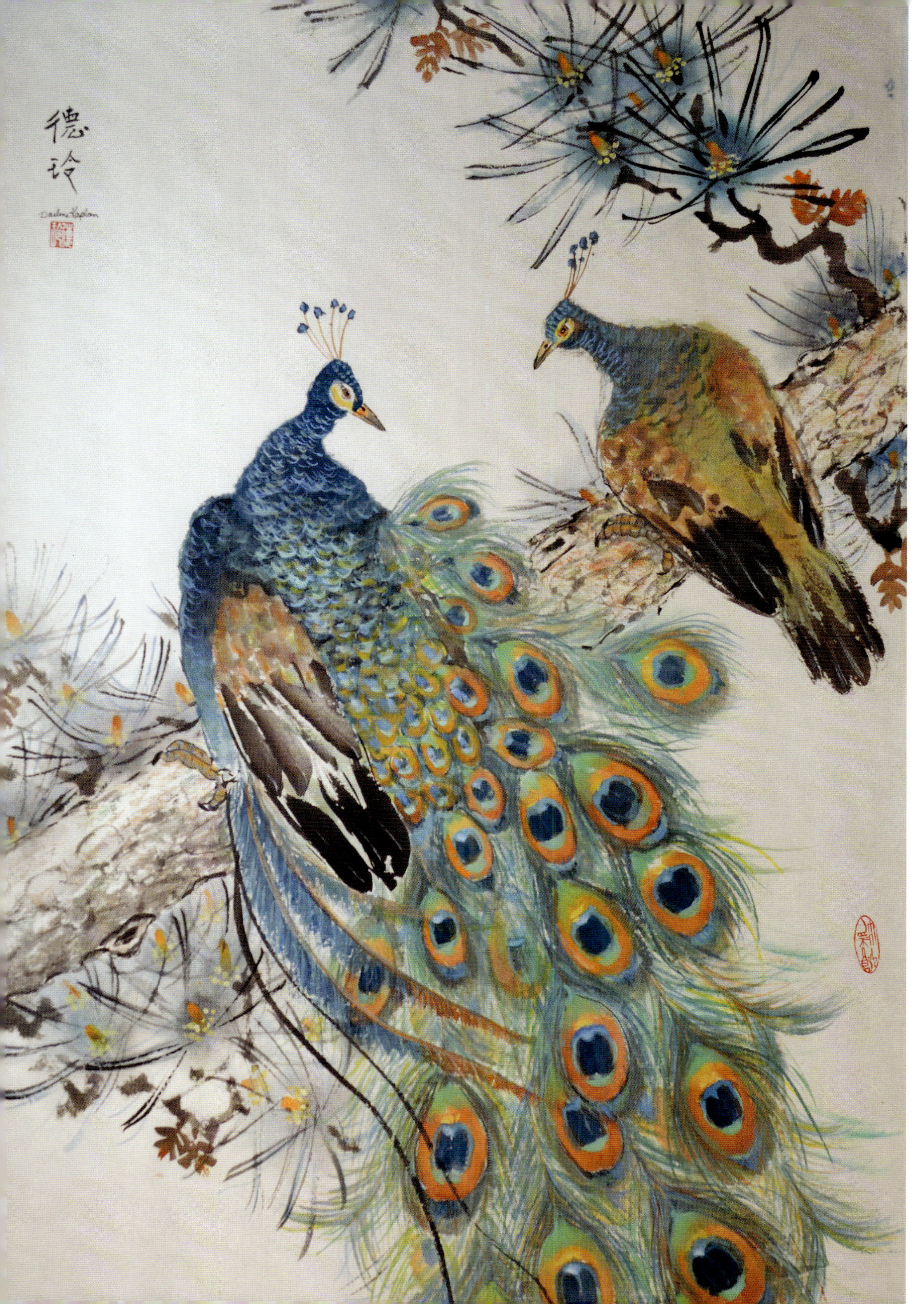
德玲
Darlene Kaplan

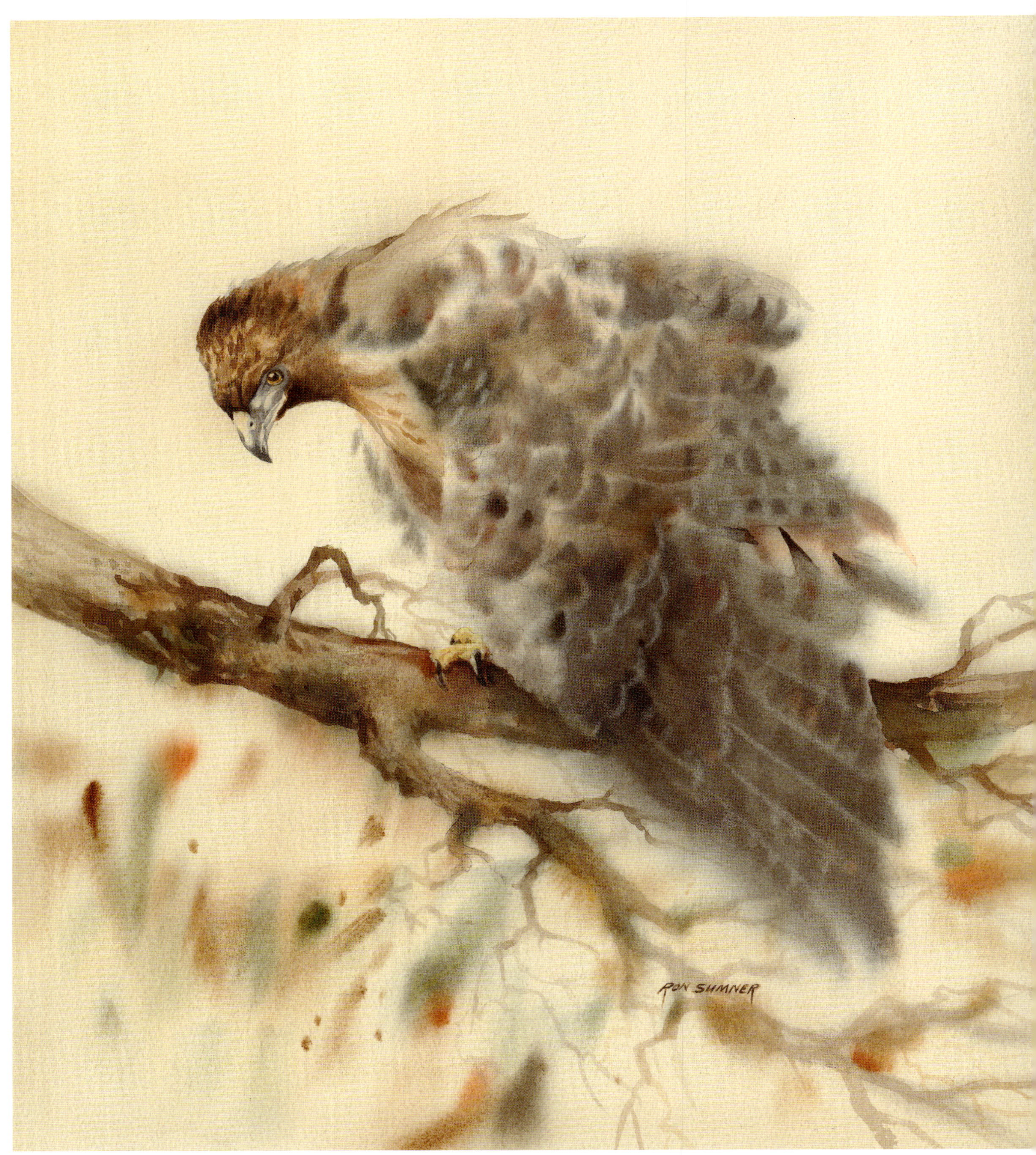

"With watercolor, the light should penetrate the pigment and then bounce back off the paper to your eye."

– RON SUMNER

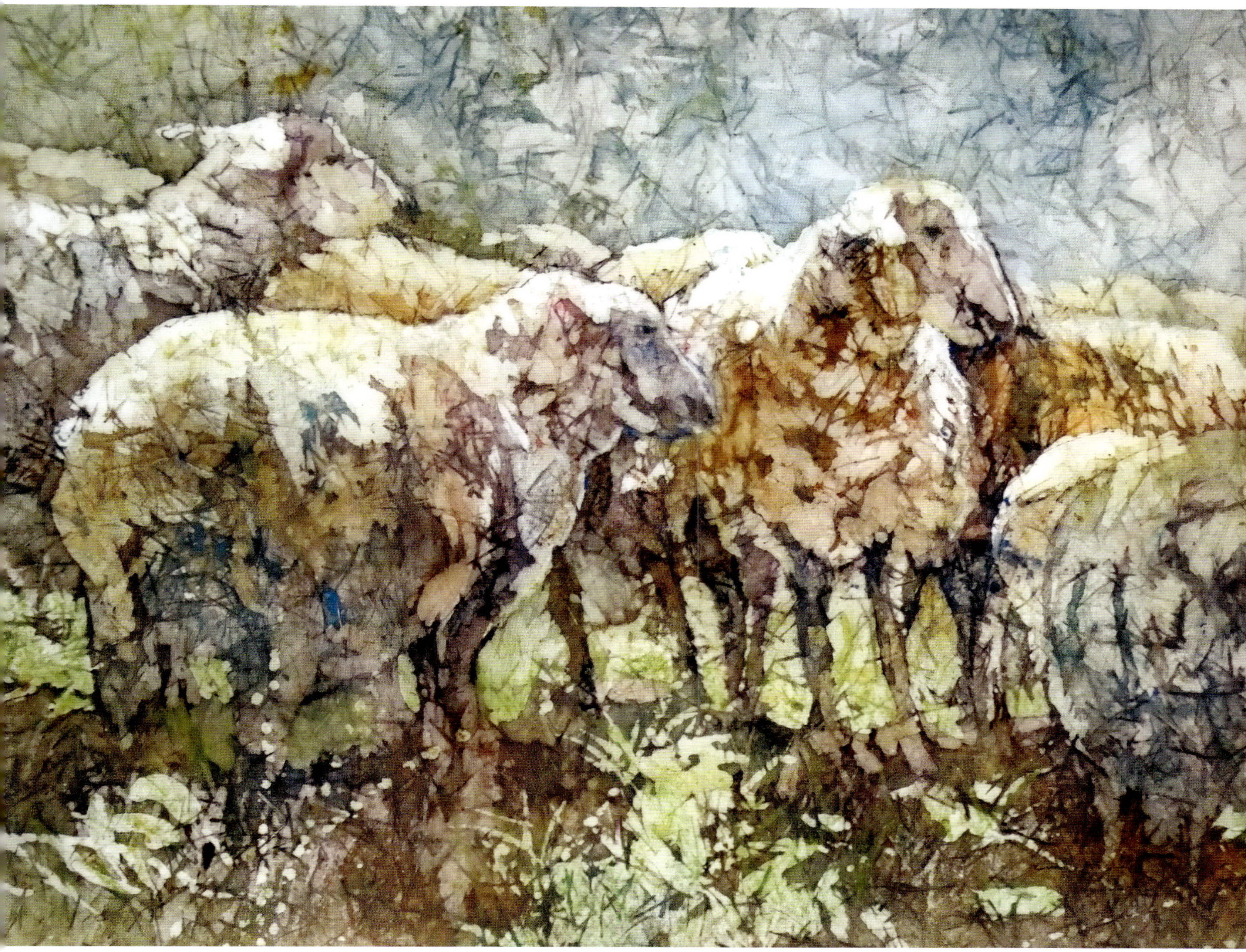

◀ RED-TAILED HAWK | Ron Sumner
18" × 14½" (46cm × 37cm) Transparent watercolor on 140-lb. (300gsm) rough Arches

I often see this rich brown, rounded-wing, short-tailed bird soaring in a circle above the grassy field behind my house. With the red-tailed hawk, the greatest challenge was the painting of the plumage. The feathers must have a feeling of softness but still keep an orderly pattern. I decided wet-into-wet was ideal for this purpose. Shapes of color of different values were added while the paper was still wet. Just before the paint dried completely, I took a small, pointed dry brush and picked up paint, giving the appearance of structural ribs within the feathers. I always keep my painting as transparent as possible, putting shapes of color down and leaving them alone.

▲ LUNCH WITH THE GIRLS | Kathie George
14" × 16" (36xcm × 41cm) Watercolor batik on rice paper

Sometimes photos don't give you all of the info you need. How do you paint several objects that all look alike? During my painting process, I layered melted paraffin wax (a resist) and watercolor washes onto rice paper. I decided to wax out some whites across the backs of the sheep. I then considered one or two of the subsequent color washes to be basic and floated them across most of the sheep. This unified the piece, but they still looked the same. At that point I saved some of the dried basic color with wax, then washed each sheep individually with different colors—those in front, brighter and more intense, and in back the color was grayed. Finally, just a touch of white pastel pencil to intensify the whites. Voilà! Not baaaaad.

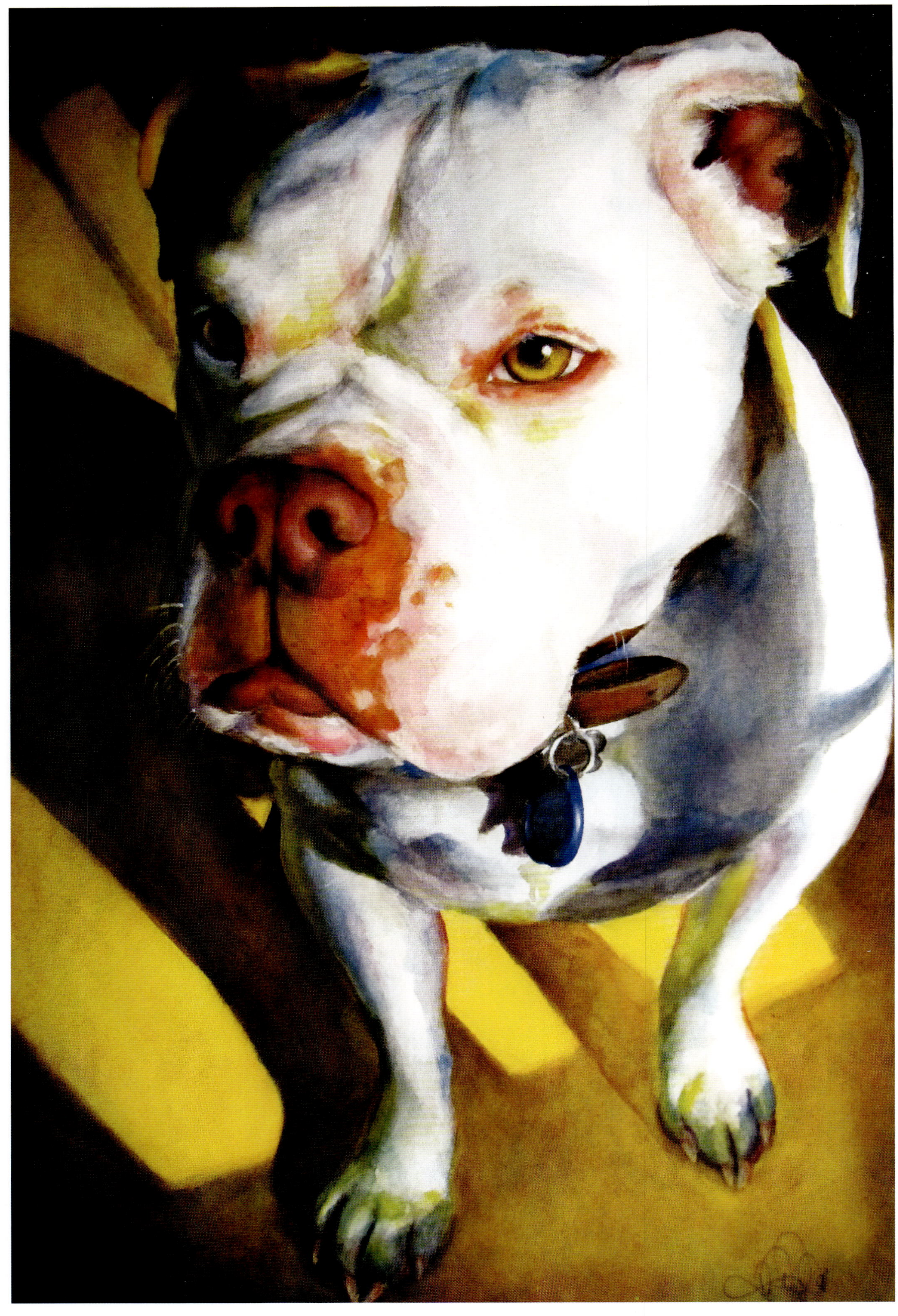

"Painters crave inspiration because their aim is to portray a phenomenon, tell a story, convey a feeling or evoke an emotion."

– DOUGLAS F. GREER

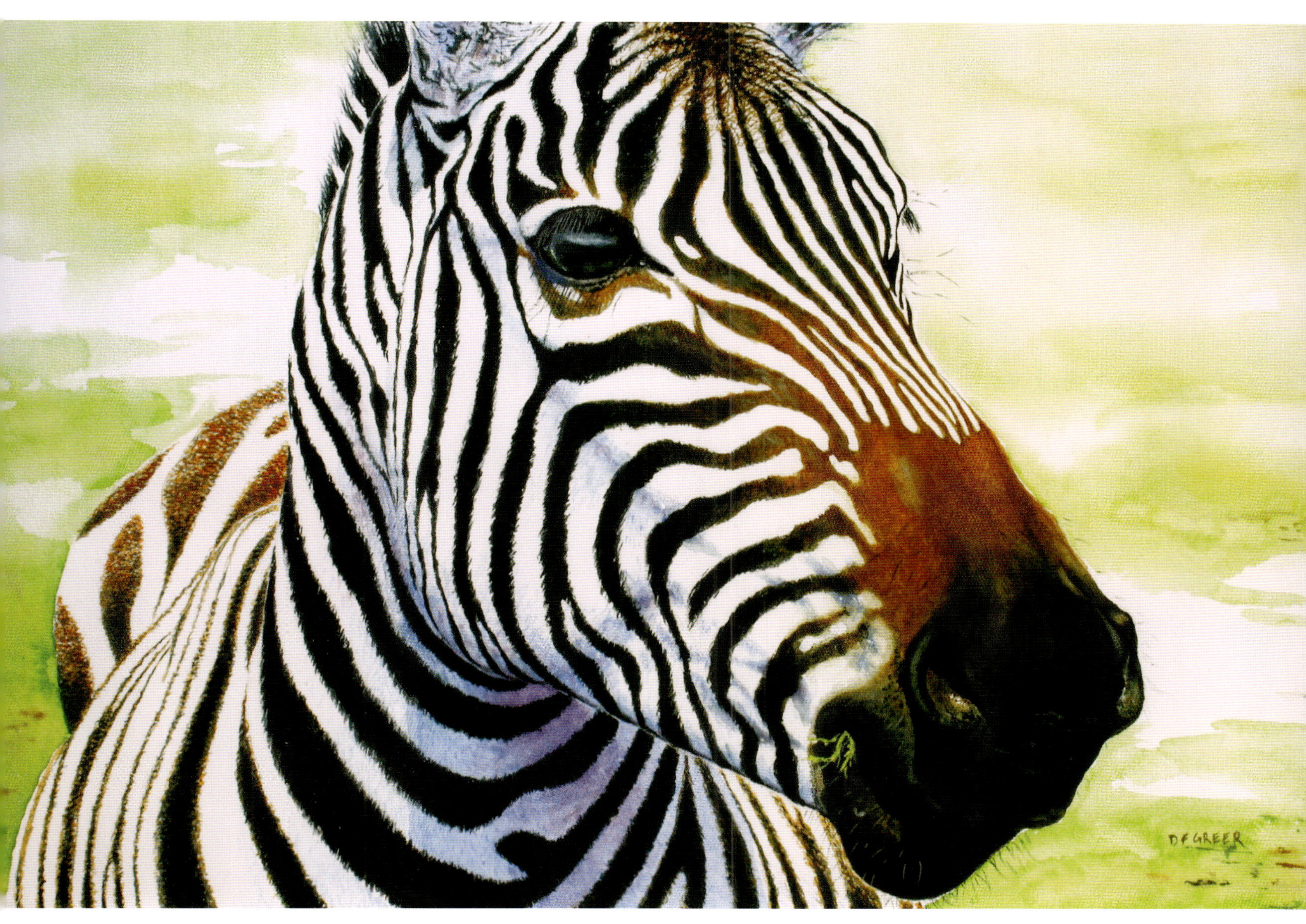

◄ BREWTUS | Jennifer C. Griffith
20" × 16" (51xcm × 41cm) Watercolor on 300-lb. (640gsm) cold-pressed Arches

When I began painting *Brewtus*, I started with a more traditional and natural color palette, laying down my mid values first. As the painting progressed, Brewtus's playful spirit was lost, and overall the painting was dusty and a bit lifeless. I became frustrated at my inability to give him weight yet keep him lighthearted. To bring his personality out I tried several very light washes of saturated yellow for both the light and reflected light surrounding Brewtus, and saturated blue for the form shadows. The result really brought him to life, the colors helping to capture his sweetness and loyalty.

▲ SERENGETI GRASS | Douglas F. Greer
18" × 27" (46cm × 69cm) Watercolor on 300-lb. (640gsm) cold-pressed Arches

It is not enough merely to reproduce an object or scene in a painting. I like to express that which inspires me. *Serengeti Grass* was never intended to be just a painting of a zebra. While visiting the Serengeti Plain in Tanzania I was taken by the splendor of the animals and the countless dramas of their lives, all dependent on this lowly vegetation: grass. This painting attempts to convey my amazement that grass routinely becomes transformed into incredible beasts. I came in close, cropping out even the zebra's ears, to draw attention to the small sprig of grass disappearing into the zebra's mouth. From that tiny bit of green, dark stripes and curves spiral outward to create a pattern of beauty and power.

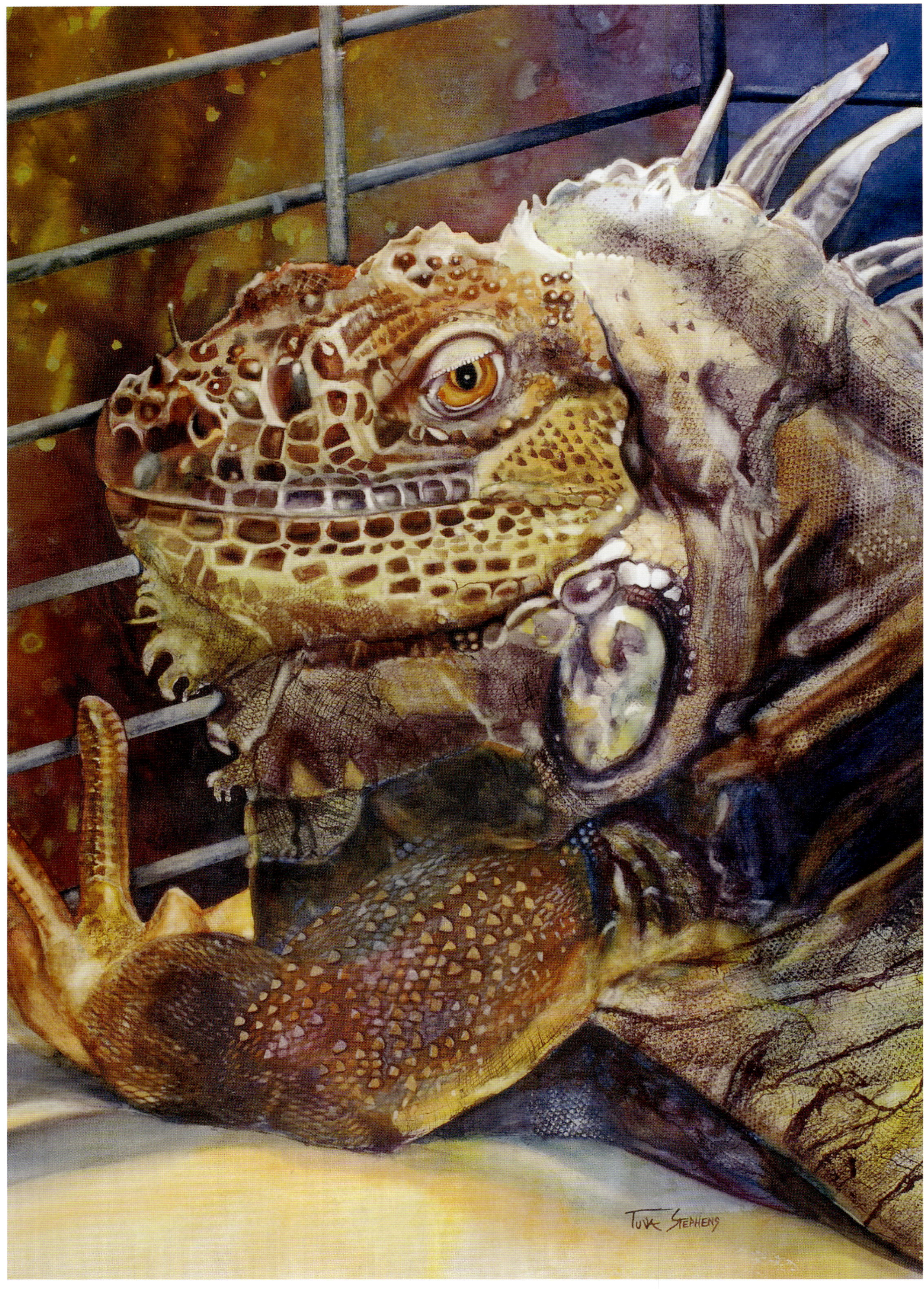

"Painting over the top of an already ruined watercolor painting eliminates the fear of making a mistake or ruining the painting, turning the watercolor process into a fun and artistic experiment."

– JANI FREIMANN

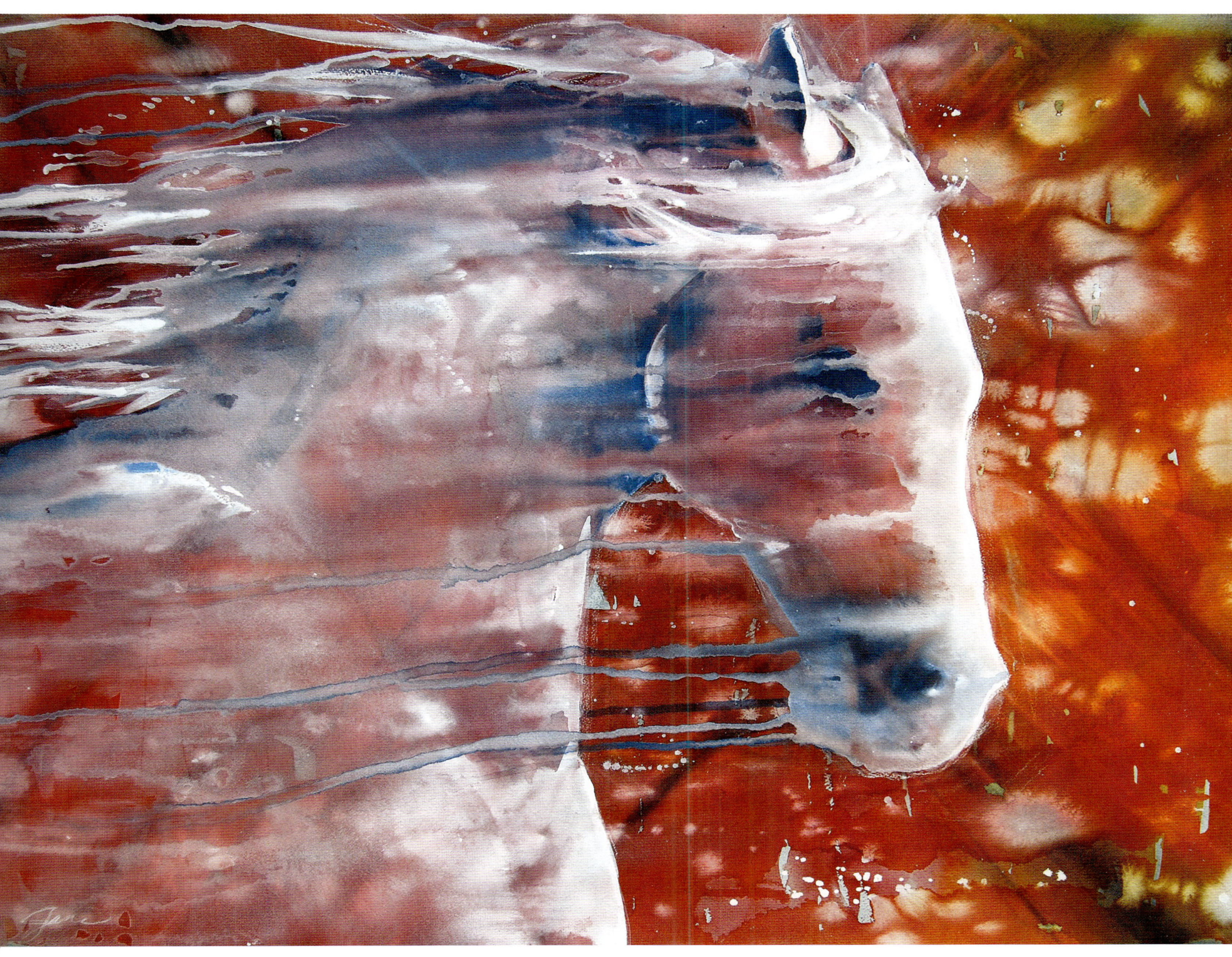

◀ **TIGGY!** | Tuva Page Stephens
28" × 19" (71cm × 48cm) Watercolor with gouache accents on 140-lb. (300gsm) cold-pressed Fabriano Artistico

The iguana's intriguing surface textures challenged me to find materials to lift or stamp complex patterns. On the upper arm area a plastic onion sack was stretched and a damp sponge was used to lift and reveal a dark pattern of lines underneath. A patterned fabric scrap was used to stamp both light and dark values. Gauze was soaked in a dark value, blotted then draped in the irregular patterned area on the throat. A metal drafting stencil was helpful in lifting details especially on the head area. Almost effortless!

▲ **PAINTED BY THE WIND** | Jani Freimann
22" × 30" (56cm × 76cm) Layered watercolor and gouache on 140-lb. (300gsm) cold-pressed Arches

This painting was originally an urban street scene from a bird's-eye view that didn't turn out well. Being someone who has a hard time throwing anything away, I recycled it by painting over the top of the ruined background with Cadmium Red and Yellow and Permanent White. You can still see remnants of the crosswalks and street corners through the red background. The white horse was painted with white gouache and Cobalt Blue. The other colors in the horse are a result of the background lifting and mixing with the white and blue. To get the windy effect, I painted the white and blue layer upon layer, letting each layer dry before another application, and stood the paper on its end after each layer to let the paint run.

"For me, half the fun and challenge of painting is exploring to find the just right object that says, *paint me*."

– TRICIA H. LOVE

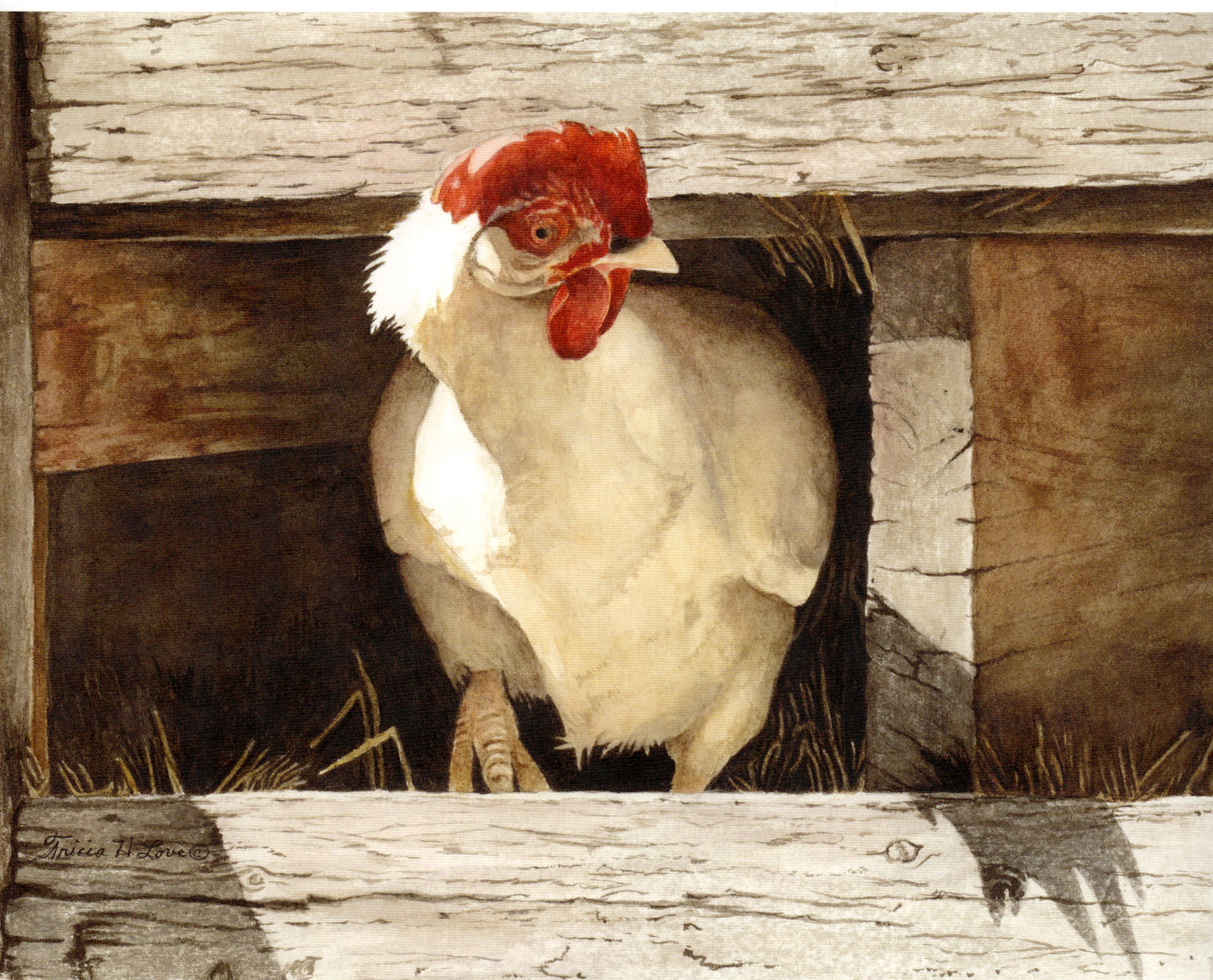

THE CHICKEN COOP | Tricia H. Love
9½" × 12" (24cm × 30cm) Transparent watercolor on 140-lb. (300gsm) cold-pressed Arches

Using a photo from one of my photo adventures, I painted *The Chicken Coop* in my studio. Being a painter who likes detail, I wanted to capture the weathered look of the wood. After painting the coop with a thin wash and letting it dry, I rubbed a piece of fine sandpaper lightly over the area. The sandpaper removed enough of the paint to make the wood look weathered. I added additional layers of paint, leaving some of the sanded areas untouched. Then I painted the chicken and added additional details.

GUESS WHO CAME TO DINNER | Claudia Rutherford

11½" × 14½" (29cm × 37cm) Watercolor on 300-lb. (640gsm) hot-pressed Arches

This roving band of domesticated white ducks was created in my studio working from a photographic image. I boldly painted the ducks on dry hot-pressed paper using a magnifying glass, teeny-tiny liner brushes, and transparent paint mixed with newfound patience. The trampled snowy background was added next, wet-into-wet. My enthusiasm for color and quest for detail had by this time darkened and over-defined the ducks. After proven methods of removing pigment failed, I lightly blotted the ducks with a damp Mr. Clean Magic Eraser sponge. Depth now restored, the white ducks radiate as an unknown free-spirited duck joins them in their meal.

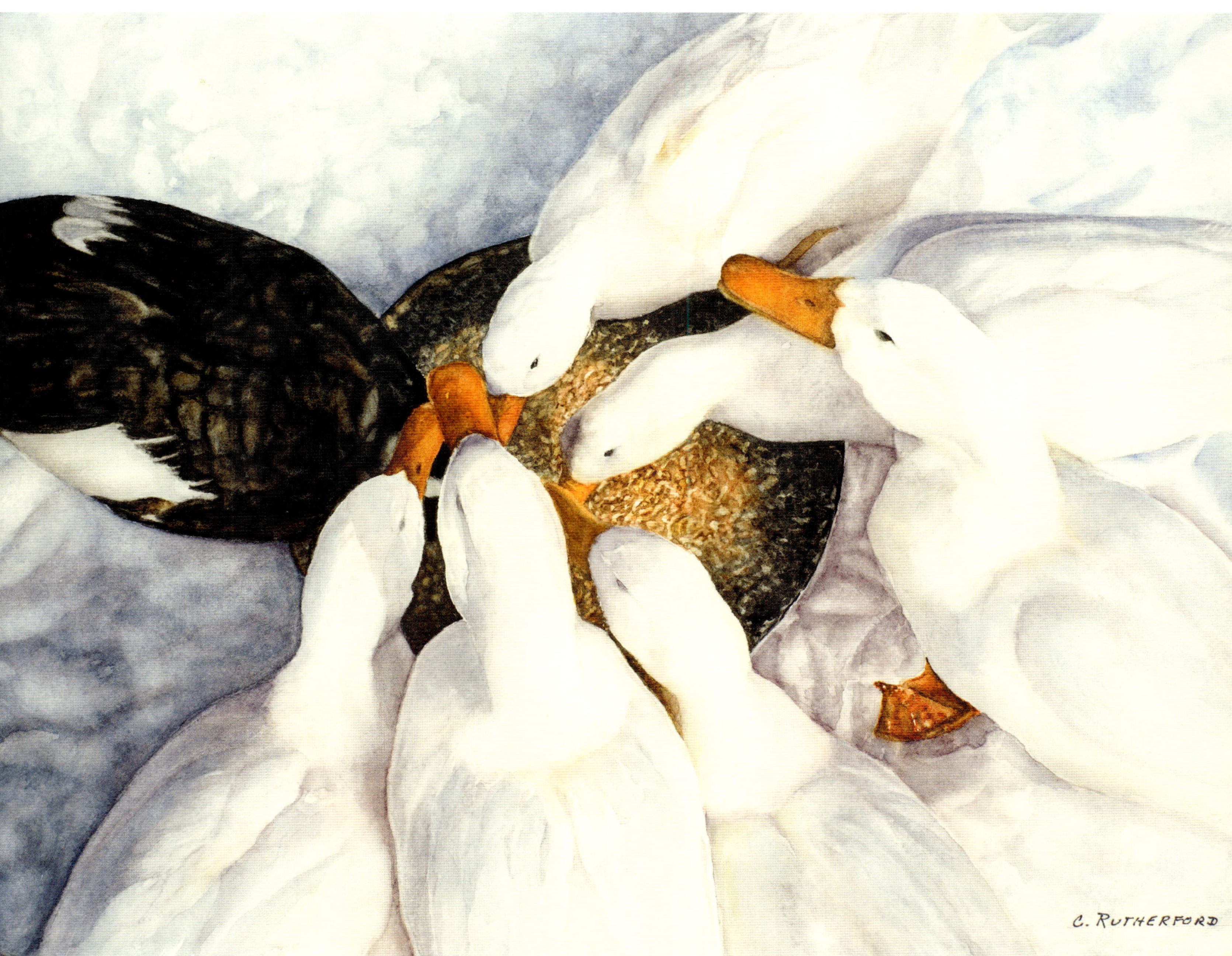

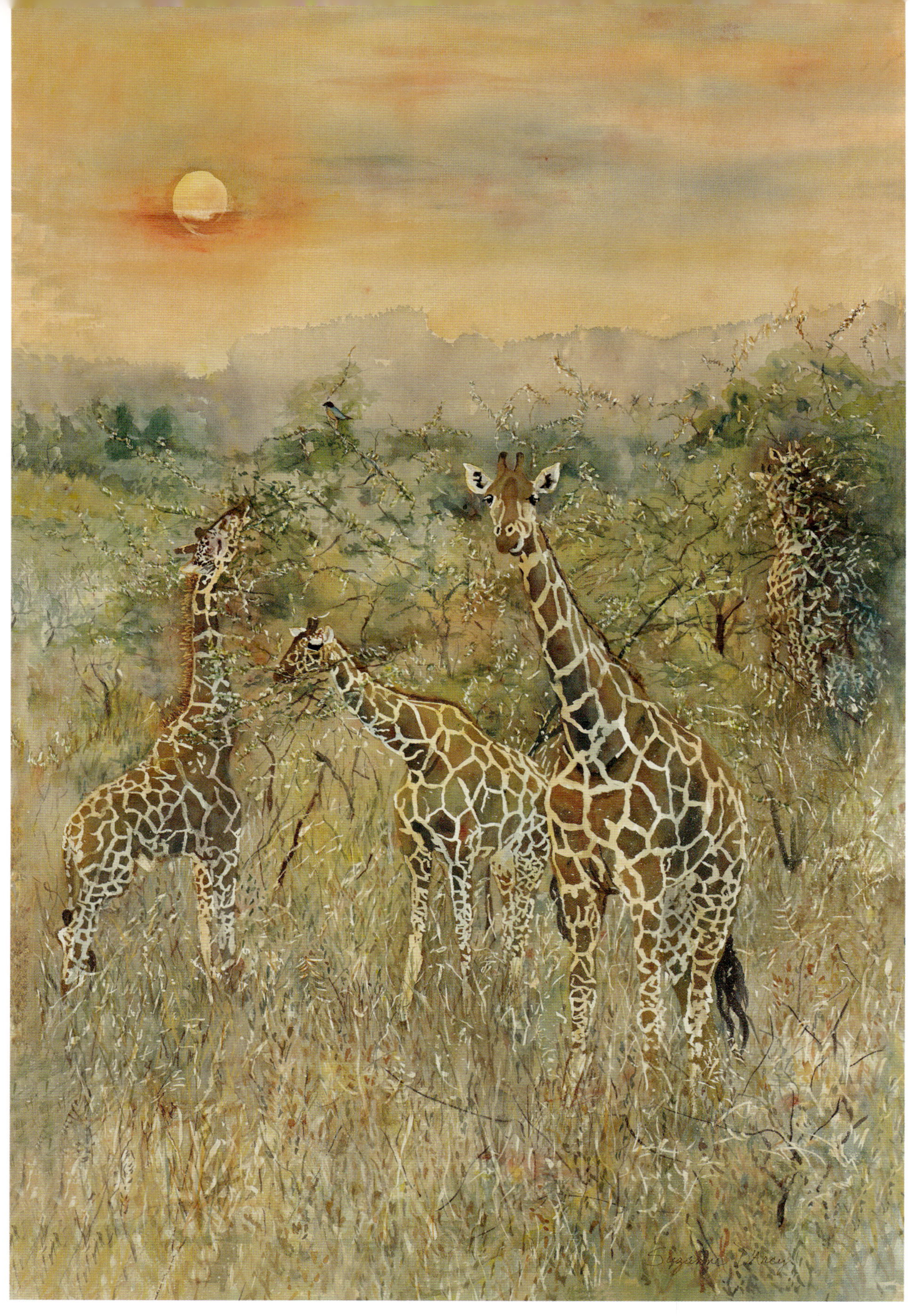

▲ **GIRAFFES** | Suzanne K. D'Arcy
40" × 26" (102cm × 66cm) Transparent watercolor with gouache on 260-lb. (550gsm) Arches

The painting was done from a combination of photos that I took on a trip to Africa. Only three colors were used: M. Graham's Prussian Blue, Hansa Yellow Deep and Pyrrol Red. Gouache was used at the bottom of the painting to create a feeling of thick underbrush. Initially the white areas were masked out to allow the freedom of being able to pour and splash the colors on the wet paper. This creates a sense of atmosphere. I always paint the background first and then the figures. If the background works, then I know the painting will work.

"If something is not working, it's usually because there's not enough water. If I can control the water, I can control the color." – MICHAEL FERRIS

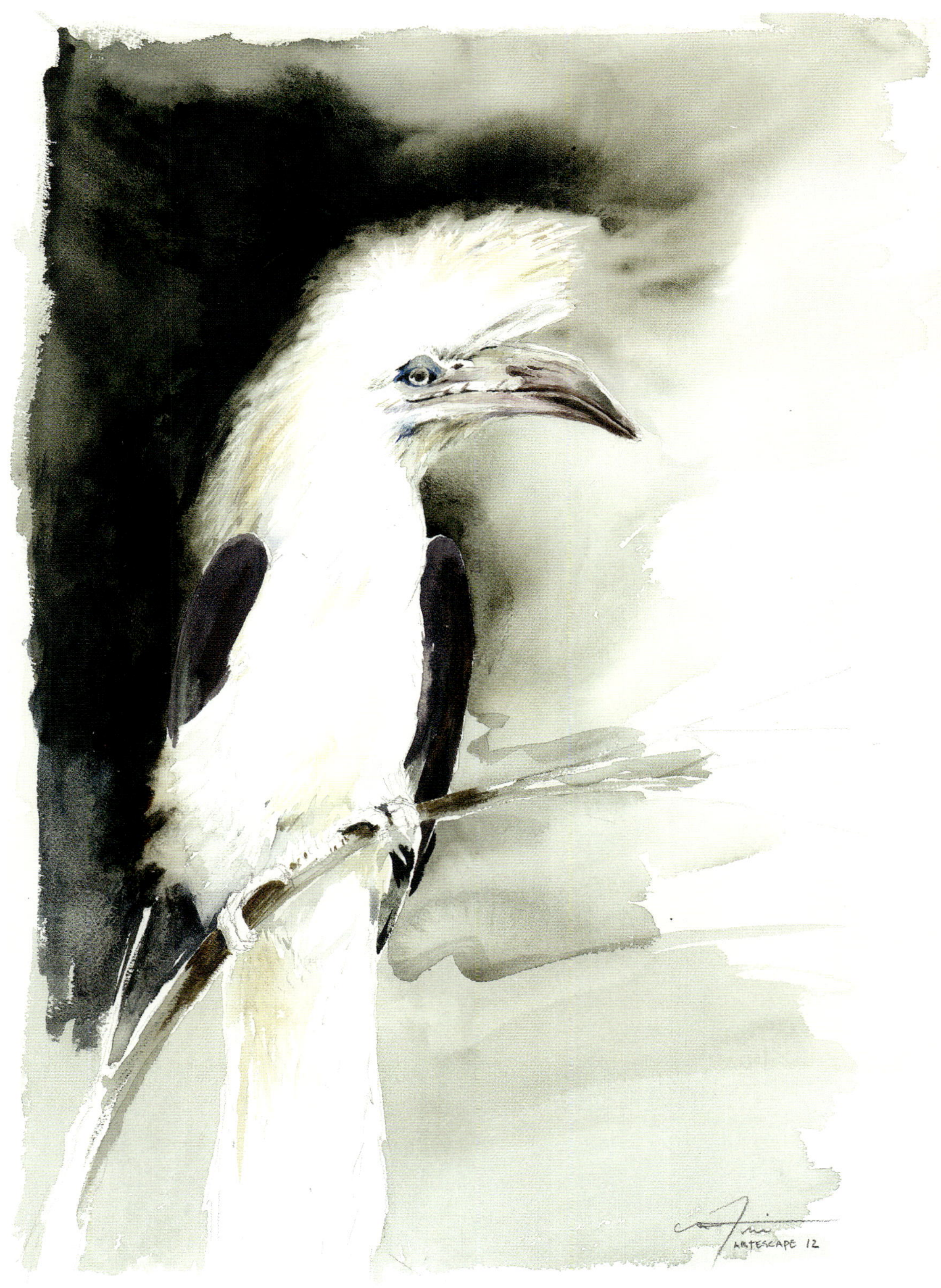

▲ **HORNBILL** | Michael Ferris
20" × 16" (51cm × 41cm) Transparent watercolor and pencil on 300-lb. (640gsm) cold-pressed Arches

This painting was done as a demonstration painting using several photographs. I started with a loose pencil outline, giving special attention to the eye and the bill. I used lots of water around the fuzzy parts of the neck and head, and let a surrounding mix (Indigo and Burnt Umber) bleed into the water. Once dry, I repeated this technique a little farther away from the body of the bird. The hornbill's character is conveyed in its eye and bill, and this required some controlled blending and the introduction of very subtle uses of Cerulean and Alizarin. The lines are sharp in contrast with the fuzzy feathers.

JOURNEY | Jennifer C. Griffith
20" × 16" (51cm × 41cm) Watercolor on 300-lb. (640gsm) cold-pressed Arches

I had several different photographic references of *Journey* to work from, but none seemed to stand out and show how beautiful this greyhound is. In all the sketches I drew she seemed to become lost in the composition, so I played around with cropping. I tried a few different designs and loved how this one really brought focus to her poised attentiveness. Even though I kept the background simple, *Journey* still seemed lacking. Two green-based quick-drying salt washes across the whole background really made the warm colors on her face stand out and her collar pop.

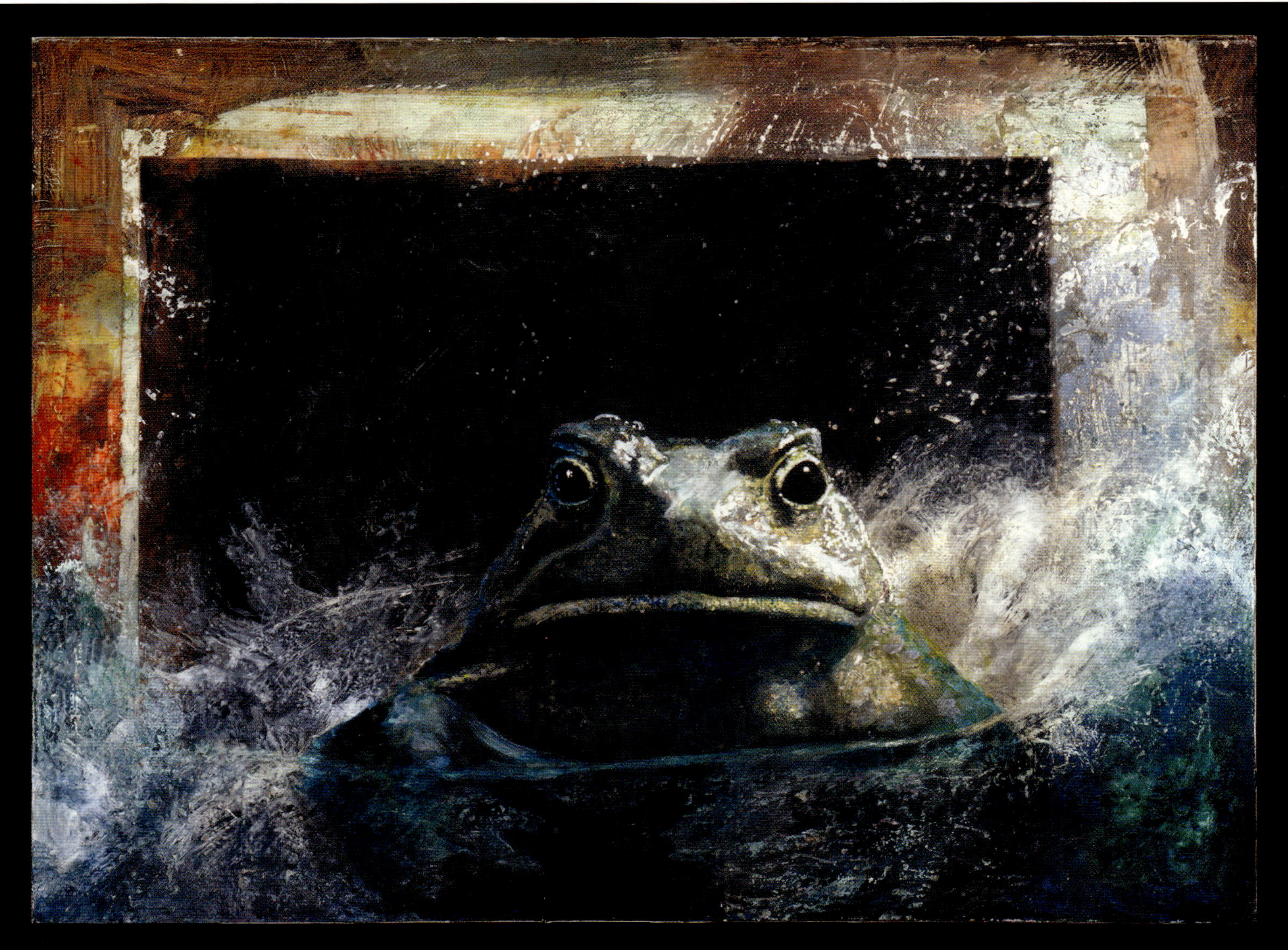

AT YOU (FROG) | Hugh F. Baker
34" × 36" (86cm × 91cm) Watercolor with acrylic accents on handmade 800-lb. (1600gsm) paper

I started with a large white handmade watercolor paper imported from Spain. I used one of my large Japanese brushes to randomly splash waterproof colors to achieve an abstract effect that suggested a frog image to me. I researched frogs and a few sketches later came up with this guy. After experimenting with textures using gesso, sandpaper and a craft knife, the frog emerged on my painting. I wanted the dichotomy of an organic frog against a graphic background, yet keeping it free and loose. A fellow artist bought this painting out of my studio, paint still wet. That is why I submitted this painting for *Splash*.

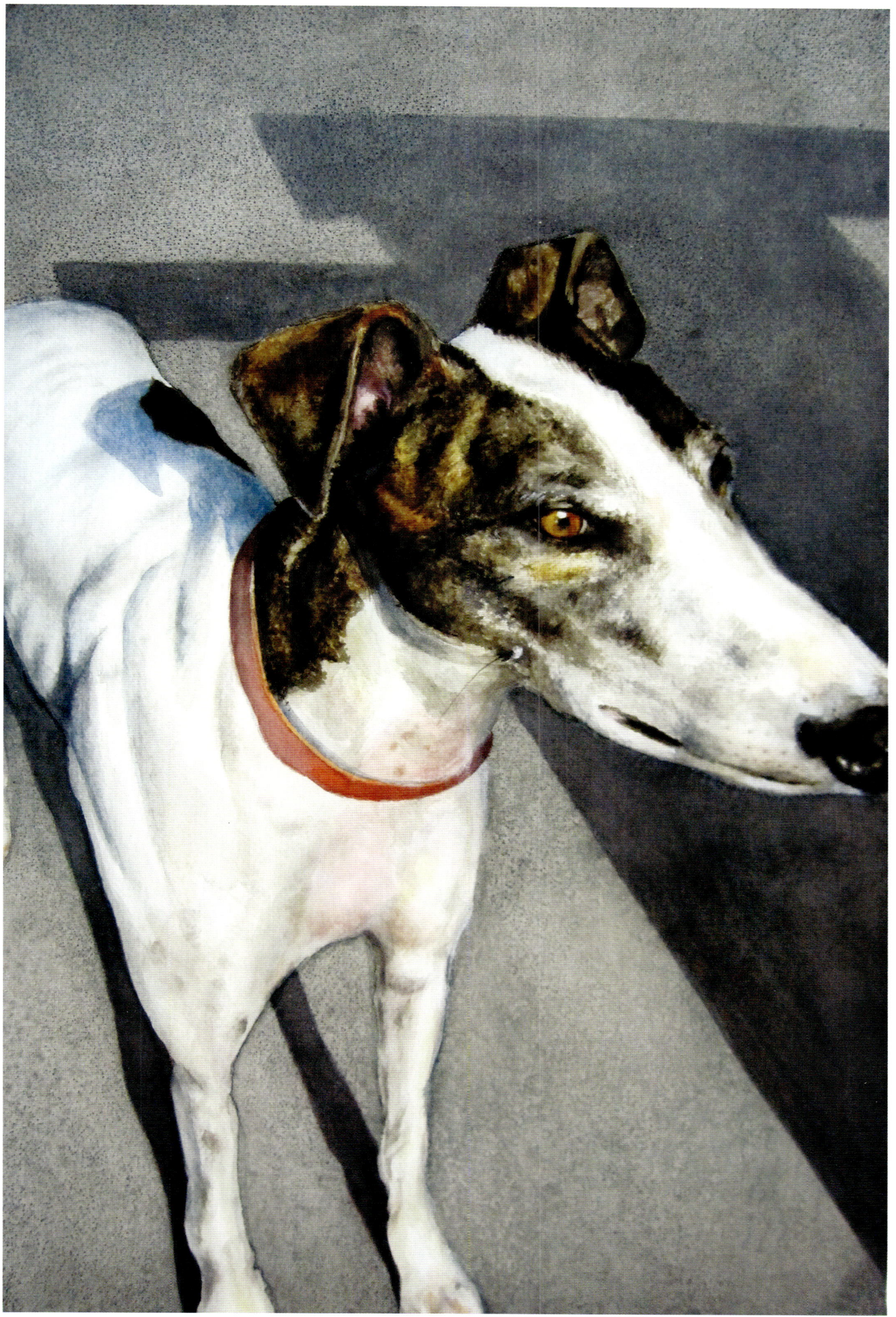

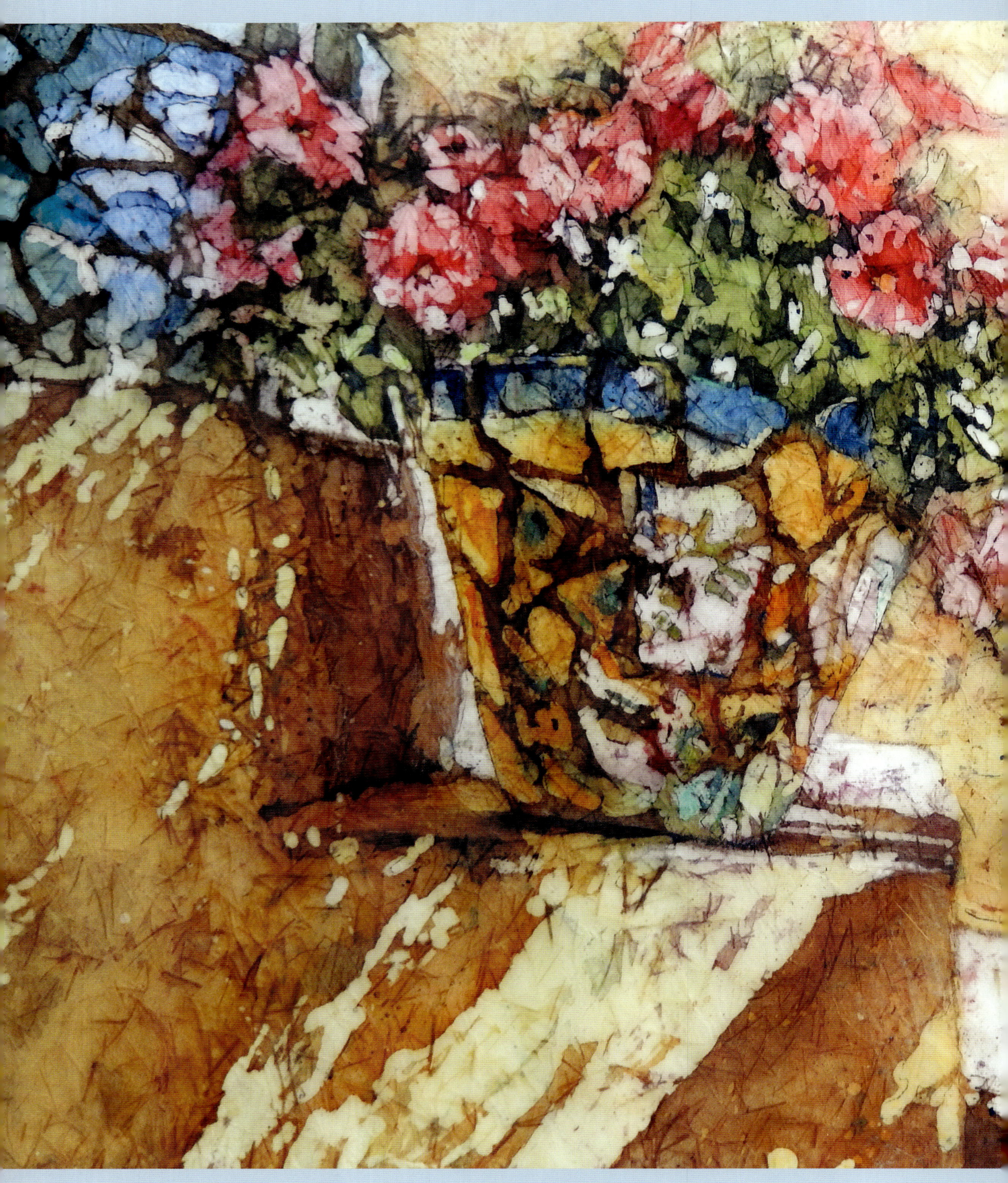

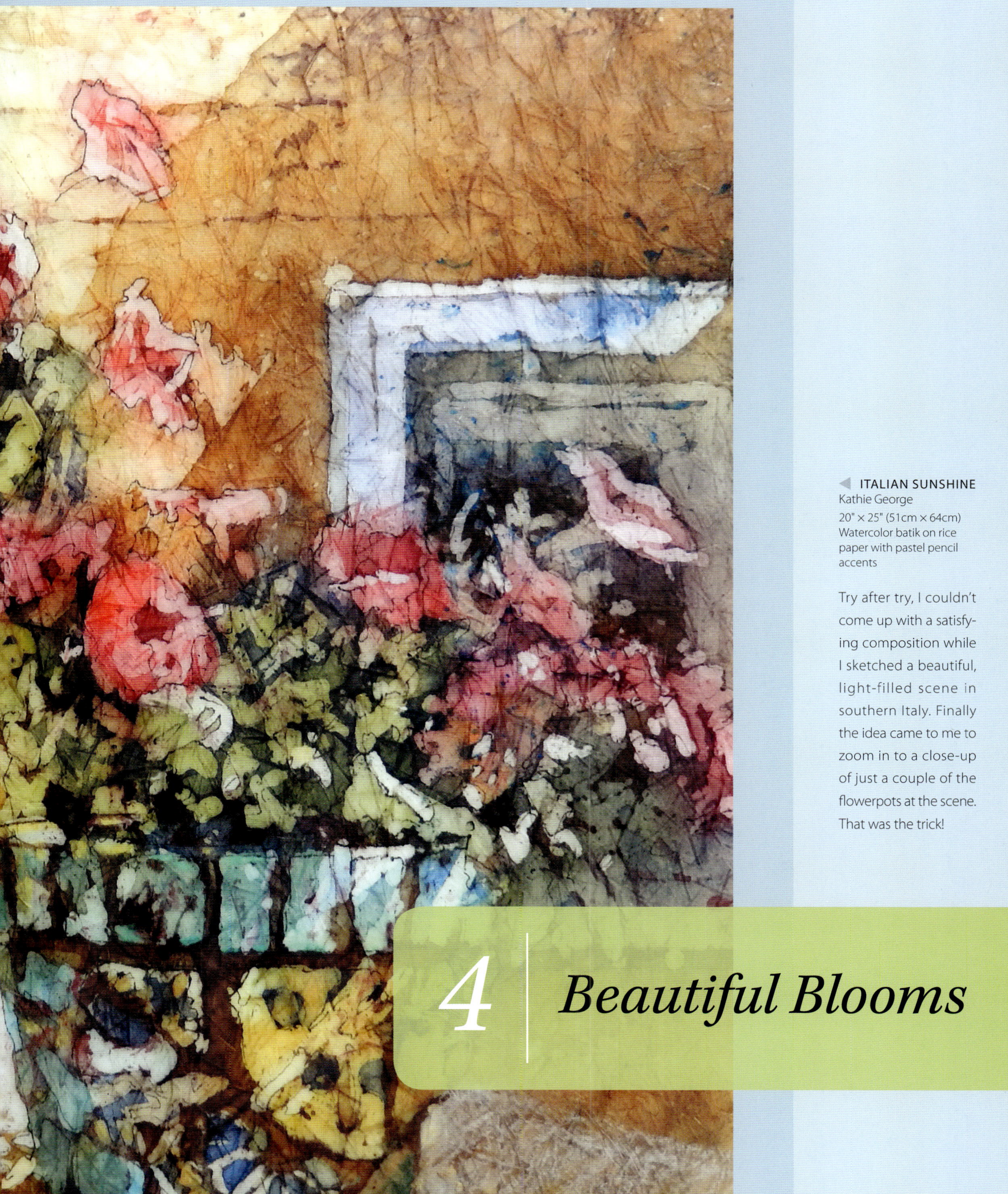

ITALIAN SUNSHINE
Kathie George
20" × 25" (51cm × 64cm)
Watercolor batik on rice paper with pastel pencil accents

Try after try, I couldn't come up with a satisfying composition while I sketched a beautiful, light-filled scene in southern Italy. Finally the idea came to me to zoom in to a close-up of just a couple of the flowerpots at the scene. That was the trick!

4 Beautiful Blooms

▼ **IN THE SPOTLIGHT** | Keiko Yasuoka
10" × 15" (25cm × 38cm) Transparent watercolor on 300-lb. (640gsm) cold-pressed Arches

This peony brought the challenge of being nearly pure white. I used a limited palette of four colors: Raw Sienna, Brown Madder, Indigo and Quinacridone Gold, choosing a black background to highlight its luminosity. To create the visual impact, I had to focus on capturing the lost edges of the flower and the crystal vase. To ground the painting I placed it on a white tabletop with black shadows and white highlights. I wanted to convey a soft mood and story.

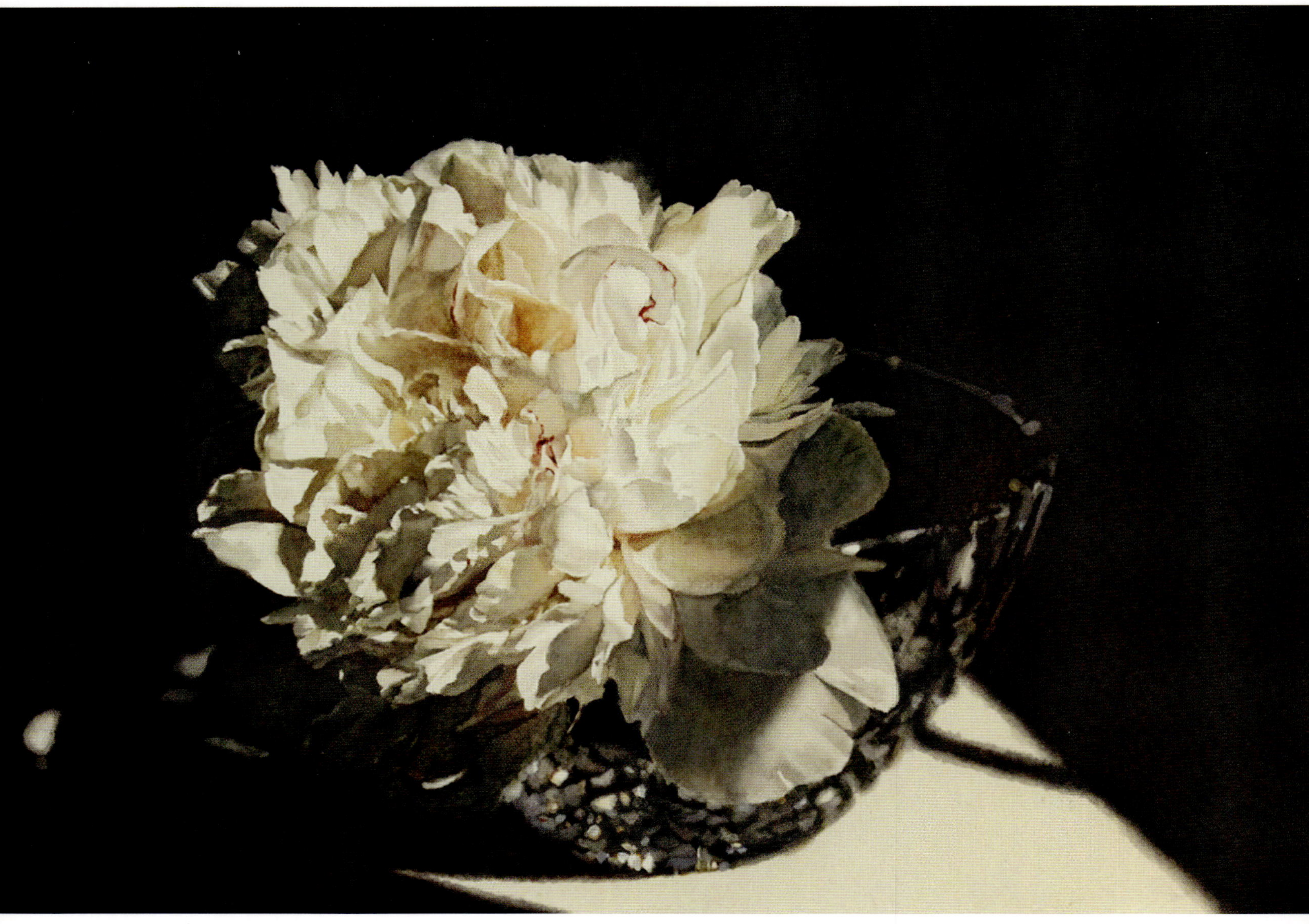

▶ **ROMANCE IS IN THE AIR** | Keiko Yasuoka
25" × 19" (64cm × 48cm) Transparent watercolor on 300-lb. (640gsm) cold-pressed Arches

This bouquet of flowers, crystal and red cherries presented a great opportunity for creative solutions both to set up and to paint. I first think through my objective of creating an elegant painting before selecting my palette of colors: New Gamboge, Cadmium Red Deep, Permanent Rose, Ultramarine Blue and Hooker's Green. There were many problems to solve such as balancing the weight of the top portion with the lower portion. Further, I wanted to have the pieces connect in a triangle of flowers, crystal and cherries.

"Work through some of your creative solutions before beginning the painting."

– KEIKO YASUOKA

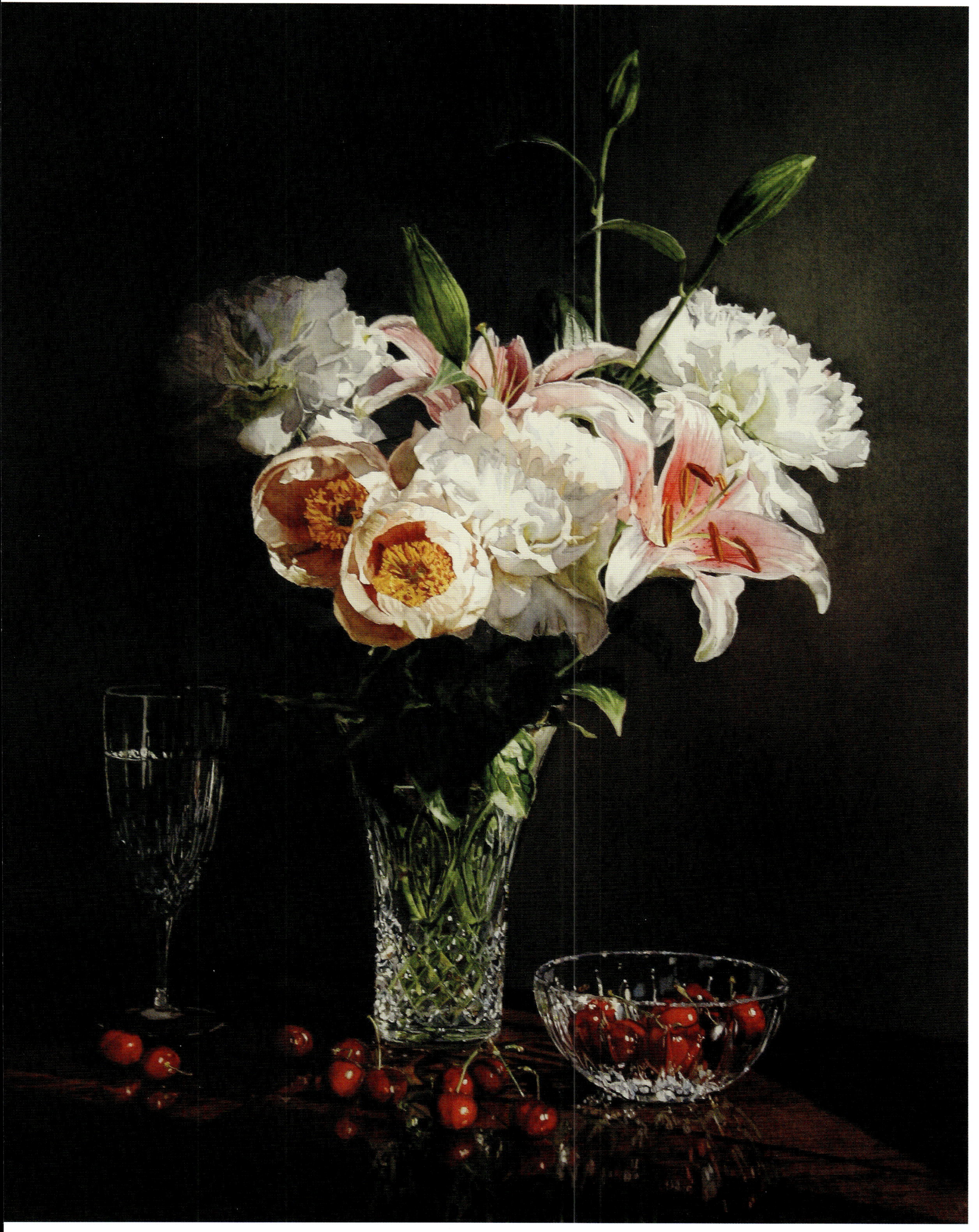

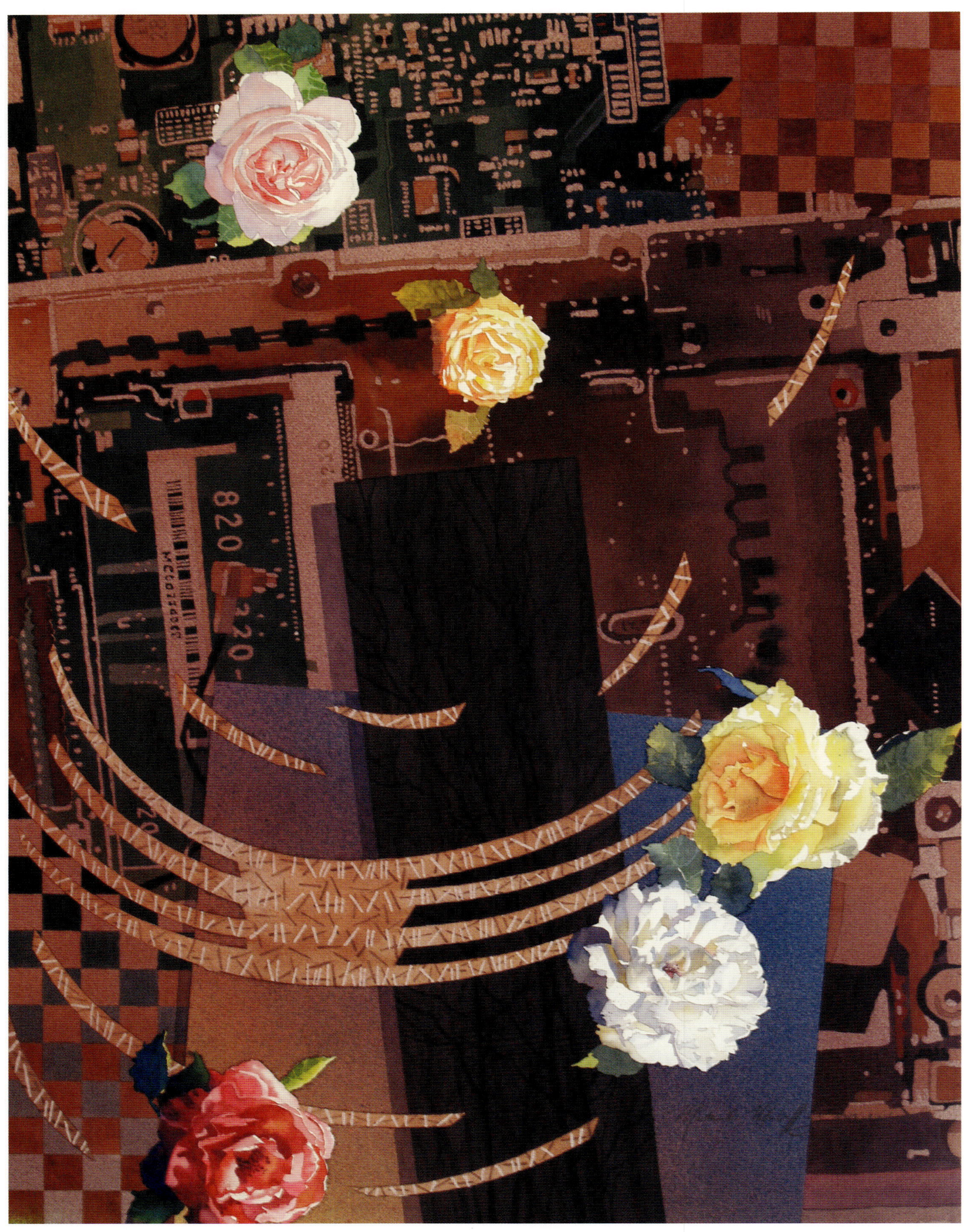

"An old tool—the mouth atomizer—which I was used to using for one purpose, I applied to another and it became my creative solution. Just what I was after!" – MARK E. MEHAFFEY

"When you're stuck, try letting your intuition overrule your planning." — MARIE LAMOTHE

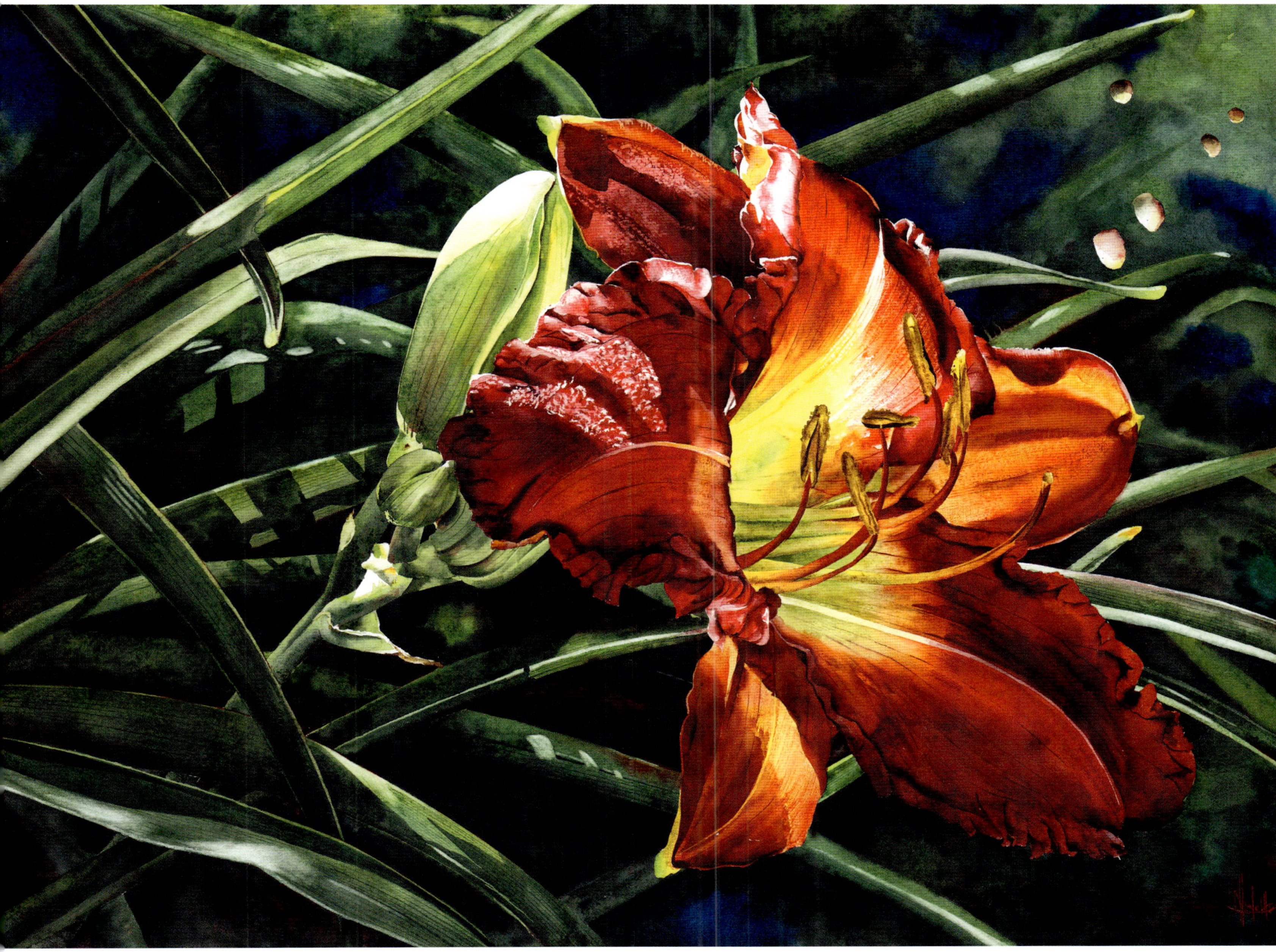

◀ **ROSE DICHOTOMY** | Mark E. Mehaffey
35" × 27" (89cm × 69cm) Transparent watercolor on Arches 140-lb. (300gsm) cold-pressed paper

My paintings are concept driven, so my process differs for each painting. *Rose Dichotomy* addresses the big gap between our man-made digital world and our natural world. For this complex painting I did the drawing starting from the surface layer (the roses) and gradually down into the deeper layers of the composition (the flying curves), then the geometric shapes and finally the computer motherboard. Everything was then painted in reverse order from the most background layer up to the flowers. Nearing completion I realized that the rest of the painting was competing with the roses. My solution? Mouth atomizer! For years I have been doing mouth atomizer spray paintings in watercolor, but I never thought to use it as a fix-it tool. I protected the roses with liquid mask and sprayed the rest of the painting with a neutral brown. When I removed the frisket and finished the roses, they really popped!

▲ **A DAYLILY DALLIANCE** | Marie Lamothe
22" × 30" (56cm × 76cm) Transparent watercolor on Twinrocker heavy art weight cold-pressed paper

At times I've struggled to create a background that complements and sustains a brilliant backlit subject. This time, intuition overtook planning. By closing my eyes momentarily and disregarding sketches, photographs and even memories, other impulses came forward. Thus, in a by-the-seat-of-the-pants moment, I dropped in saturated brushloads of Phthalo Blue while working wet-into-wet what I had intended to be a variegated green background. As the orange daylily came to life, I appreciate the vibrancy created by the unplanned use of a complementary color.

HANALEI FARMER'S MARKET II | Kathleen Alexander
12" × 40" (30cm × 102cm) Transparent watercolor on 300-lb. (640gsm) cold-pressed Fabriano Artistico

My photo reference for this painting was a wide view of an entire farmer's market scene. I cropped the photo and chose two extremely horizontal sections of flowers for this series of paintings. I began by painting the shadows to establish the structure of the flowers. When the shadow shapes were complete, I moved on to the local colors. When the painting was essentially done, I still didn't feel that the shadow on the right of the painting was deep enough, so I solved this by gently glazing over it with a mixture I call "Triad Grey." It's made up of Cobalt Blue, Permanent Rose, and Aureolin. This gray looks really bad when it's first applied, but as it dries it lets the colors beneath shine through while at the same time pushing the area back into shadow.

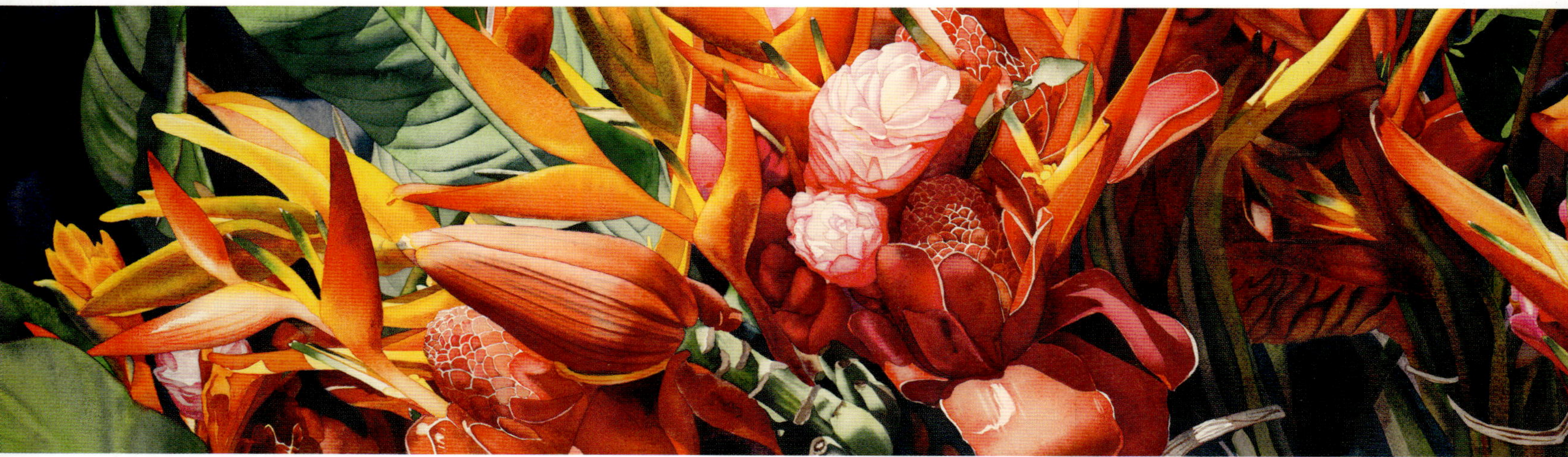

UNDER THE ARCH | Kris Preslan
27" × 21" (69cm × 53cm) Transparent watercolor on 140-lb. (300gsm) cold-pressed Arches

Searching to create my unique composition of Paris's most formidable landmark, I decided that my painting would not look like a straight-on postcard view. That's been done before. I wandered across the concrete, dodging tourists with dogs and strollers, looking … looking. I needed something organic to balance this megaton steel monolith. Several hundred feet away on a grassy patch behind a fence I saw some rosebushes. I vaulted the fence, lay down in the damp grass and squinted up through the plants. Voilà … I found my composition! Luckily the four gendarmes walking by didn't notice that I was on the wrong side of the "Stay off the Grass" sign. What we do for art!

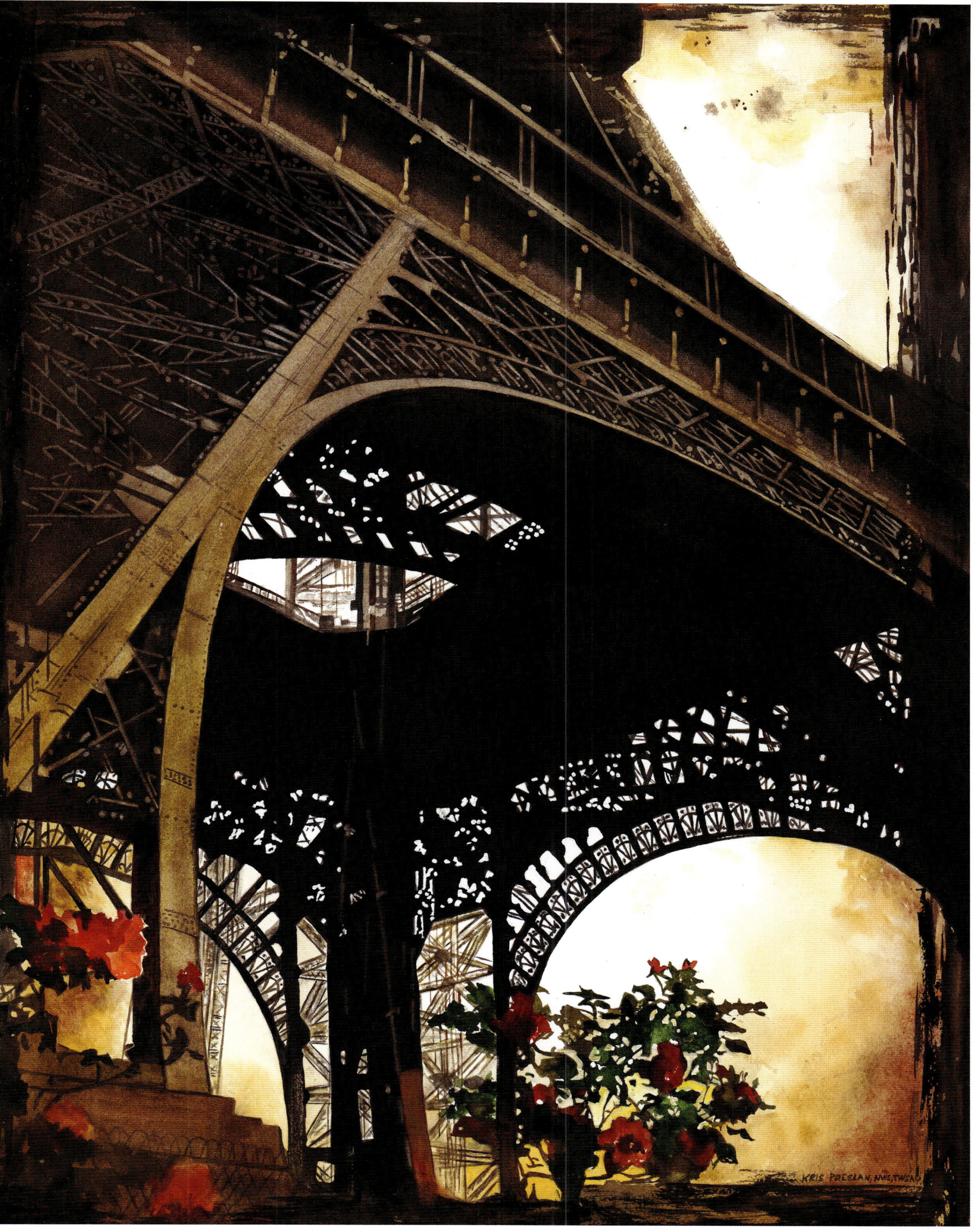
KRIS PRESLAN, NWS,TWSA

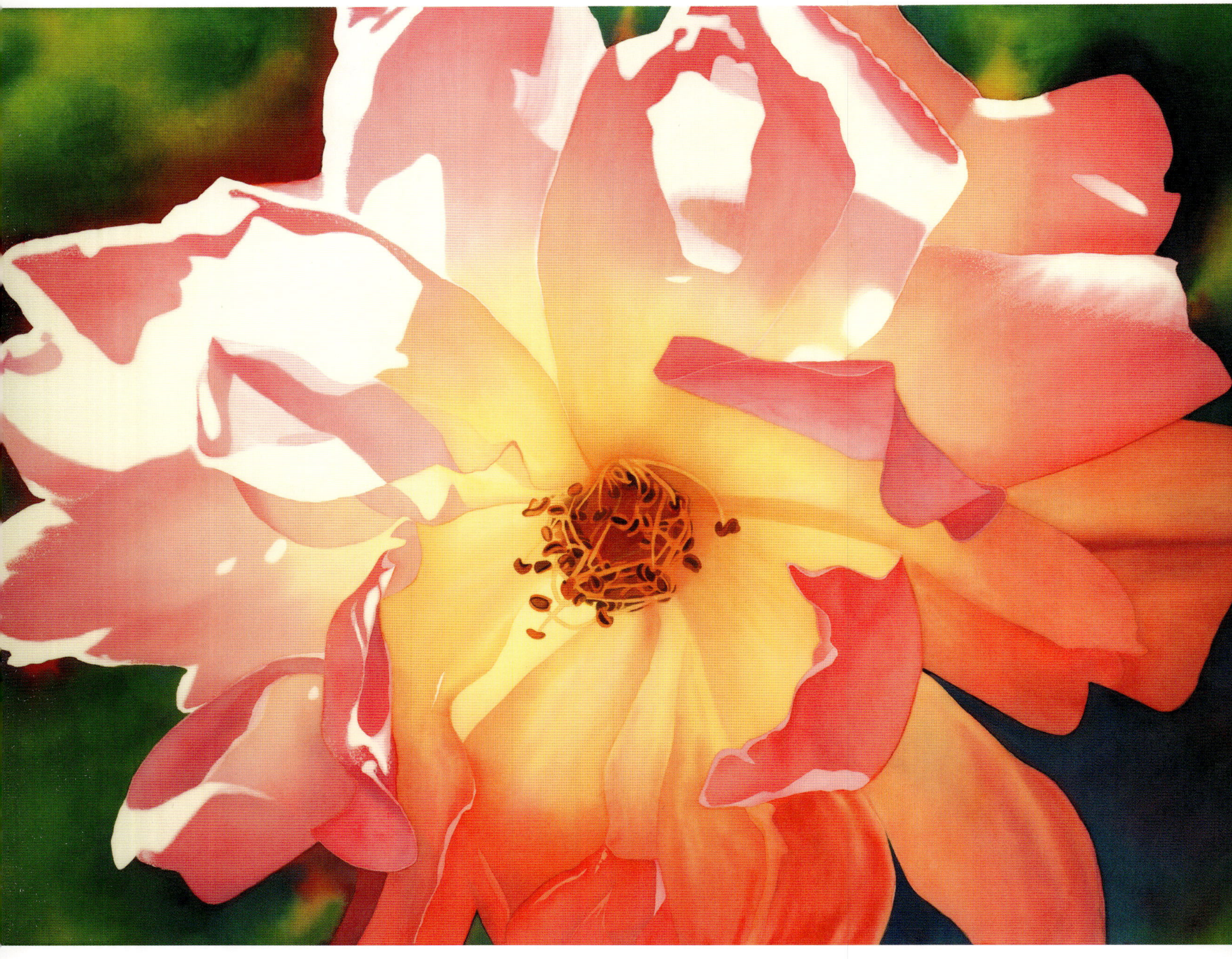

▲ **SUN KISSED** | Guy Magallanes
33" × 48" (84cm × 122cm) Transparent watercolor on 156-lb. (350gsm) cold-pressed Arches

Sun Kissed was painted on watercolor paper stretched over wooden stretcher bars after coating the wood with Kilz, which seals the wood and stops the oils from seeping into the paper. I preserved the large white areas with masking fluid, which helped when painting the big color transitions. When the paper is saturated, it sags and ripples, so I kept tilting the painting back and forth to stop the pigment from settling into the valleys. When satisfied with the image, I removed the masking, softening the hard edges by lightly scrubbing for a softer appearance. Once finished, I varnished the entire surface with a polymer varnish.

▶ **PEONY AND CHIVES** | Robert J. O'Brien
21" × 16" (53cm × 41cm) Transparent watercolor with gouache accents on 300-lb. (640gsm) cold-pressed Arches

Peony and Chives was painted in my studio using sketch and photo references. What intrigued me about this subject was how to capture in a painting the essence of the sunlit peony emerging from the deep cool shadows of late spring. I've been eager to paint a subject with a lot of dark shadow tones, and I felt this one ideal to expand my creative boundaries. I used a wet-on-dry layering process to build up the shadows on the petals while trying to maintain a fresh, clean transparent look. The dark values enhanced the light on the sunlit side of the flower. It was a rewarding outcome that only the watercolor medium can achieve.

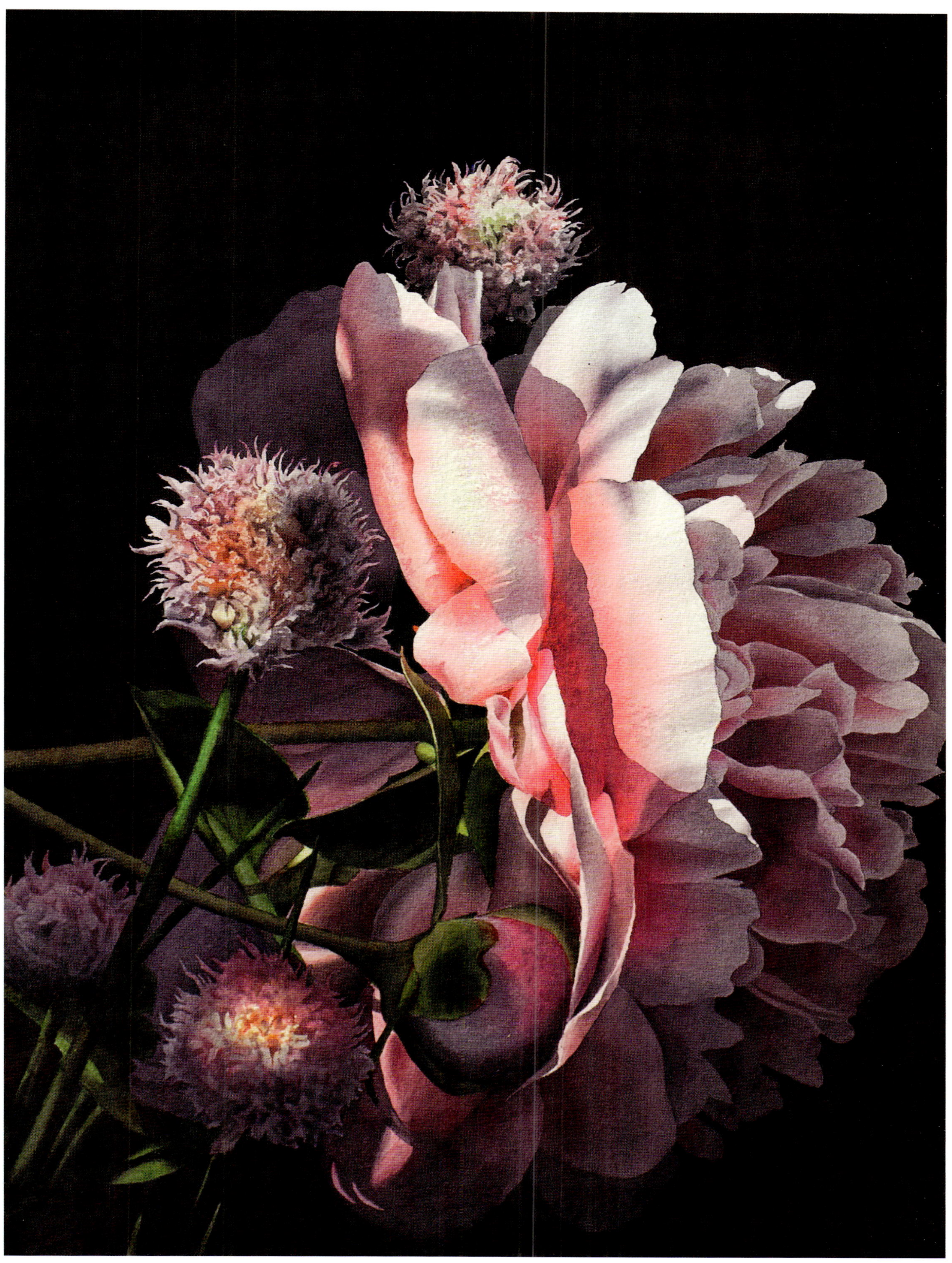

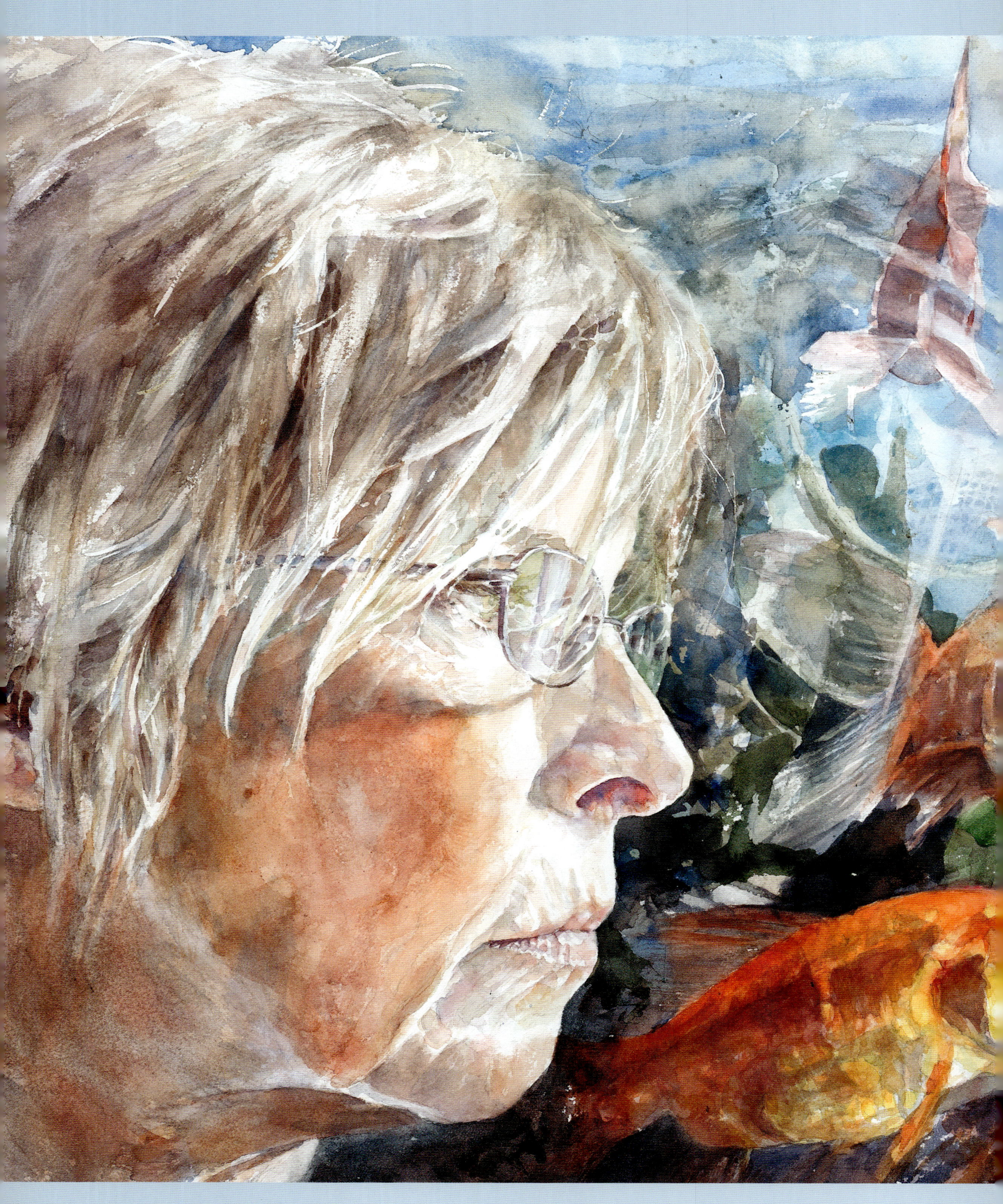

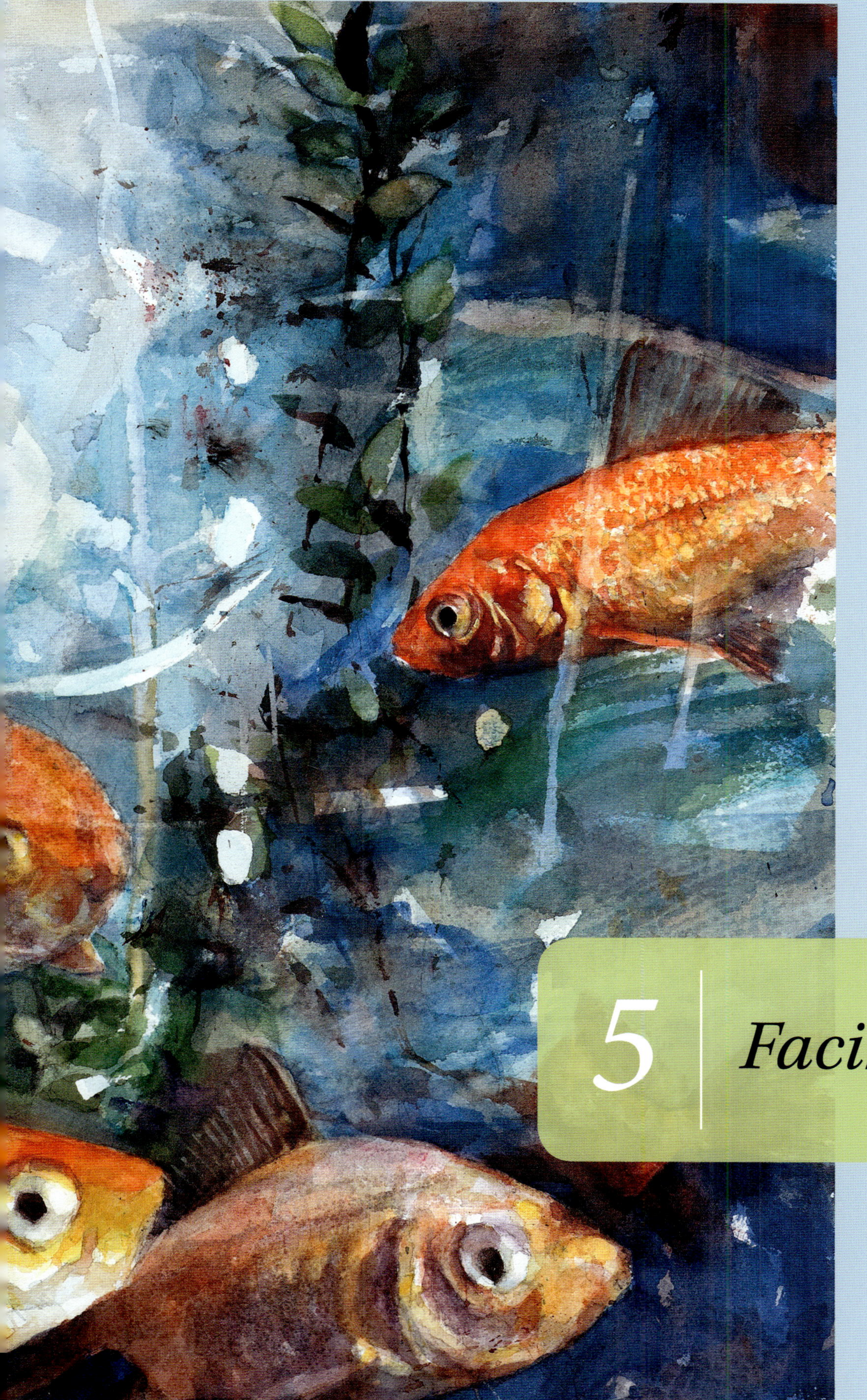

◀ **SELF PORTRAIT/PERCEPTION**
Christine Misencik Bunn
20" × 28" (51cm × 71cm) Transparent watercolor on 140-lb. (300gsm) cold-pressed Arches

I wanted to express the fish-bowl confinement I felt when caring for my husband during his illness. Painting became a kind of therapy and escape. I began by assembling a collage using my original photographs and sketches, and transferred the image onto watercolor paper. I was unsure how to paint the fish, so one by one I completed each with the utmost detail. I soon realized that the fish were too perfect—just images on a page without emotion. So I loaded a large cat's tongue brush and dropped color in, around, and through the fish, allowing colors to mingle and interact on the paper. Once dry, I used masking tape and a Magic Eraser to lift out highlights and define new patterns of light and shadow.

5 | *Facing the Soul*

"Taking the perfection out of my painting gave it life. Life is not perfect. Life just happens."

– CHRISTINE MISENCIK BUNN

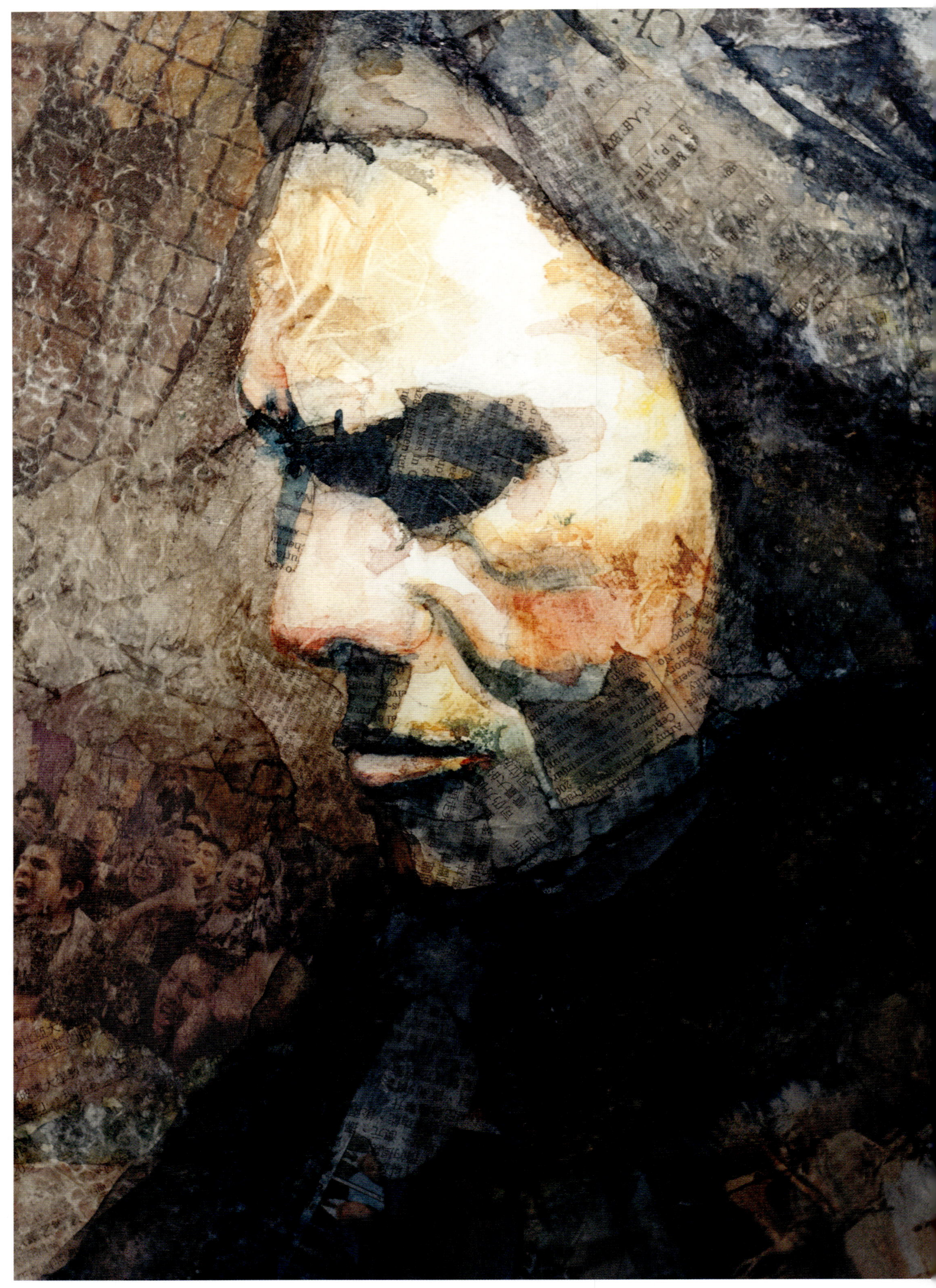

"My solution to creating luminous and lively darks is to use a mix of transparent colors. Never use black straight from the tube."

– ROBIN VAN DEN BARSELAAR

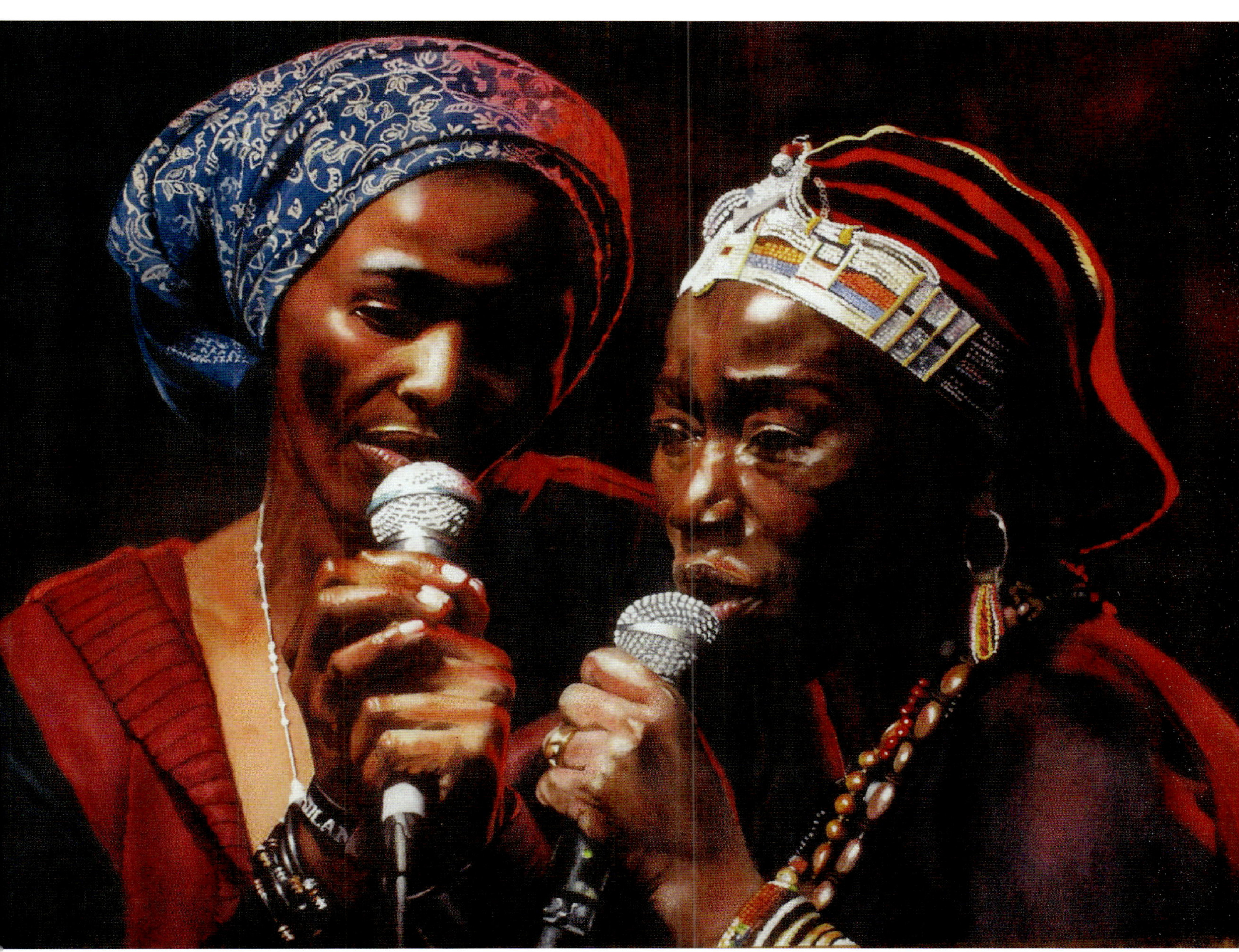

◀ SORROW | Dorothy W. Lee
16" × 12" (41cm × 30cm) Transparent watercolor with collage on 140-lb. (300gsm) cold-pressed Arches

Seeing the plight and suffering of the Haitian people in Habitat for Humanity's story inspired me to create a figure in portraiture to represent their sorrow. As I progressed through the painting, I realized that the emotions I sought to capture were universal and decided to expand its scope to include all of humanity. The work itself also evolved as I used collage material to layer textures and color onto the original painting, which added varying levels of depth and mood that each subtly altered the portrait and created a sense of universality.

▲ AFRICAN SINGERS – SIMPHIWE DANA AND BUSI MHLONGO | Robin Van Den Barselaar
42" × 56" (107cm × 142cm) Transparent watercolor on 140-lb. (300gsm) cold-pressed Arches

People are my main subjects—I try to capture their stories and emotions in my work. I was inspired to paint this picture from a photograph of Simphiwe and Busi because of the beautiful highlights and the way the luminous darkness seems to enfold them. It is suggestive of intimacy and deep emotion. Busi's death from cancer shortly after I completed the painting adds real poignancy. I applied masking fluid to protect some of the light areas so I could layer the darker colors on freely.

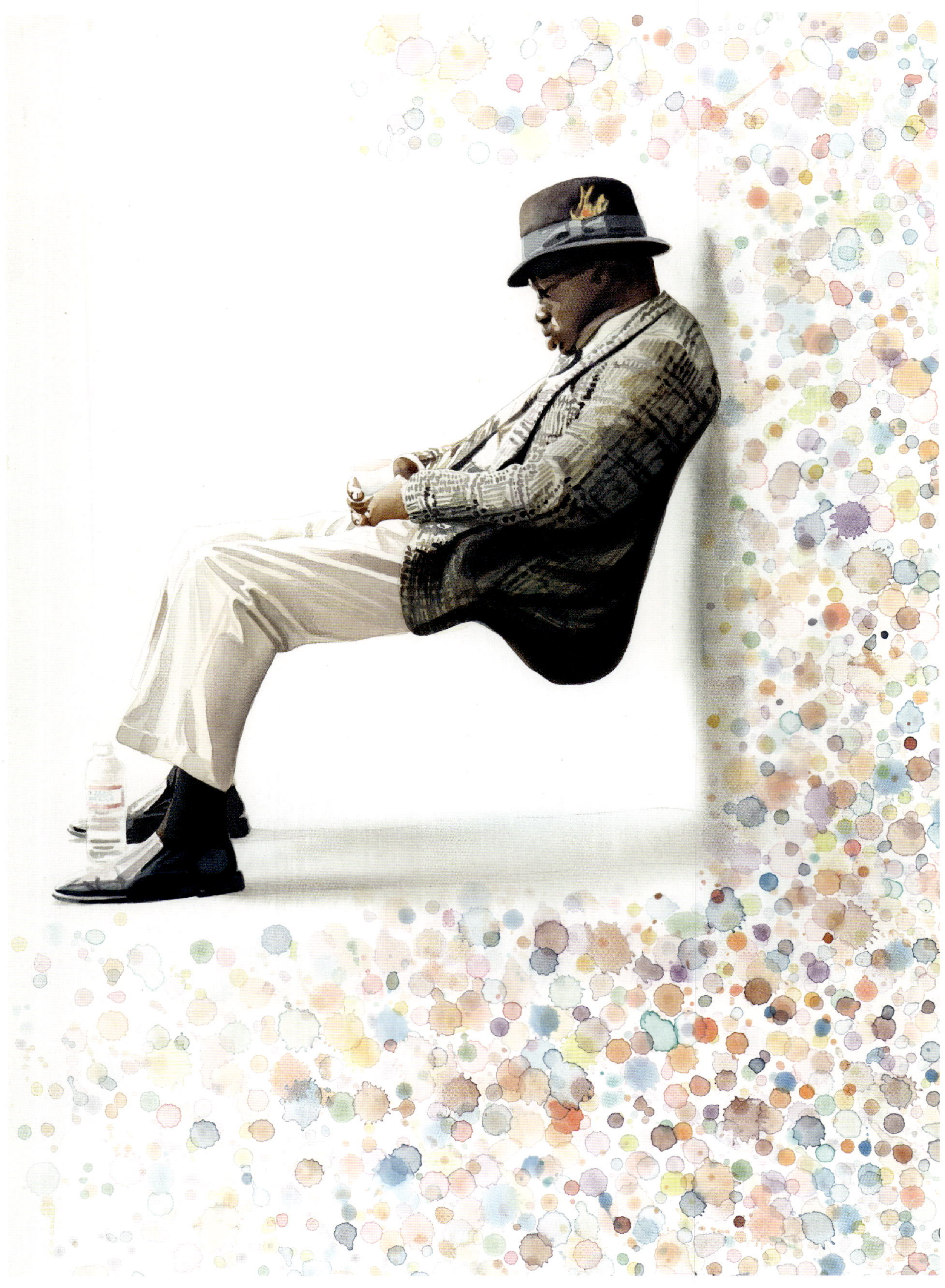

▲ **SUSPENSE** | Paul Jackson
26" × 20" (66cm × 51cm) Transparent watercolor on 260-lb. (555gsm) cold-pressed Arches

When I was informed that the judge for a big show was a fellow who admittedly disliked my work, I set out to change his tune. I had this piece of watercolor paper that I was using to shield another painting from my palette drippings. I just needed to fill the given space with something that would be a surprise. I spent only a little time painting this off-the-wall masterpiece and never signed it. When the judge discovered that he had given my work Best of Show, he was speechless.

"Create visual emphasis with contrast between straight and curved lines." – ROBERT STEINMETZ

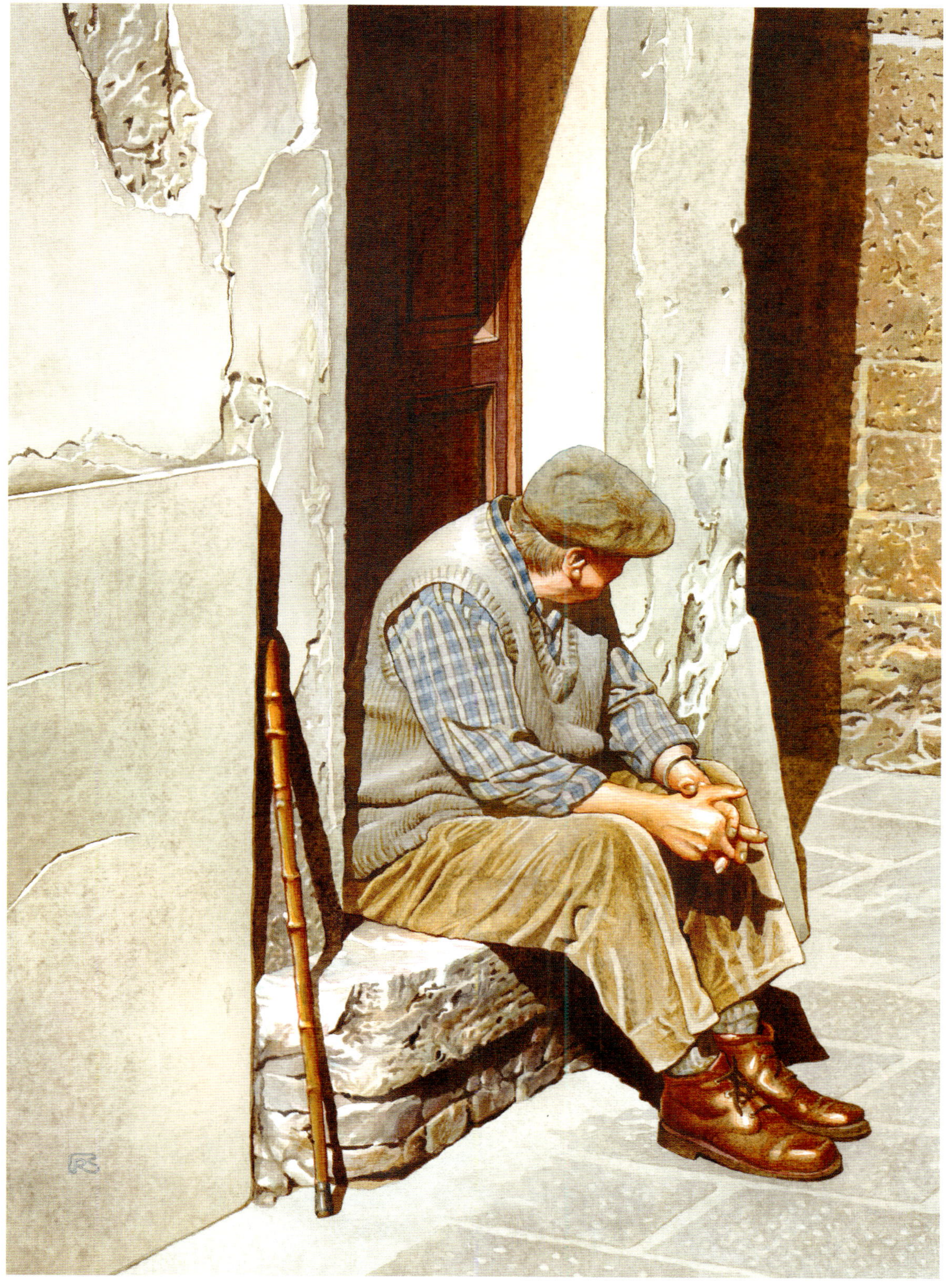

RIPOSO | Robert Steinmetz
14" × 10" (36cm × 25cm) Transparent watercolor and drybrush on 300-lb. (640gsm) hot-pressed Arches

A serendipitous photo by my wife on an empty back street in the Italian hill town of Pitigliano was the basis for this candid figure study. Seconds later the subject noticed us and the natural moment was lost. Judicious cropping facilitated a strong composition. My first step is always to develop a monochromatic underpainting of two or three values using a projected photograph. I establish this initial image with water-thinned acrylics, because the values won't bleed or lose definition when I overlay them with multiple color glazes of transparent watercolor to develop and finish the painting.

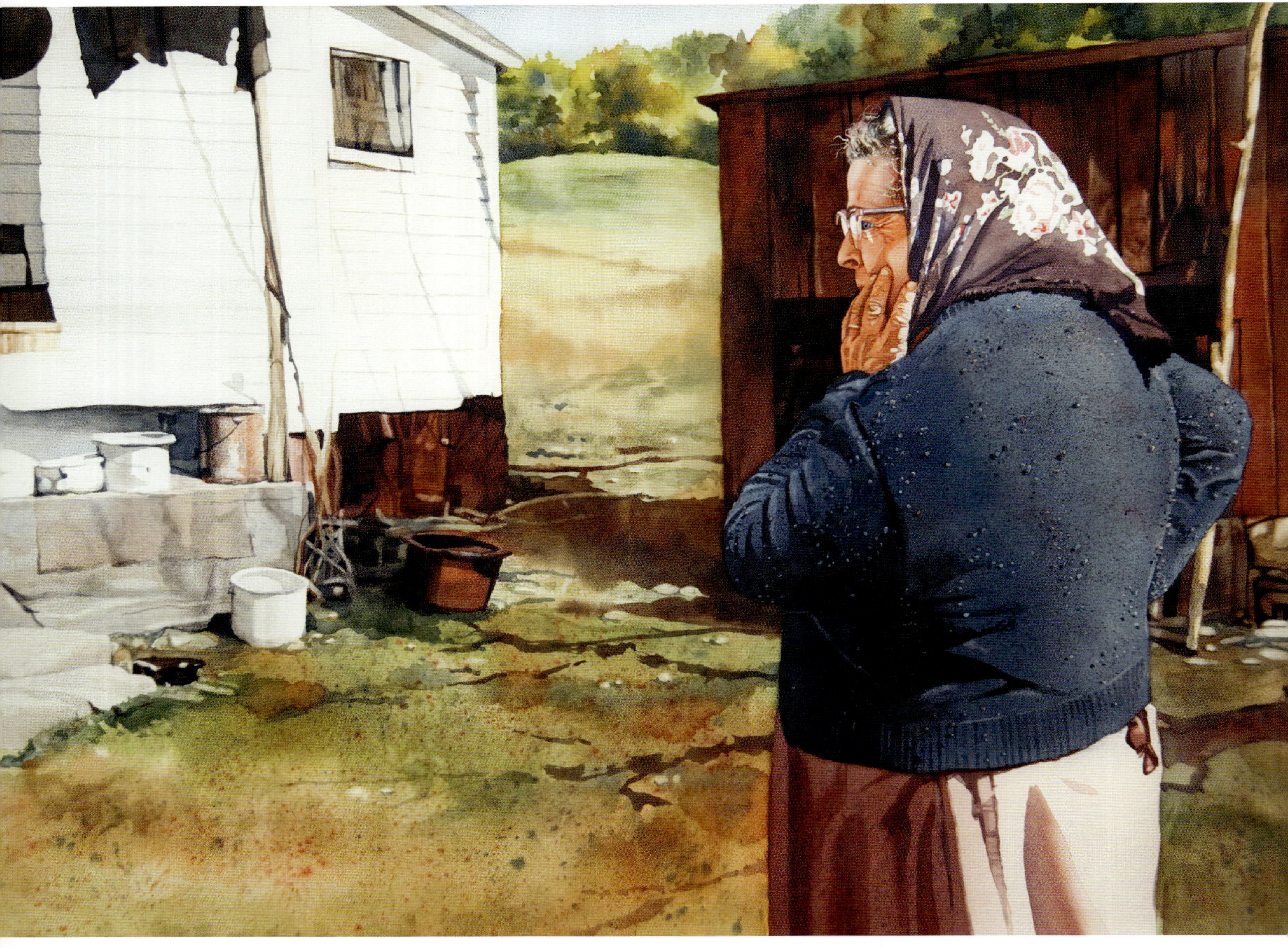

▲ **AUNT MARION** | Catherine P. O'Neill
20" × 28" (51cm × 71cm) Transparent watercolor on 300-lb. (640gsm) cold-pressed Arches

I was delighted to discover the busy black-and-white photos my father had taken years ago during a family visit to Aunt Marion's farm. As my ideas for a painting developed, however, I became distracted by the action and movement of the many figures shown in the images. In the end, it was the singular quiet stance of Aunt Marion herself I found most compelling. This was the story I wanted to tell.

RICE PADDY | Kris Freslan

19" × 25" (48cm × 64cm) Transparent watercolor on 140-lb. (300gsm) cold-pressed Arches

Being a representational artist, I decided this time to step outside the box and attempt an abstract painting. I was in Bali and saw this rice paddy. It had pleasing shapes, value contrasts, balance and color. This would become my abstract watercolor painting! But while creating the image on my Arches paper, something happened. A Balinese man walked right into my composition, toting his heavy rice bag on his shoulder after toiling for hours in his rice paddy. A real person had walked into my abstract, and it was good.

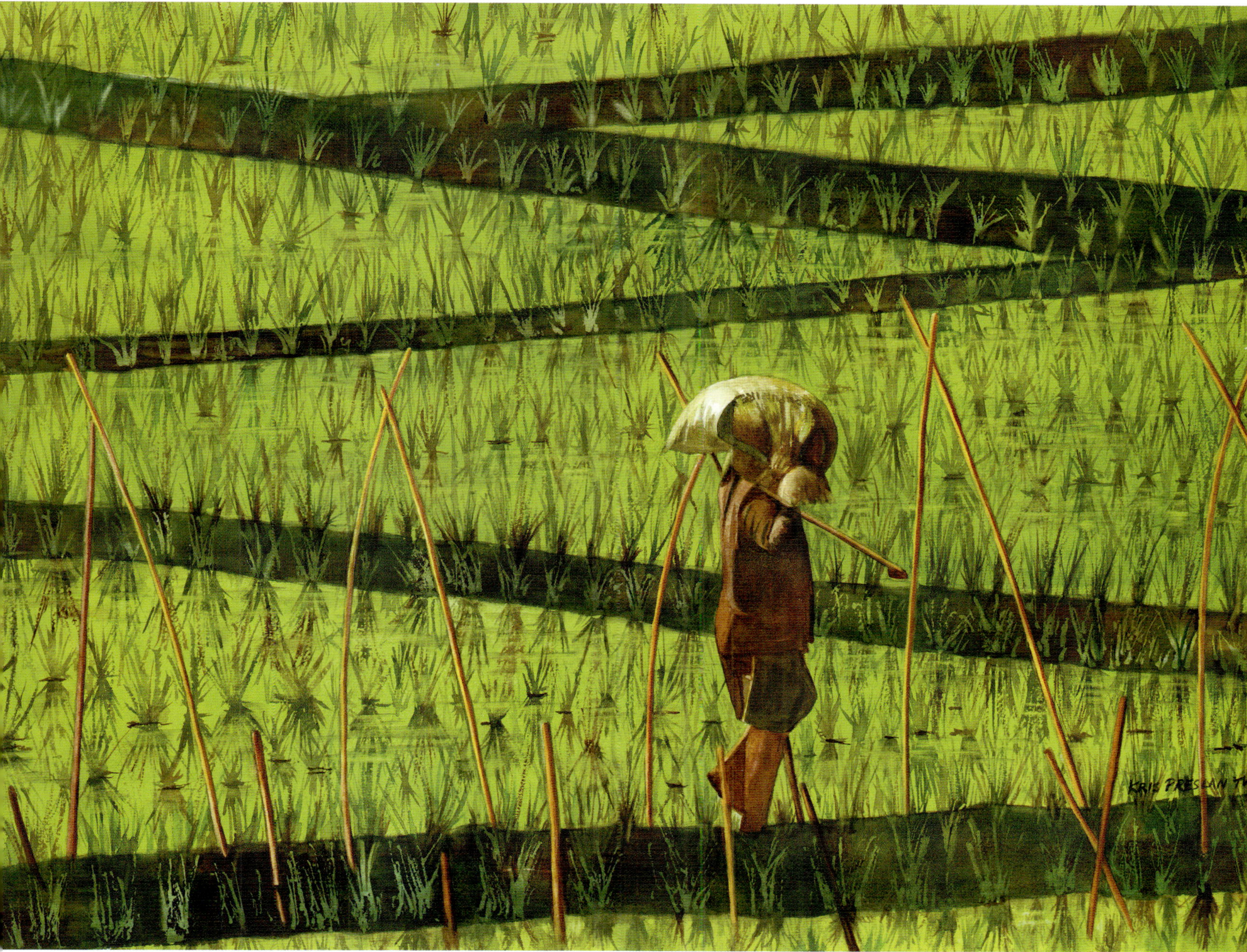

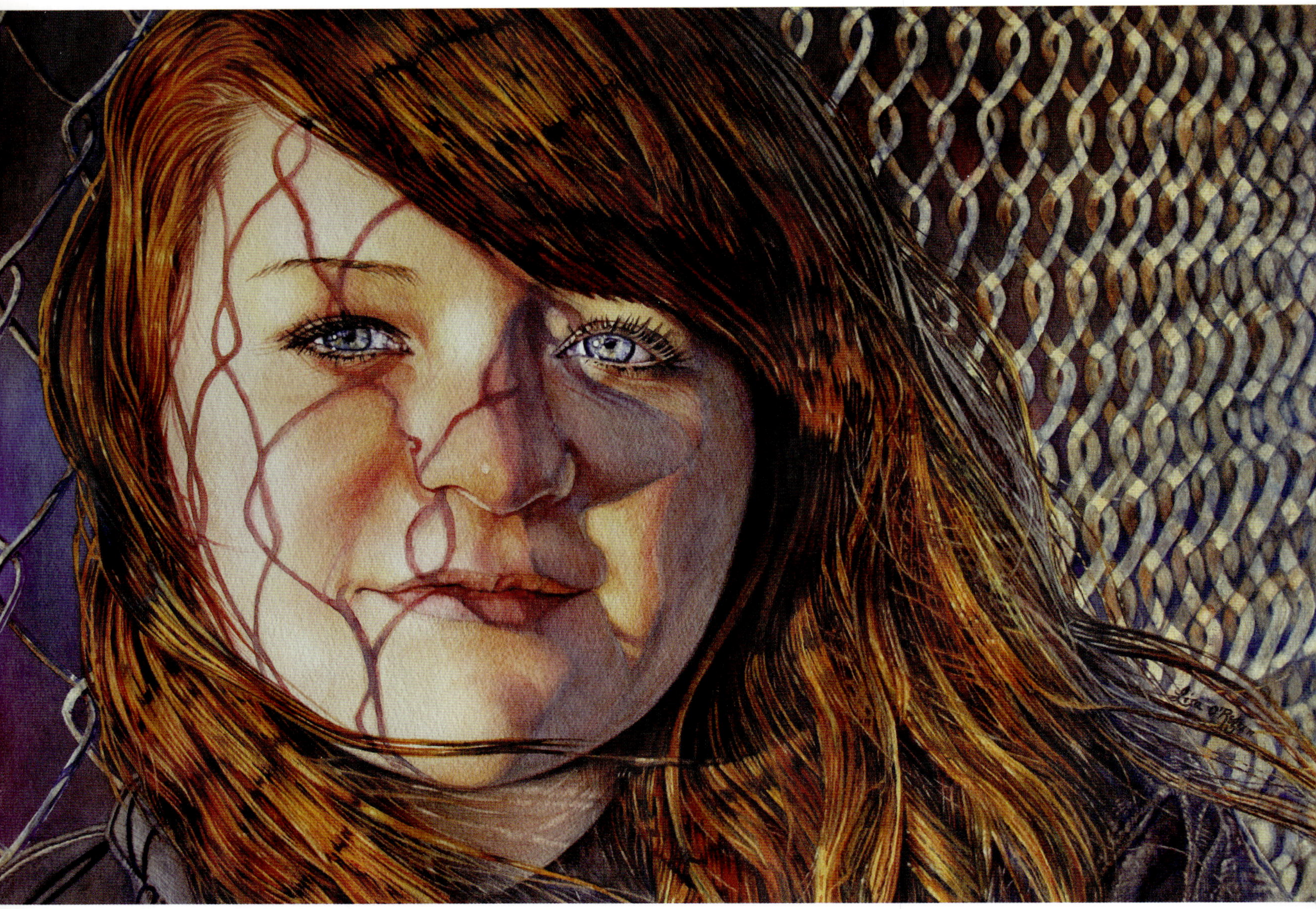

▲ **INSIGNIFICANT BOUNDARIES** | Lisa O'Regan
18½" × 27½" (47cm × 70cm) Transparent watercolor on 300-lb. (640gsm) cold-pressed Arches

My daughter Robin's red hair is what usually pulls me in, but the chain-link shadows created on her face in this photo drew me to paint this portrait of her. After several starts, I wasn't sure how to proceed with the fence. I remembered I had recently purchased a masking pen that was on sale. I thought I might use it to block out pieces of the fence so I could retain the whiteness of the paper. After filling in some of the gaps inside the chain links with color, I decided that the masking had no purpose, and I needed to work on the fence and background in unison. Struggling to scrub away the glue-like masking fluid brought me to the verge of tears. I finally managed to remove it, only to reveal an orangey tinge where it had been applied. I hoped that the discolored paper would subside with the other colors. It didn't. What happened instead was that the fence was adorned with the perfect light source cast from an early-evening setting sun, and finally I was relieved and grateful for my mistake.

▶ **RAINING FISH** | Lynn Ferris
28" × 21" (71cm × 53cm) Transparent watercolor on 140-lb. (300gsm) cold-pressed Arches

A painting student, Ron, with a passion for fishing was the inspiration for *Raining Fish*. As he described his ideal fishing day, an image began to form in my mind. I asked him to pose, holding a fold-up chair in a bag as though it was his big catch. In the painting I turned that fold-up chair into a fish. To express Ron's joy, my creative solution was to remove everything except him and his catch. I then used multiple layers of negative space to fill the background with the fisherman's dream of raining fish.

> "In order to convey the essence of an idea, narrow the focus."
>
> – LYNN FERRIS

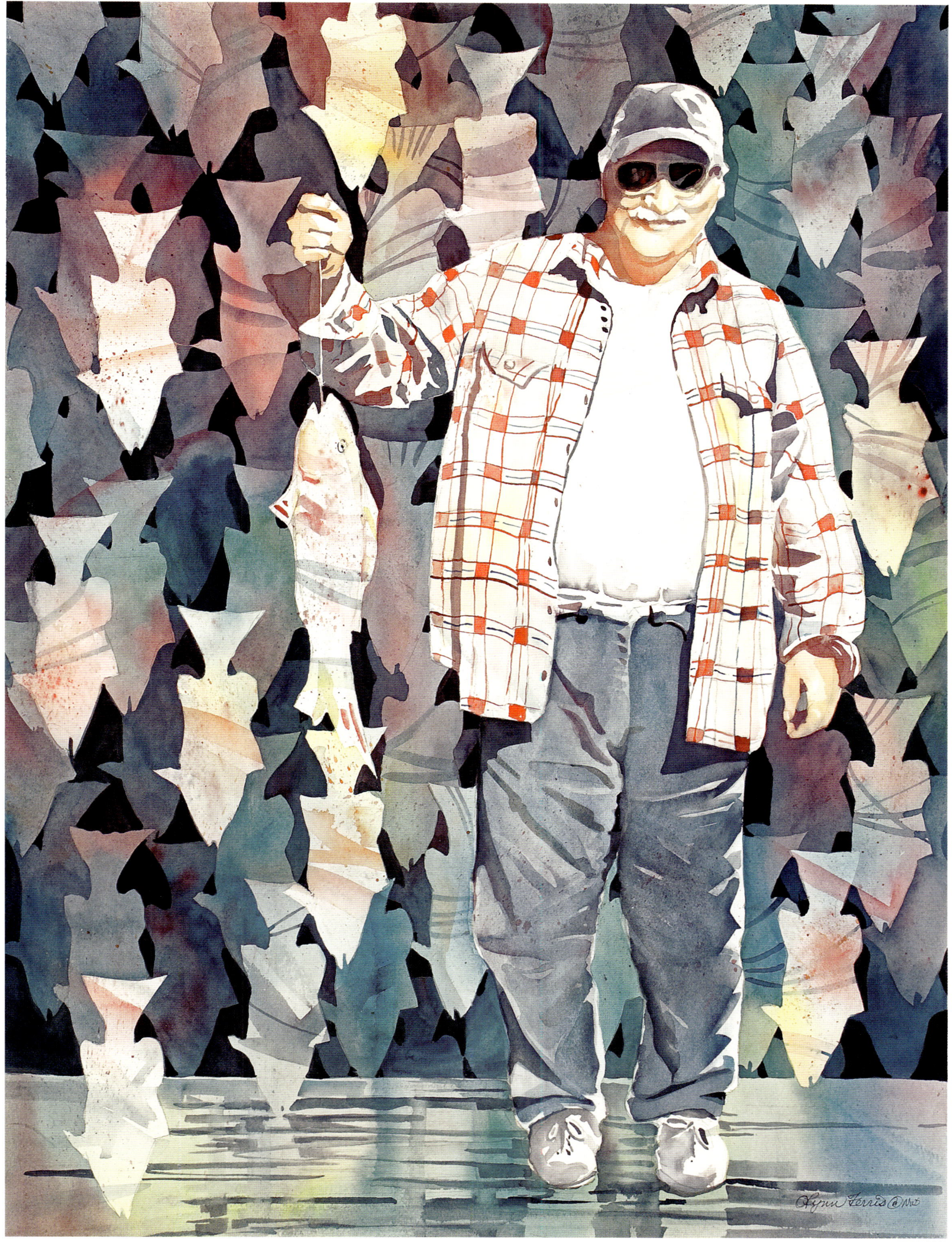
Lynn Ferris

▶ **SOUS CHEF** | Bev Jozwiak
22" × 17" (56cm × 43cm) Transparent watercolor on 140-lb. (300gsm) hot-pressed Fabriano Artistico

As beginners, we often start with a photo and believe a painting should be rendered to match it. As we grow and develop, we learn to use the brushstrokes to make an image say what we want it to say. Look at the utensils behind the chef; they are put in with a minimal amount of strokes, focusing only on the essential darks and a few highlights. The same is true for the pots and pans and the wine bottle. I want the chef to be the focal point, so more details were added there.

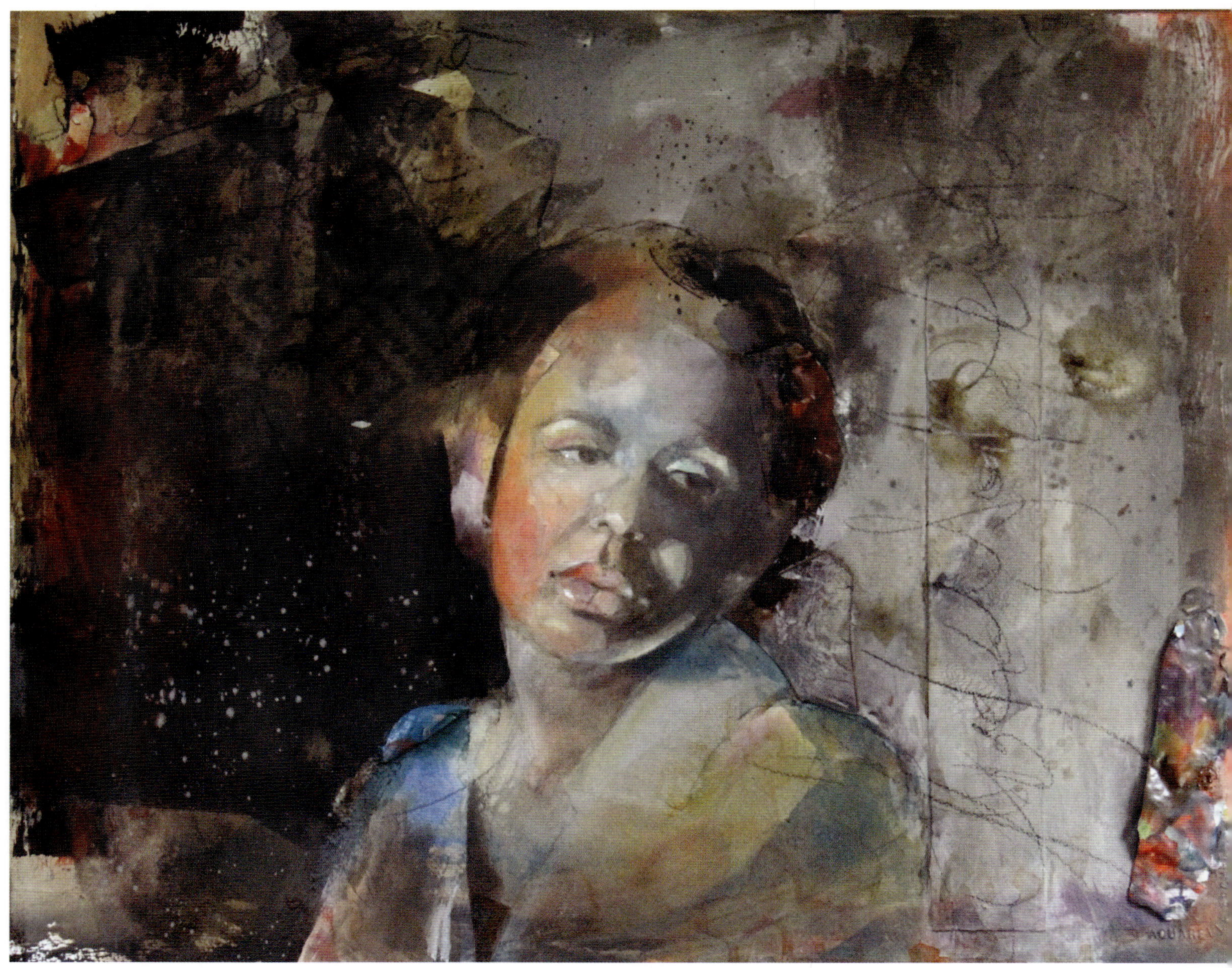

▲ **THE LIBRARY** | Jean Pederson
16" × 20" (41cm × 51cm) Mixed media on 140-lb. (300gsm) Arches

Painting is an ever-evolving personal journey. A lot of small breakthroughs that go unnoticed eventually result in big changes. The biggest step for me was to learn to look at the work objectively and ask, *What are my intentions? What is my story and how am I going to tell it? What elements of design will I emphasize?* In my early paintings I had a tendency to paint the same area over and over with similar results. I finally passed the IQ test by realizing that I had to try something completely different to make a positive change. Now if something isn't working, I will do the opposite of what was painted in the bothersome area. A busy area becomes calm, one that is high in color intensity becomes neutral, and so on.

"Breakthroughs are the result of fearless exploration and problem solving!"

– JEAN PEDERSON

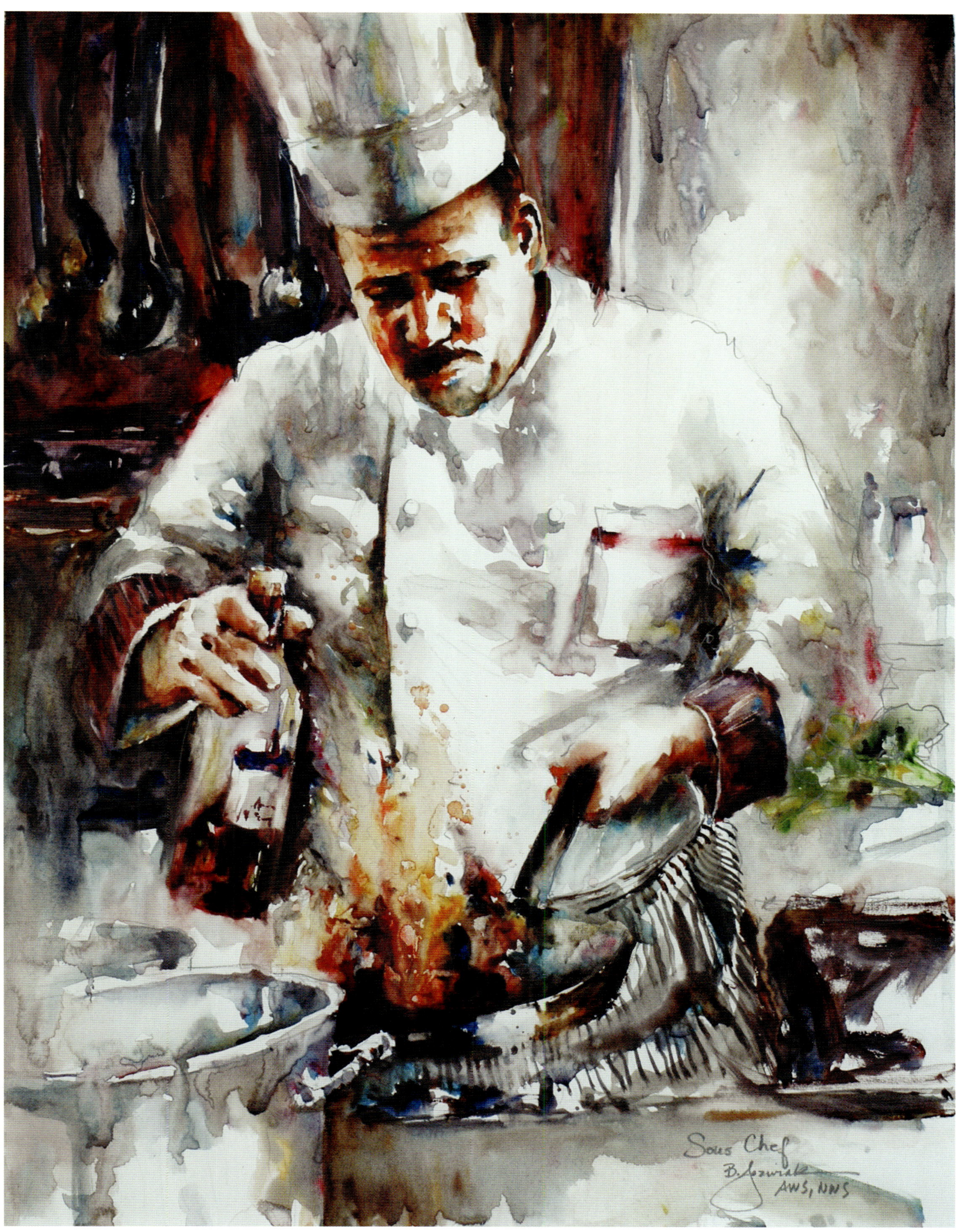

"When painting stripes, a creative solution to keep them from looking cut out and stiff is to paint them first, then add the shadows. This smears the paint underneath in a just-right way." – BEV JOZWIAK

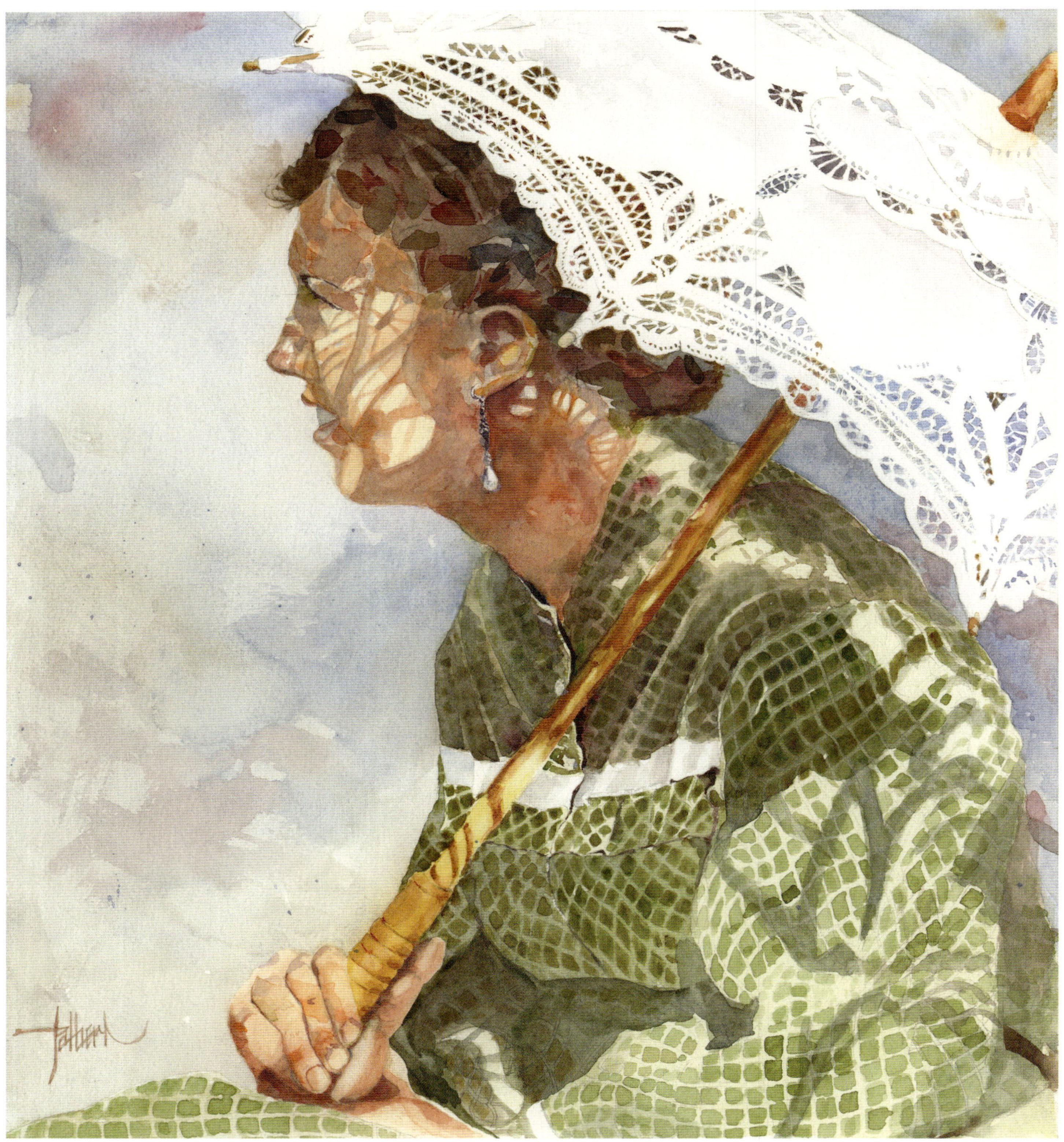

▲ UNDER HER PARASOL | Robert N. Talbert
15" × 13½" (38cm × 34cm) Watercolor and gouache accent on 300-lb. (640gsm) hot-pressed Arches

I spent several days drawing a detailed contour directly on 300-lb. (640gsm) Arches, which was challenging due to the many varied shapes in the parasol and clothing. I used a large monitor to zoom in and out so I could see both the large shapes of the figure and shadows as well as the small ellipses and trapezoids that define the dress and parasol.

After laying in the main washes, I was uncertain about what to do with the background. I wanted to accent the face and balance the white parasol. Although I had never used white pigment before, I decided to mix a small amount of transparent watercolor with white gouache to paint the wispy cloud shape surrounding her face. The experiment worked and achieved the desired effect!

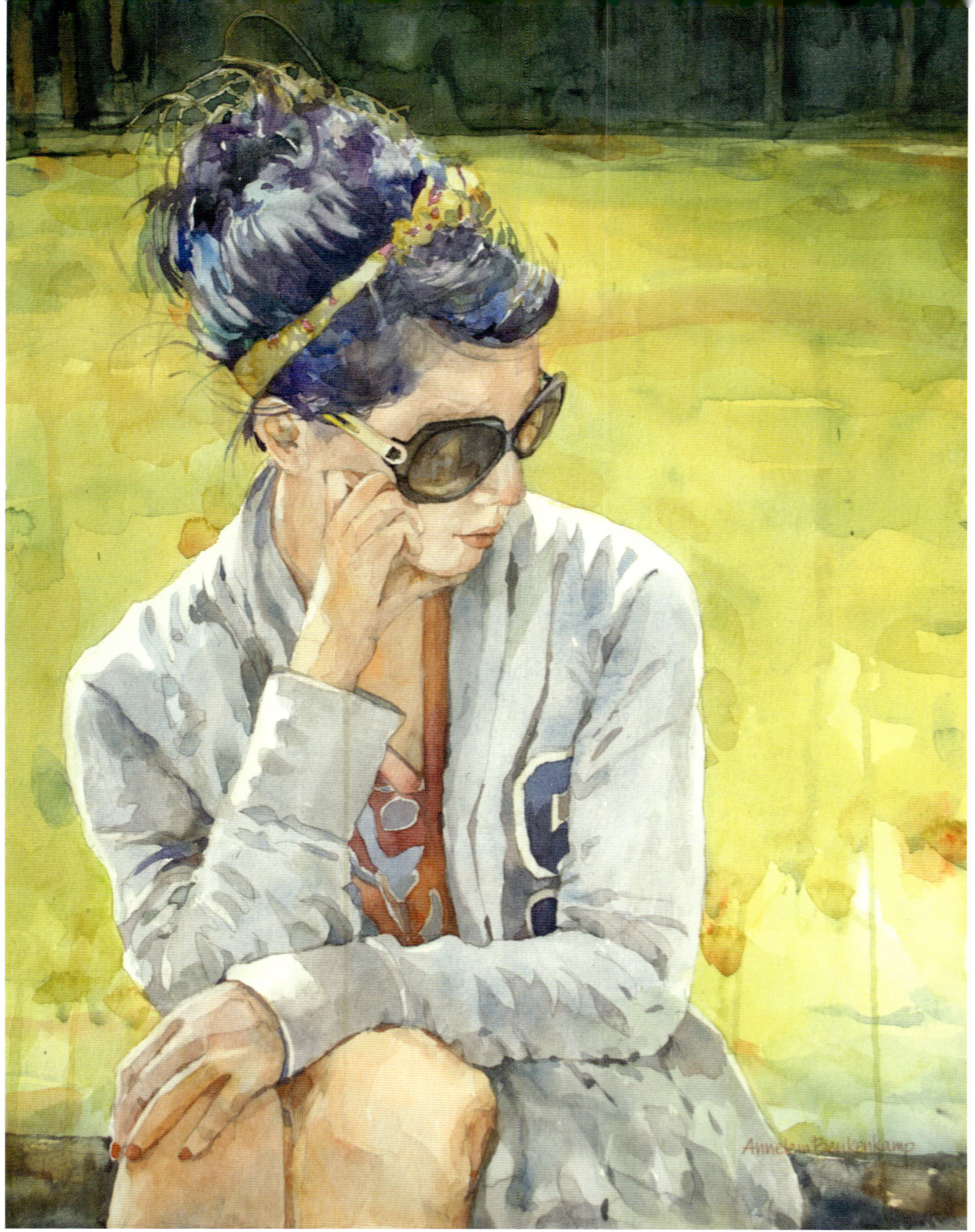

LETTER SWEATER | Annelein Beukenkamp
17" × 11" (43cm × 28cm) Transparent watercolor on 260-lb. (555gsm) hot-pressed Saunders Waterford

My painting was created from a photograph I took while walking through a park in Paris on a beautiful sunny day. The young lady who is the subject of *Letter Sweater* was actually seated on the edge of a large fountain wedged between two other people. My creative solution was to eliminate extraneous detail and invent a background consisting of a green field with dark trees. A quote by van Gogh always rattles around my brain as I paint to try to push myself to be unique and create work that uses my initial inspiration as simply a launching pad.

"Do not quench your inspiration and your imagination; do not become the slave of your model."

– VINCENT VAN GOGH
VIA ANNELEIN BEUKENKAMP

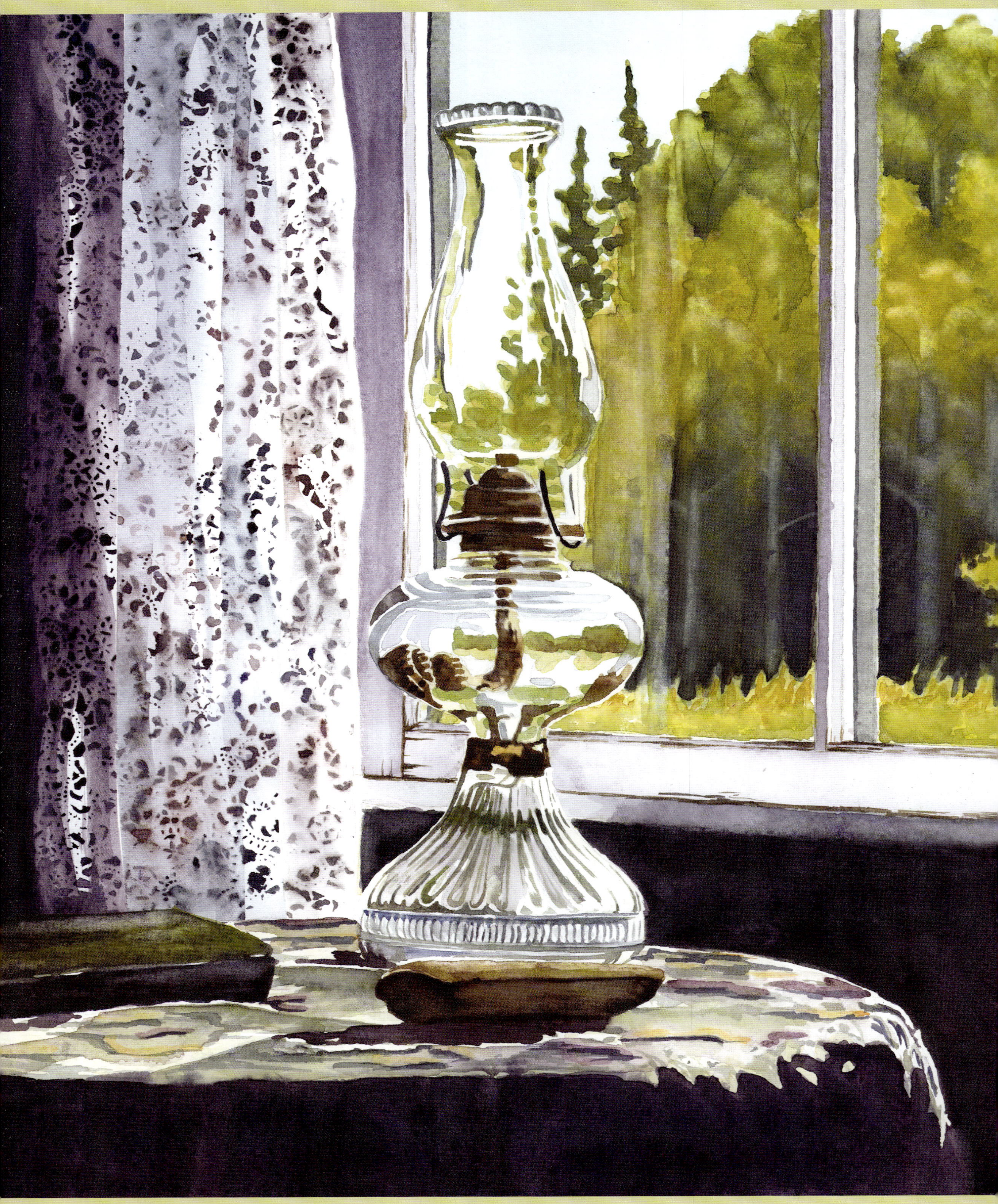

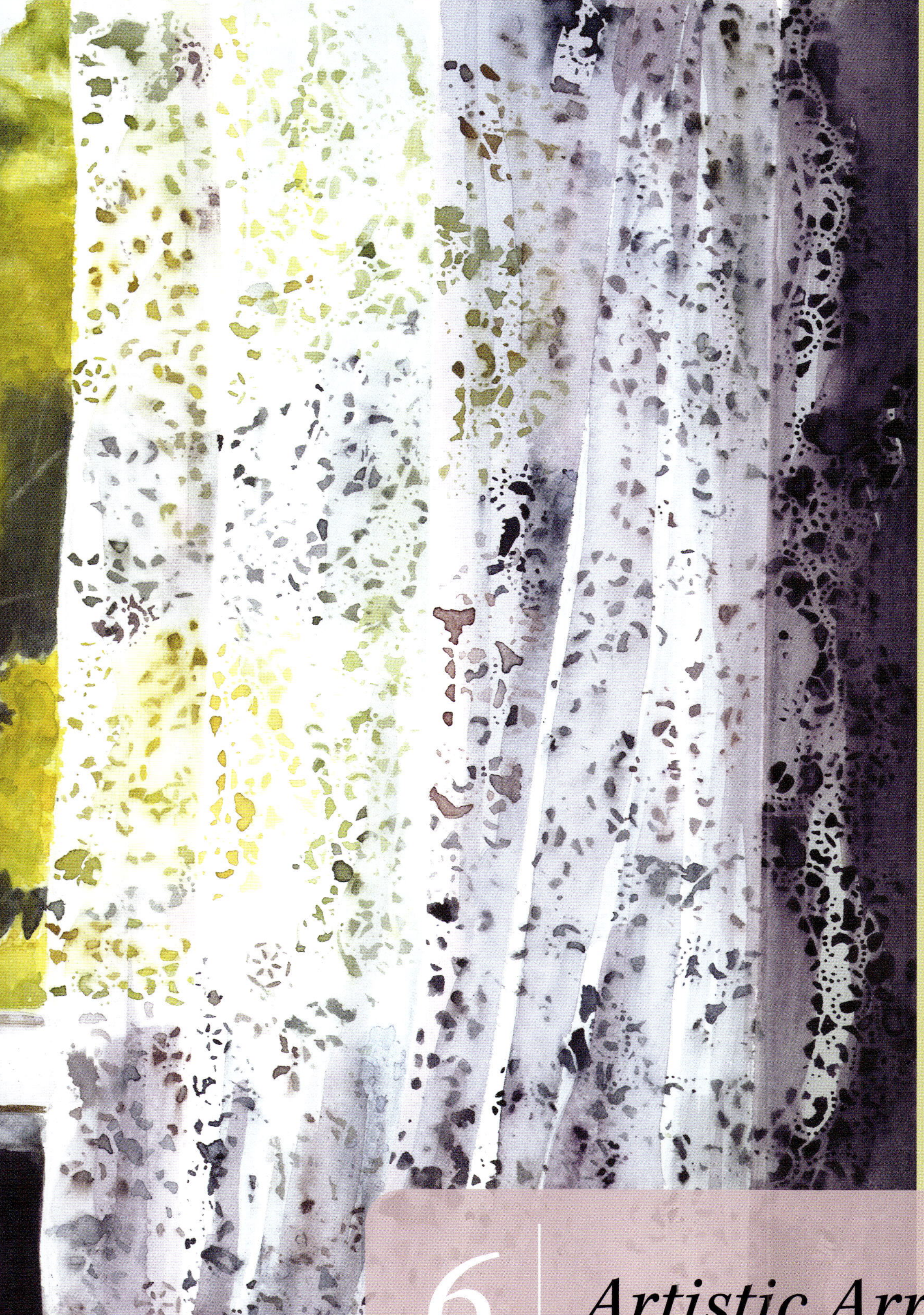

TIMELESS VIEW
Cliff Mann
15" × 22" (38cm × 56cm)
Watercolor on 300-lb. (640gsm)
cold-pressed Arches

This piece was painted from a photograph I took of the interior of Huble House, a historic homestead built in 1912 near Prince George, British Columbia. The fine lace curtains were central to portraying the vintage impression. Capturing the weightlessness and fine texture of this lace in watercolor presented a challenge. The solution: After masking off sections of the curtain, I used a paper doily to stencil in the curtains using the background color. After the initial application of paint, I used a clean wet brush to create hard and soft edges, giving shape and depth to the lace. With this technique the painting really took on the feeling I was looking for.

6 | *Artistic Arrangements*

"Don't ever give up on a painting. This still life took me over six years, on and off, and at one point I was ready to throw it out. It turned out to be one of my favorite still lifes!"

– DANIEL K. TENNANT

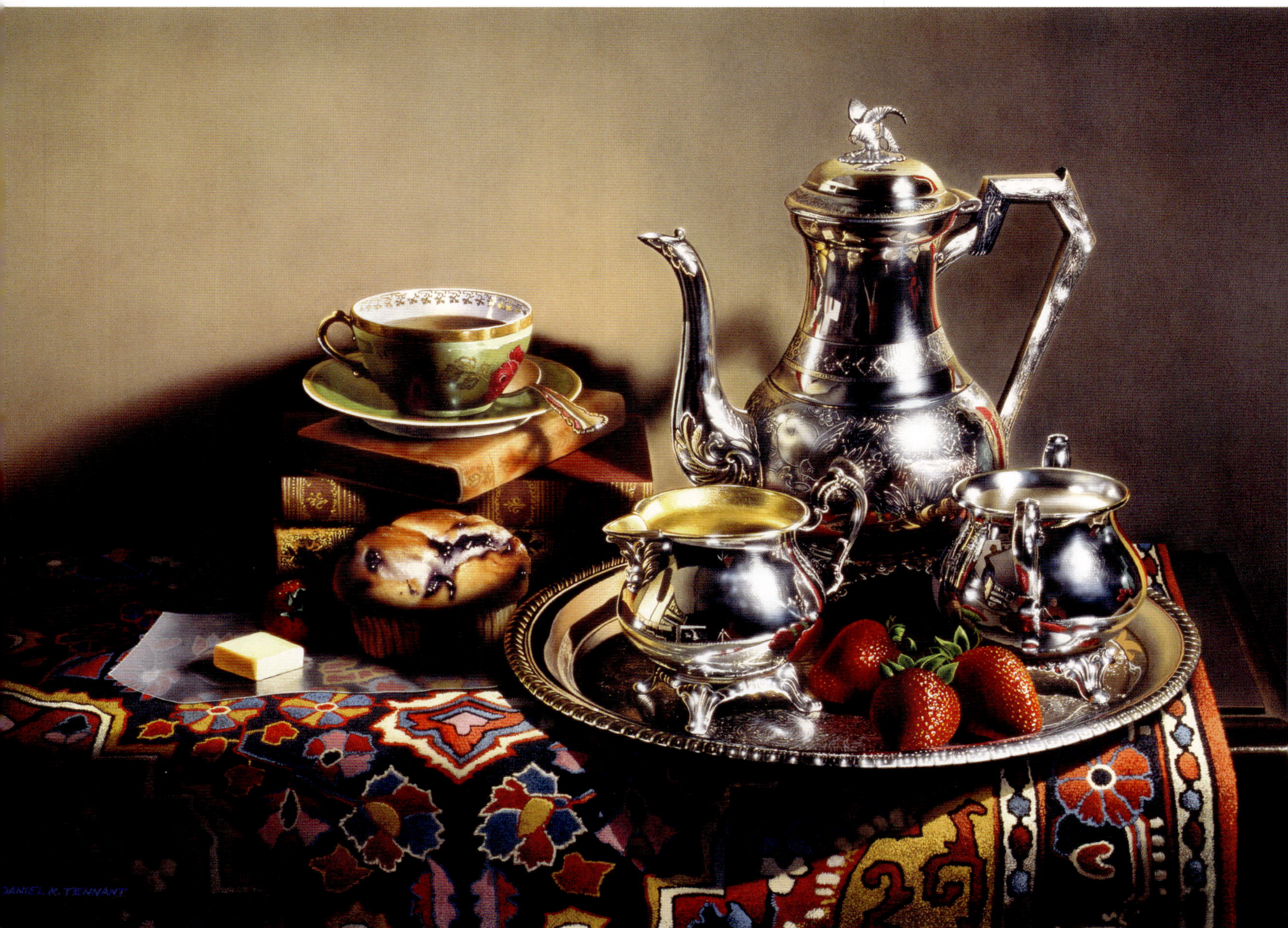

▲ **STILL LIFE WITH BLUEBERRY MUFFIN** | Daniel K. Tennant
26½" × 37" (67cm × 94cm) Gouache on museum board

A friend of mine has over 300 teapots and this is a particular favorite. The eagle on top of the teapot inspired the painting. I always photograph the still life in my studio as fruit is perishable and I like the consistent lighting achieved in my medium format slides. I was interested in the compositional repetition of ellipses and also in placing the color red throughout the painting. I use traditional watercolor brushes as well as an airbrush for certain effects. Gouache continues to be my favorite medium after 35 years.

ESSENTIAL INGREDIENT | Linda Erfle

16" × 20" (41cm × 51cm) Transparent watercolor on 300-lb. (640gsm) cold-pressed Arches

I love garlic and consider it an essential ingredient in many dishes, so my objective was to have anyone who viewed this painting be able to feel the papery outer layers and practically smell the bouquet of garlic. I placed my subject outdoors in the morning sun and shot multiple photos from which my composition was sketched onto watercolor paper before beginning my painting using a limited palette. I knew I would have to create both soft edges and hard edges to give the illusion of both smooth and brittle textures. The solution was the amount of water used on the paper—very damp for smooth and barely damp to dry for the brittle textures.

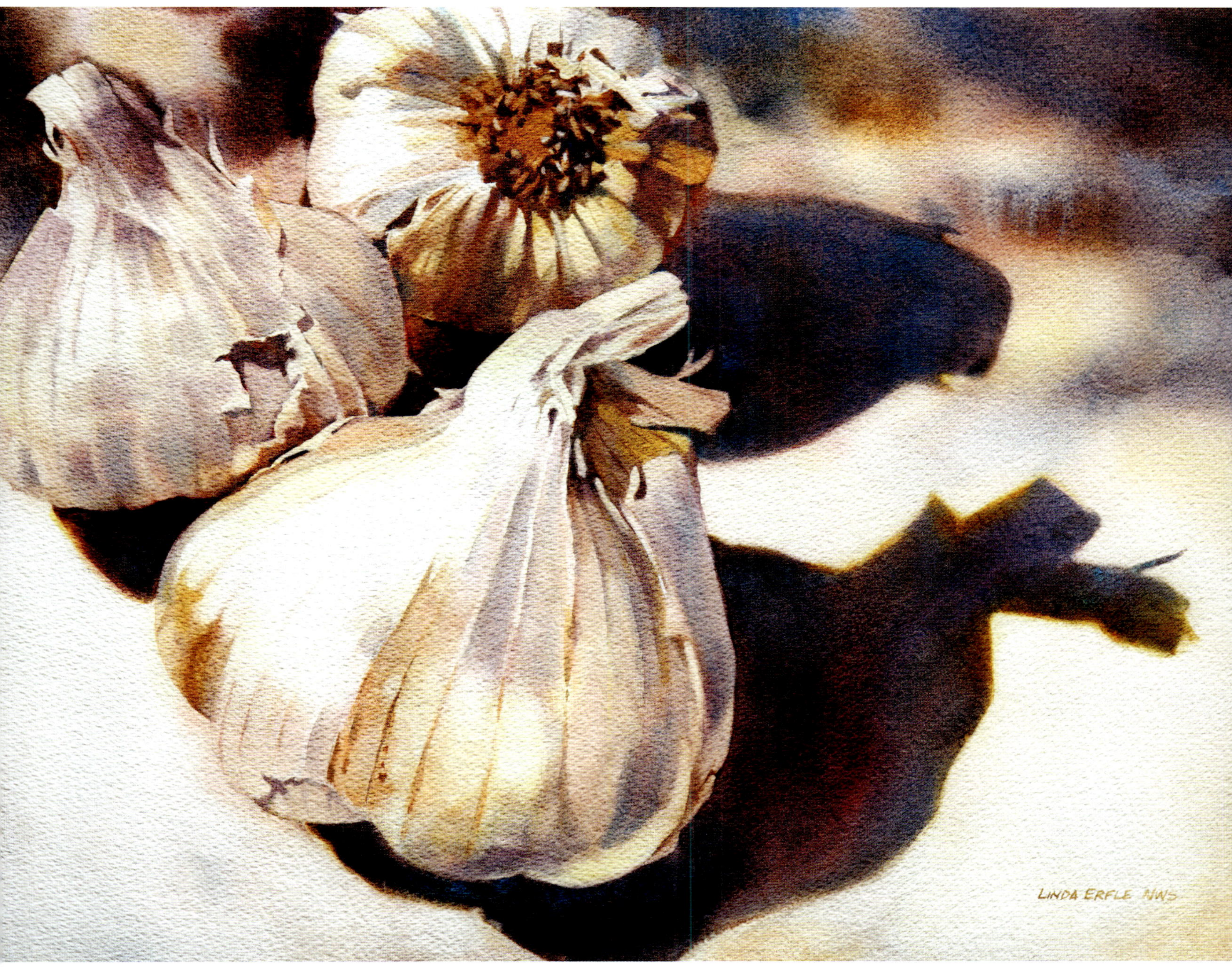

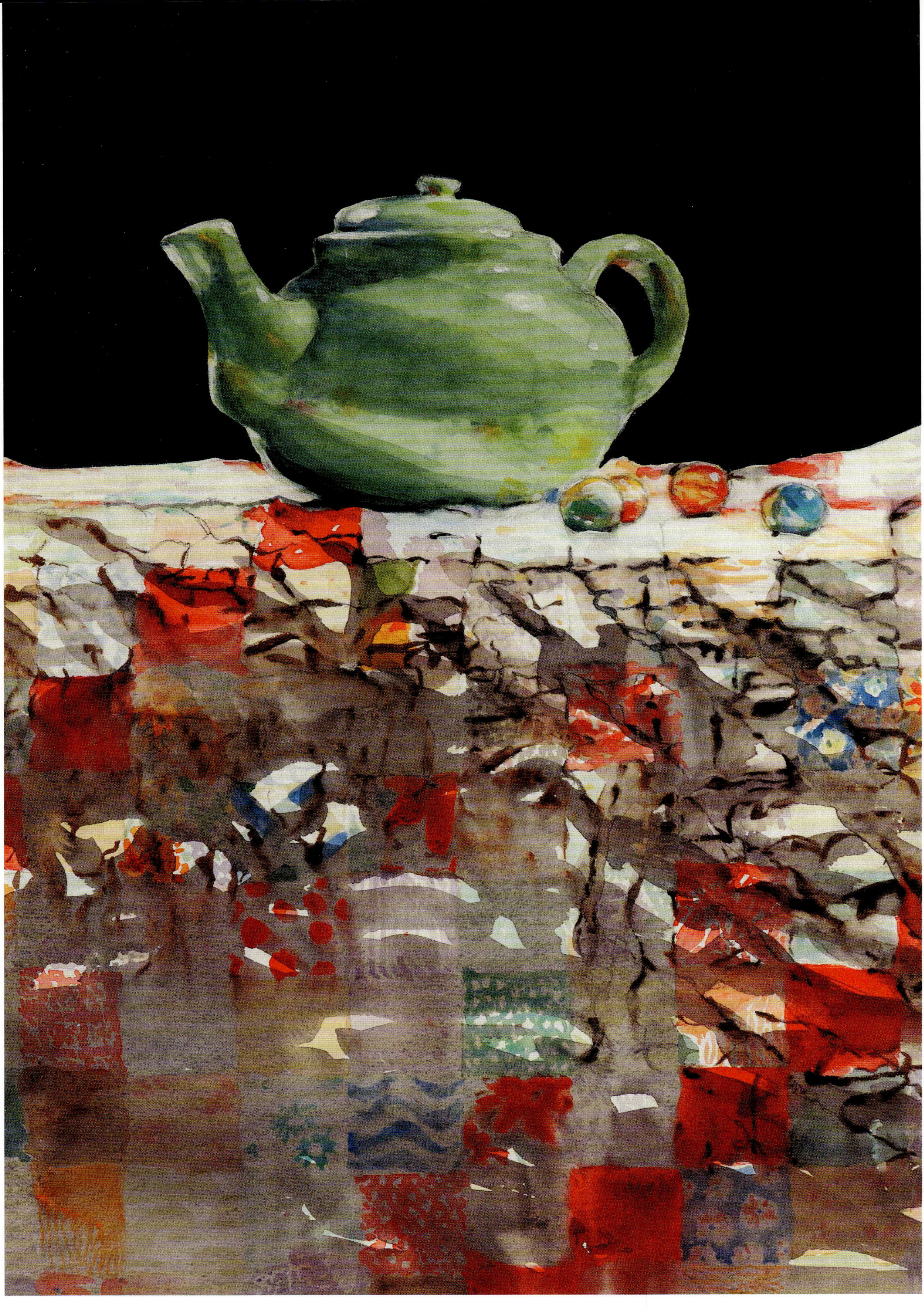

◀ STILL LIFE WITH QUILT | Jennifer Polnaszek
18" × 12½" (46cm × 32cm) Watercolor on 140-lb. (300gsm) cold-pressed Arches

This work was painted from a photo of a still life I had set up in my studio. I love rich bright color and dramatic shadows and wanted a subject that would allow me to play with both elements. I was struggling with how to introduce shadow to my intricately painted quilt. In a leap of faith, I applied a watery wash to the areas of shadow. In horror I watched my carefully and painstakingly painted pattern melt and run. What a joyful accident, in hindsight, and one I hope to be able to apply purposefully in other work!

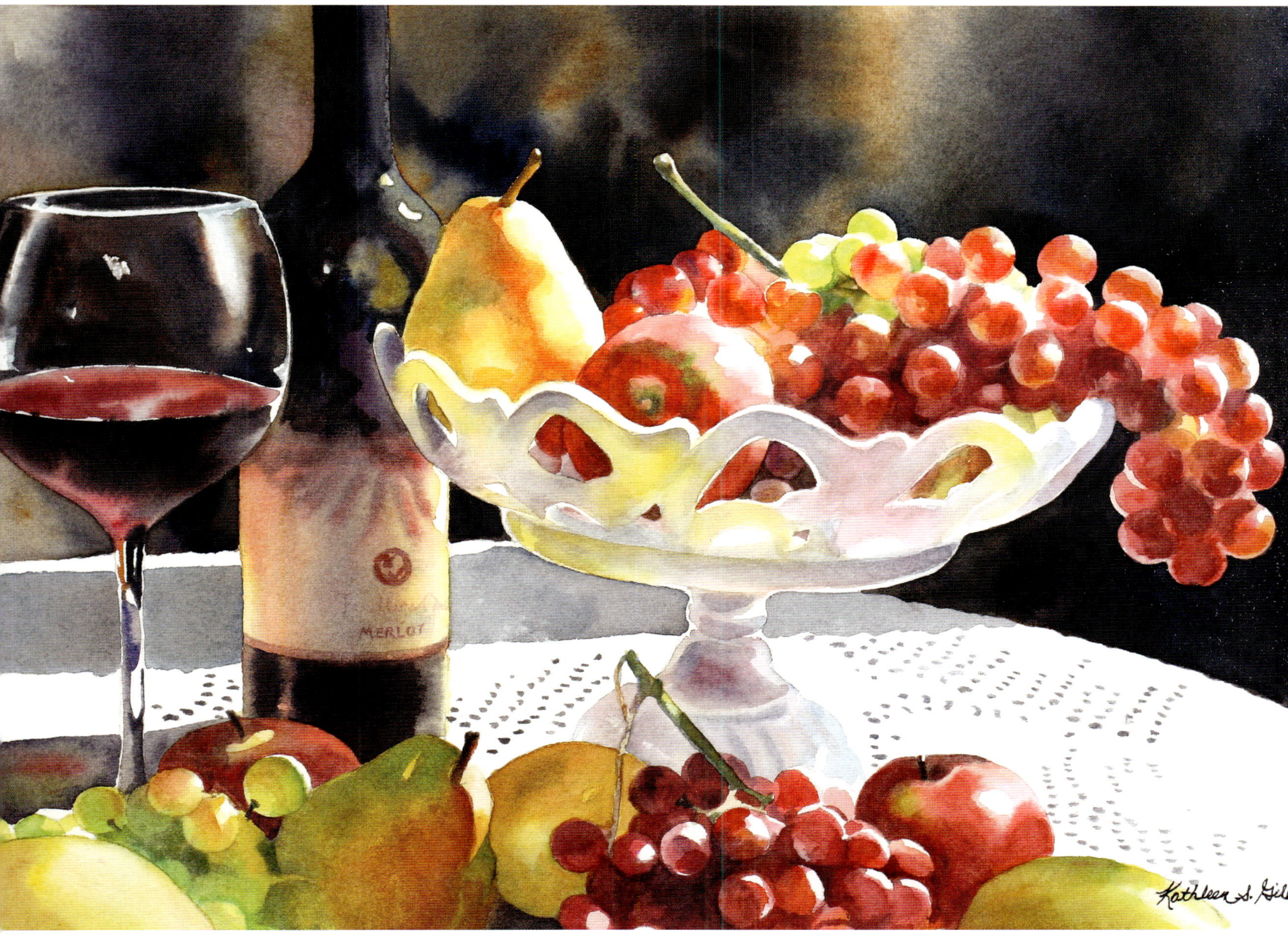

▲ GRANDMA'S MILK GLASS | Kathleen S. Giles
10½" × 14½" (27cm × 37cm) Transparent watercolor on 300-lb. (640gsm) cold-pressed Winsor & Newton

I had only a few hours to paint this still life for a show and simplified it with some extreme cropping of my photo. My time crunch forced me to leave soft edges and not paint every grape. The fruit in the bowl was painted as one shape. I worked quickly, dampening a small area with a color-saturated brush on dry paper. Working right to left (I'm left-handed), I continued to add color and deepen value. The white areas were left dry. The wine bottle was also done wet-into-wet. I always paint white shadows with reflected color as on the antique bowl. I chose the simple background to further highlight the fruit and repeated the bottle color for unity.

"I want my paintings to interpret what I see rather than just illustrate a scene precisely as it may appear."

– THOMAS W. SCHALLER

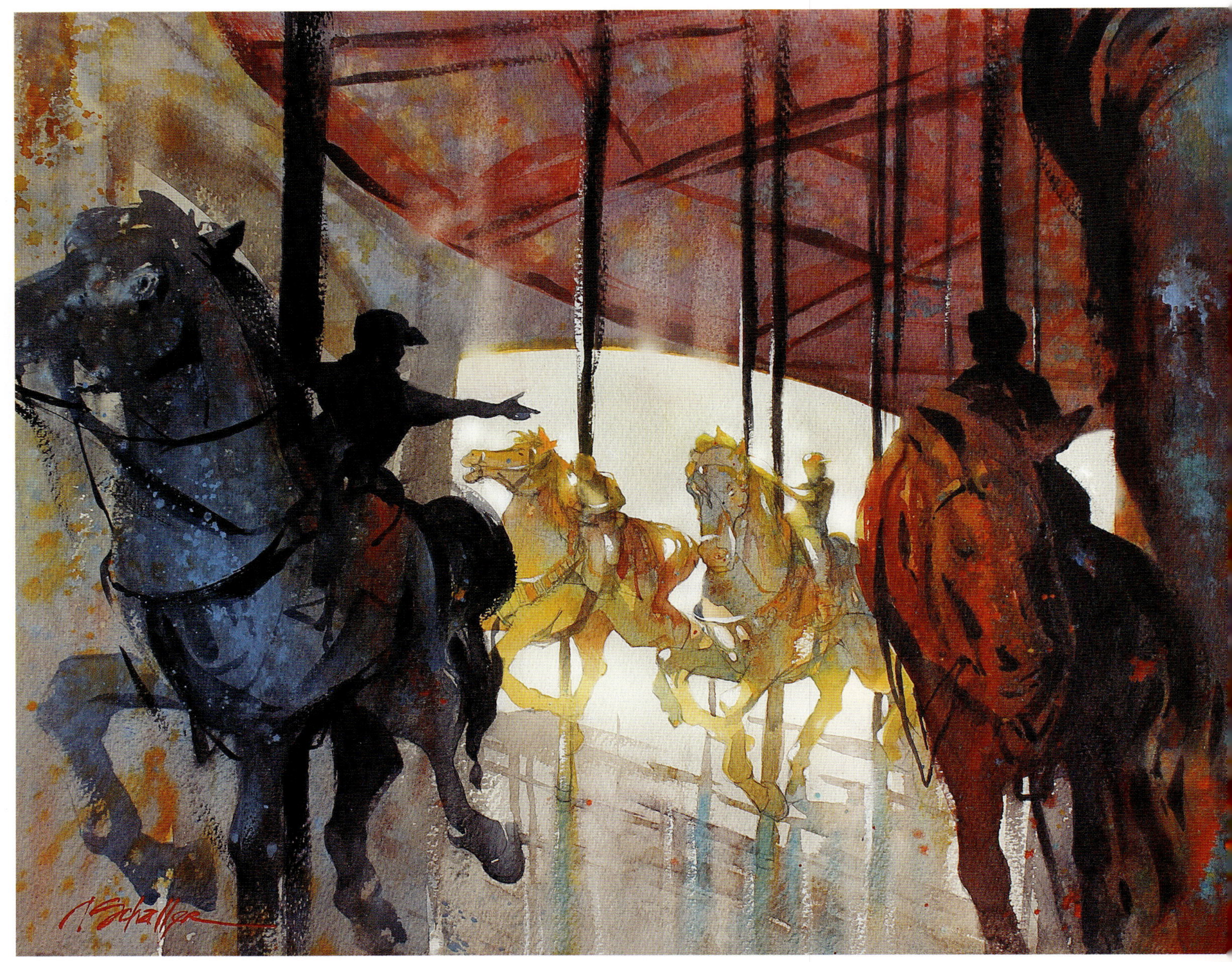

▲ **CAROUSEL, CENTRAL PARK – NYC** | Thomas W. Schaller
18" × 24" (46cm × 61cm) Watercolor on 140-lb. (300gsm) rough Saunders

This painting was intended to be less about specific details and more about the movement and joy embodied in the very idea of a carousel. Typically, my work is less reliant on color than upon value. But in this case I felt it appropriate to use color as value and to apply color in an extremely loose and vigorous manner. Complementary colors for vibration and splattered paint were critical to create the appropriate atmosphere.

RED 31 | Mel Grunau

21" × 29½" (53cm × 75cm) Transparent watercolor with acrylic accents on 140-lb. (300gsm) cold-pressed Arches

Everyday objects, especially those related to industrial manufacturing, provide unlimited inspiration for me. This painting was created from my photograph of a manhole cover. My challenge as a painter was to incorporate this flat, round, ordinary object into a painting. I wanted the manhole cover itself to be the center of interest. The dark geometrical forms in the surrounding pavement provided depth for the otherwise two-dimensional object. The painted daisies and the number 31 created additional interest. Together these elements—manhole cover, pavement, paint—tell an aesthetic story of ordinary life.

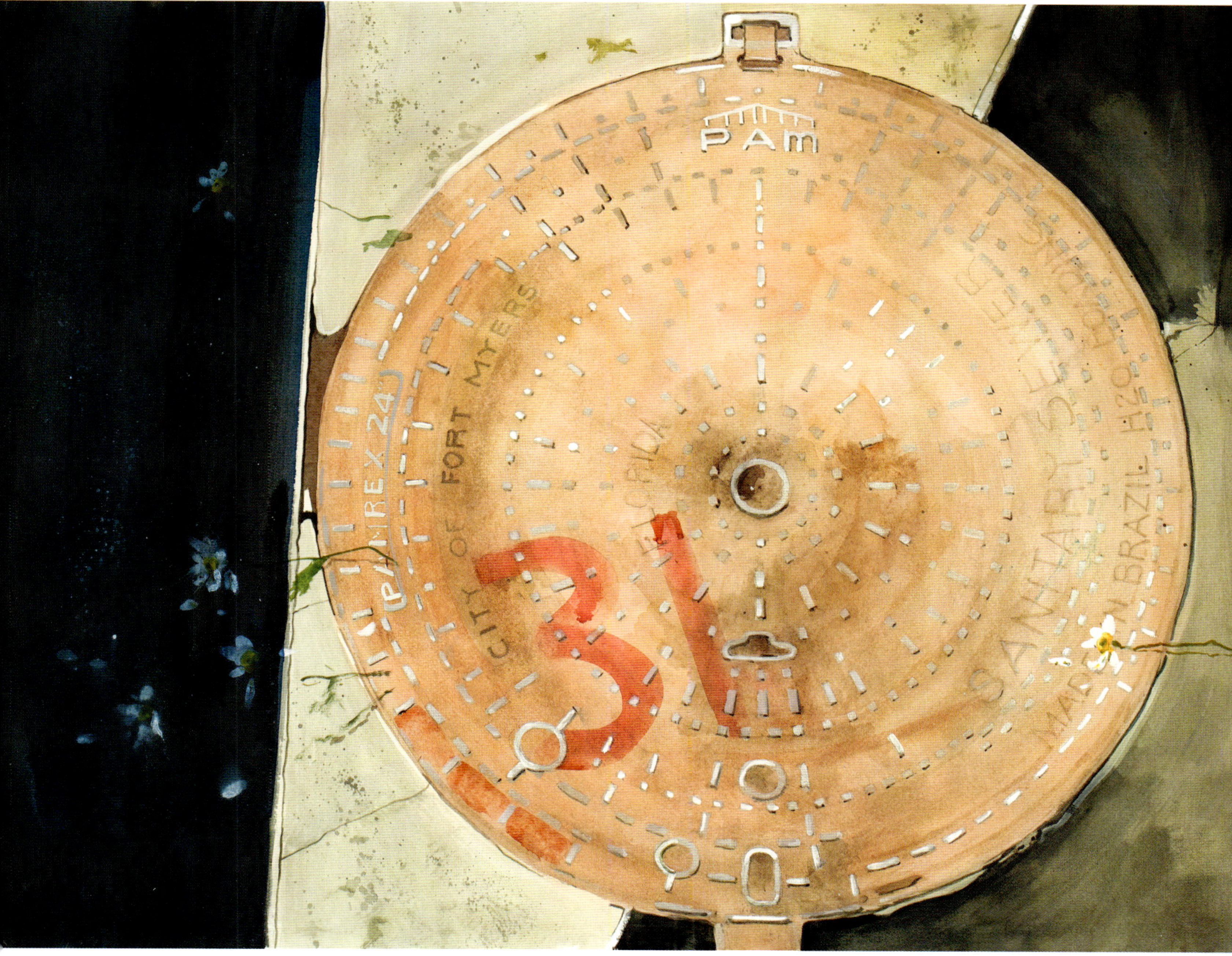

▼ **SECOND COCKTAIL** | Charlene Collins Freeman
27" × 41" (69cm × 104cm) Watercolor on 140-lb. (300gsm) cold-pressed Arches

Neon draws me in visually. I like the challenge of learning how to make it glow in watercolor. It would be easy to let all the bottles and bar paraphernalia take over the painting, but instead I chose to paint those details first as the background to the main subject, the glowing cocktail sign. I made the bottles softer in detail and more muted in color and slowly snuck up on the neon sign. There I dropped in strong color and used water to soften as the light pulled away from the sign and blended into the background.

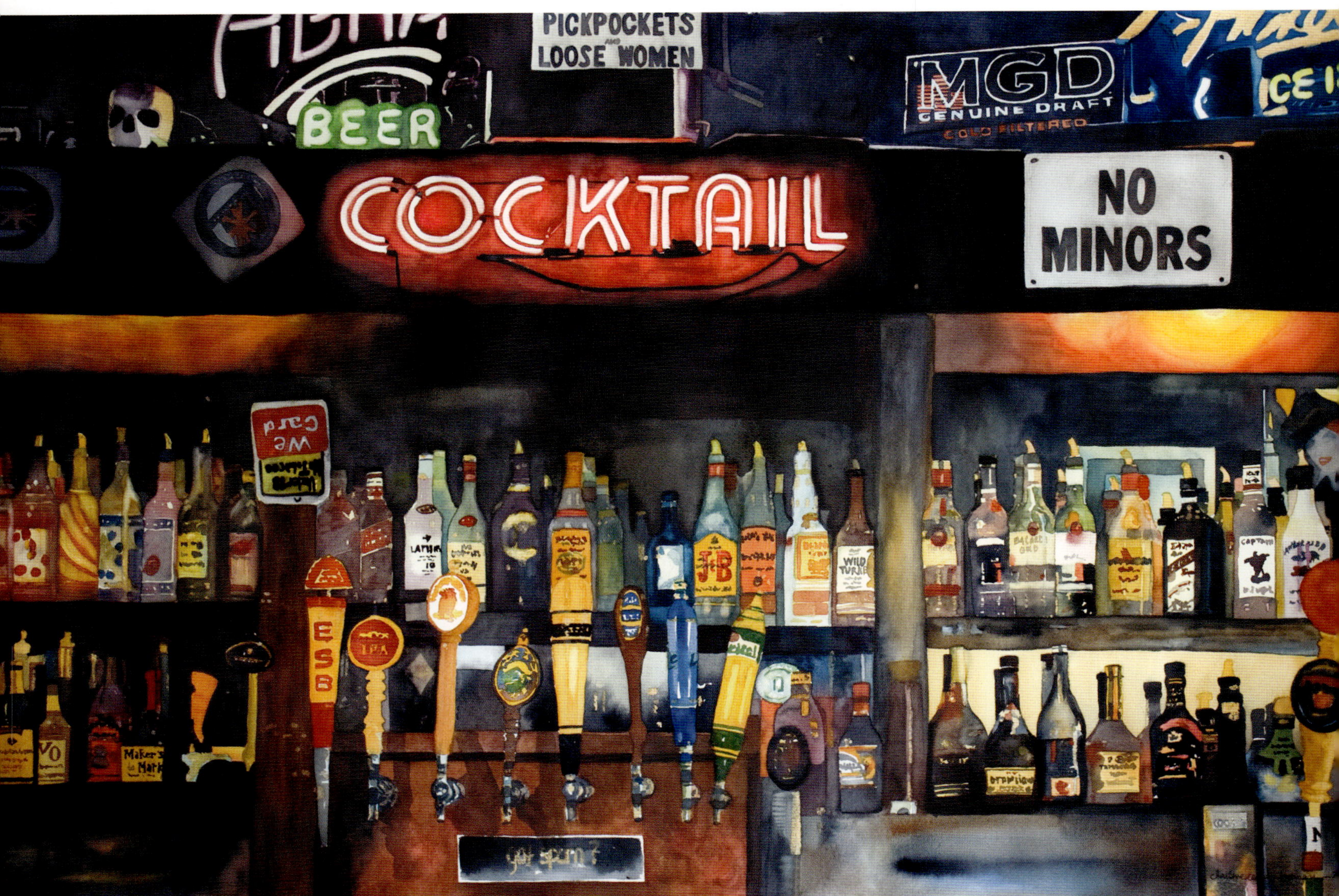

"It's important to keep your sense of humor and to persevere; the combination is unbeatable."

– SUZANNE HETZEL

▶ **RESTRAINT** | Suzanne Hetzel
30" × 22" (76cm × 56cm) Transparent watercolor on 140-lb. (300gsm) cold-pressed Richeson

Walking through a department store, I saw my kind of subject: interesting fabrics, groupings, women's issues—all in one. I snapped some pictures on my phone (I'm sure the salesclerks thought I was nuts). As I designed the bras on my watercolor paper I thought of some women for inspiration: Daisy Duke, Laura Ashley, Mae West, Lolita, the list goes on. I painted the bras once, cut up the first painting to arrange them to my liking, then painted the composition again with modifications to pattern, style, color, cup size and texture. The background had to be strong in contrast, so the bras really stuck out.

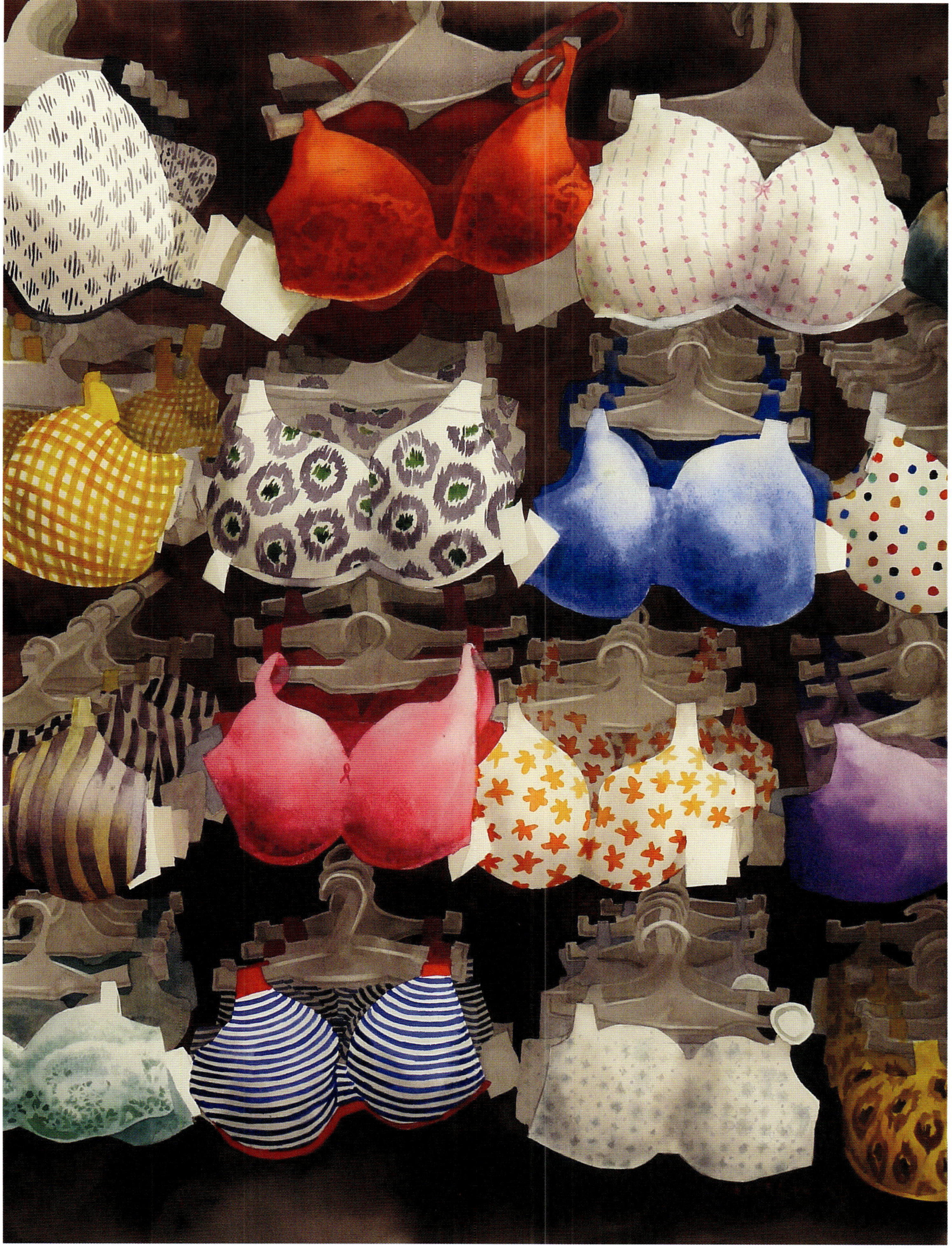

RED WALL STORY | Ran Mu
36" × 44" (91cm × 112cm) Watercolor on Arches

I tried to balance the color in this work to represent the traditional oriental culture in Beijing. I used wet-into-wet technique for the red background color to make it strong and deep. To contrast, I used dry-on-wet technique on the central figures to make these more distinctive but still simple to balance the whole painting. In addition, I put a piece of newspaper and the corner of a refrigerator on the edge of each side in order to express my experience of new Beijing (new culture mixing with traditional culture).

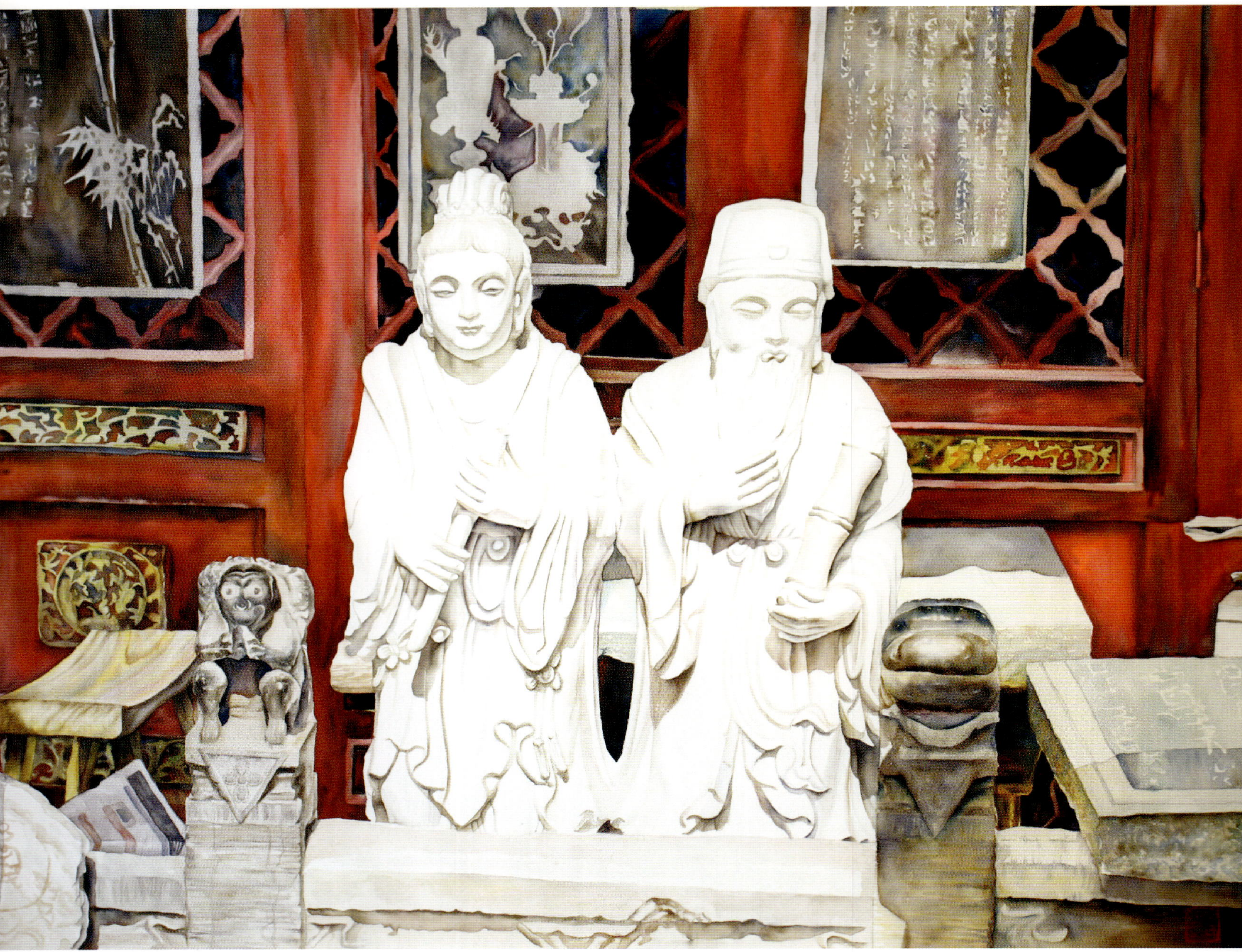

"Soft, warm colors evoke memories of a simpler life that's worth preserving."

– J. HENDERER BURNS

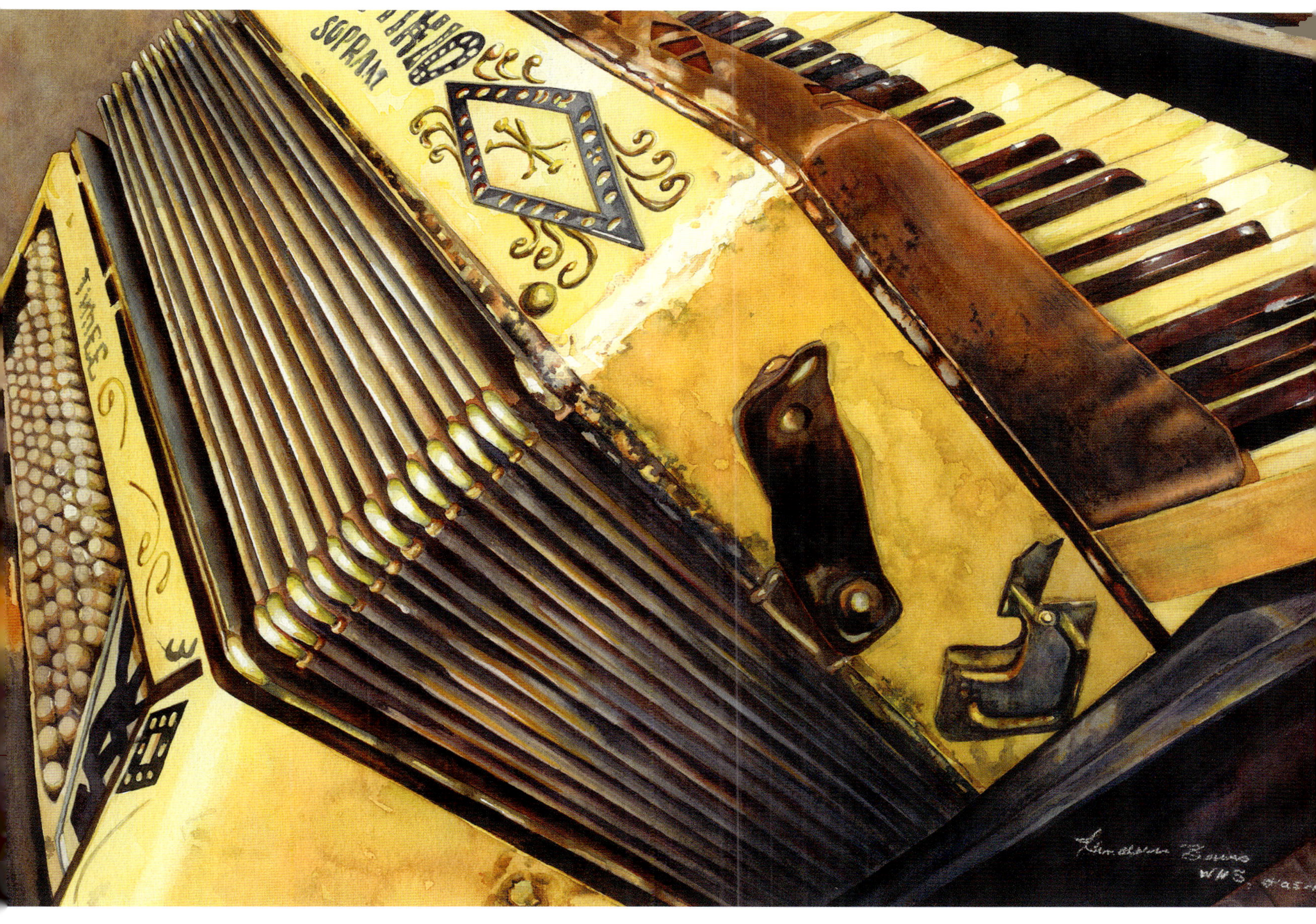

▲ **SQUEEZE ME** | J. Henderer Burns
15" × 22" (38cm × 56cm) Watercolor on 300-lb. (640gsm) paper

While I was wandering through a dusty antique shop in Texas Hill Country a few years ago, this well-used accordion started to tell me its story. Later, as I studied its photographs in the quiet of my studio, I easily imagined the gentle chords of "Waltz Across Texas" played by its owner's capable hands … and the weathered but loving faces moving through the dance hall in Gruene to its refrain. Problem: Find a way to portray the instrument's intricacies, so popular in an earlier age, and the musty world it so quietly inhabits today. Solution: I chose soft, dusty colors with brighter highlights to enhance its once shiny keys and metals.

"It is the little observational touches that bring a painting to life."

– ONA KINGDON

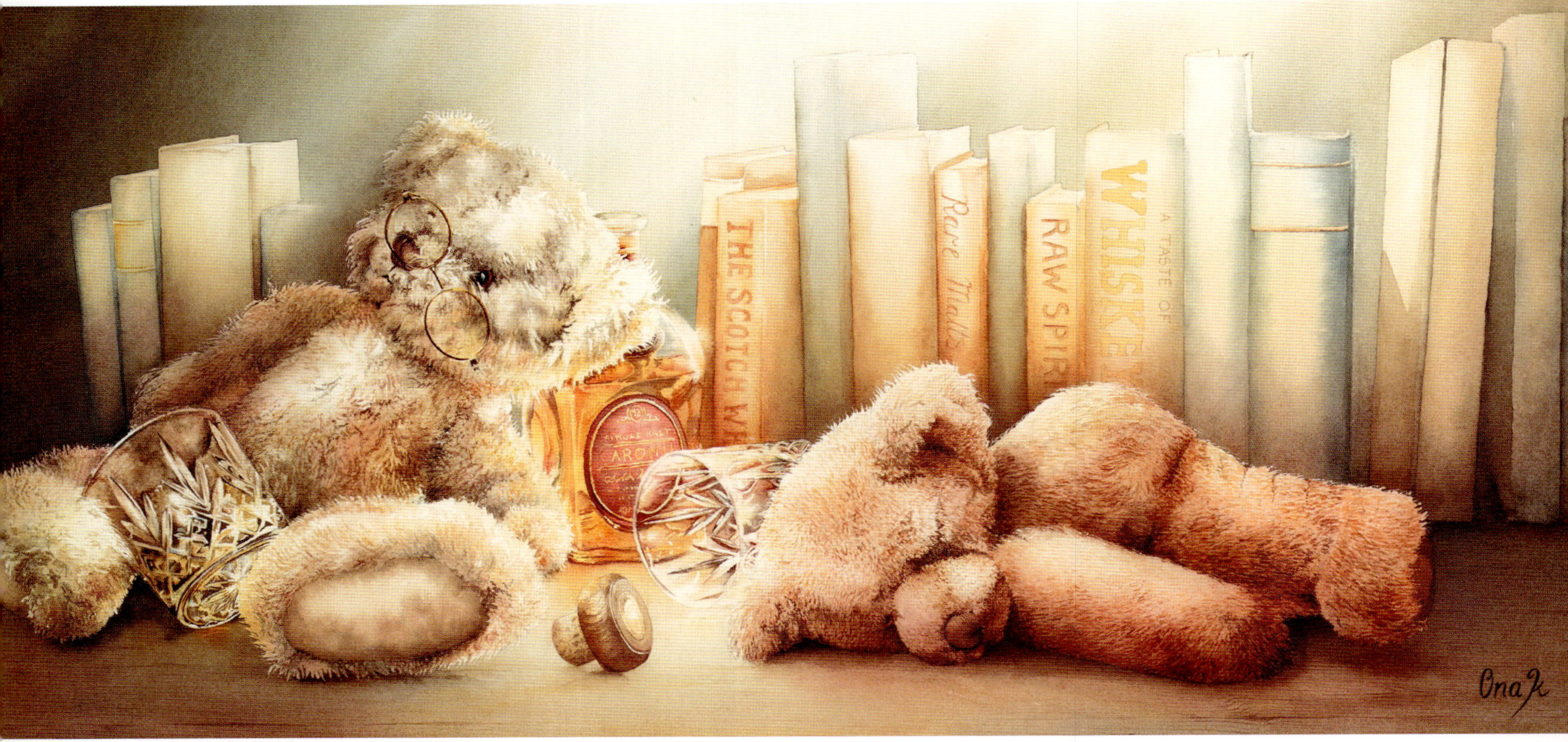

▲ **INTOXICATE-TED AND INEBRIATE-TED** | Ona Kingdon
13½" × 30" (34cm × 76cm) Transparent watercolor on 140-lb. (300gsm) cold-pressed Arches

This painting is part of a series in which I give teddy bears humanlike characteristics. The setting is a gentleman's study. It's the morning after and the two small Teds represent all who have either innocently or not so innocently experimented with alcohol and suffered as a result. My bear models are sewn, safety pinned, even taped into position to get a feel for the basic composition. I then exaggerate key elements such as the off-kilter glasses as I draw the outline to help me better convey the bears' personalities. I also add features as I paint, such as the rosy-flushed color of the horizontal bear's fur and the warm glow of the morning light. Each of these small changes is meant to convey the atmosphere and emotions I am looking for.

HIP HOP BEBOP | Chris Beck

12" × 12" (30cm × 30cm) Transparent watercolor on 140-lb. (300gsm) cold-pressed paper

Searching for still-life materials, I stumbled on this long-forgotten book in my collection. With its froggy orchestra on the cover, it was the perfect setting for my anuran salt shaker band. However, I realized it would be difficult to paint the scene depicted on the book cover if I laid in the deep shadows first, yet I risked lifting the images if I were to wash a dark tone across it afterwards. My solution was to paint the cover art without shadows and then use a dry-brush technique—making multiple passes with a deep gray paint mix—to establish convincing shadows at the end.

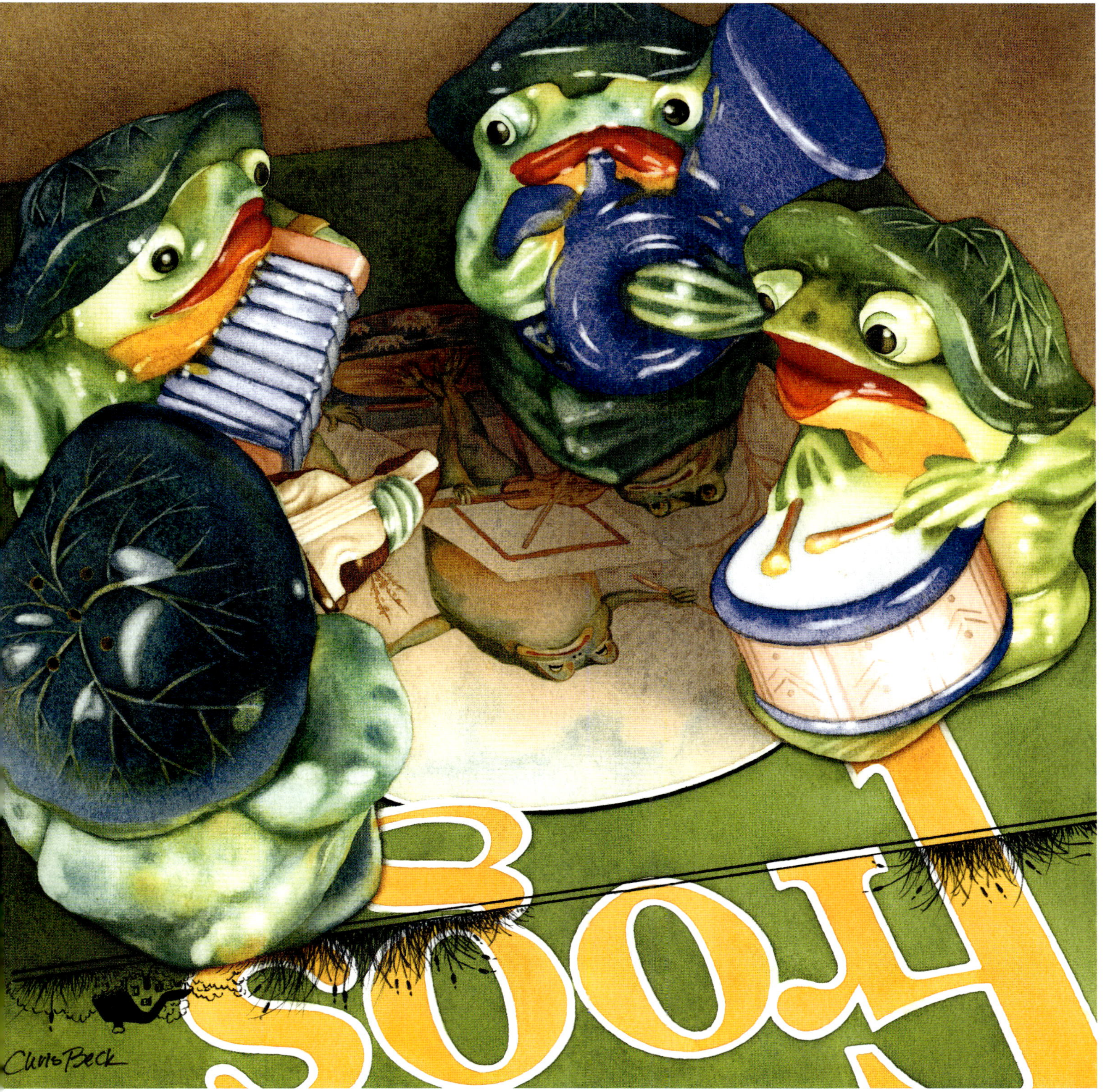

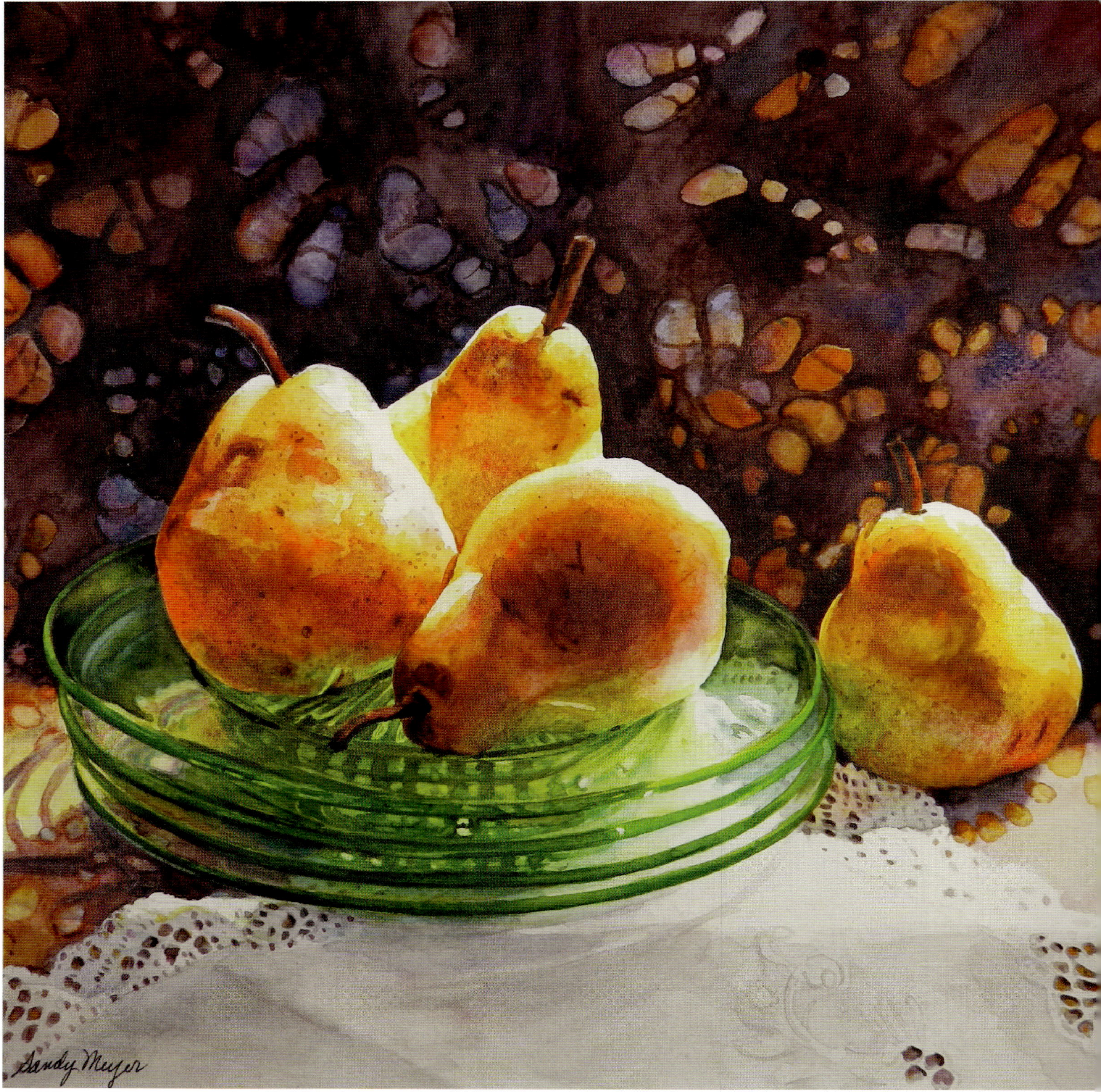

▲ **PEARS AND GREEN PLATES** | Sandy Meyer
19" × 19" (48cm × 48cm) Transparent watercolor on soft-pressed Fabriano Artistico

This is one in a series of still-life paintings in which fabric has been used to help bring unity to the composition. This fabric was chosen for its colorful shapes, which repeat the shapes of the pears. The smaller shapes are repeated in the holes of the lace doily and even in the shapes of reflected light in the center of the plates. I arranged the pears so they might seem to be dancing on the plates as the shapes are dancing across the back. The background was painted by spreading light colors across the paper using wet-into-wet technique. After it dried I came back and created the shapes by doing negative panting with a darker color.

"Using fabric as a backdrop for still-life paintings has made me aware of the many options for creating different background effects."

– SANDY MEYER

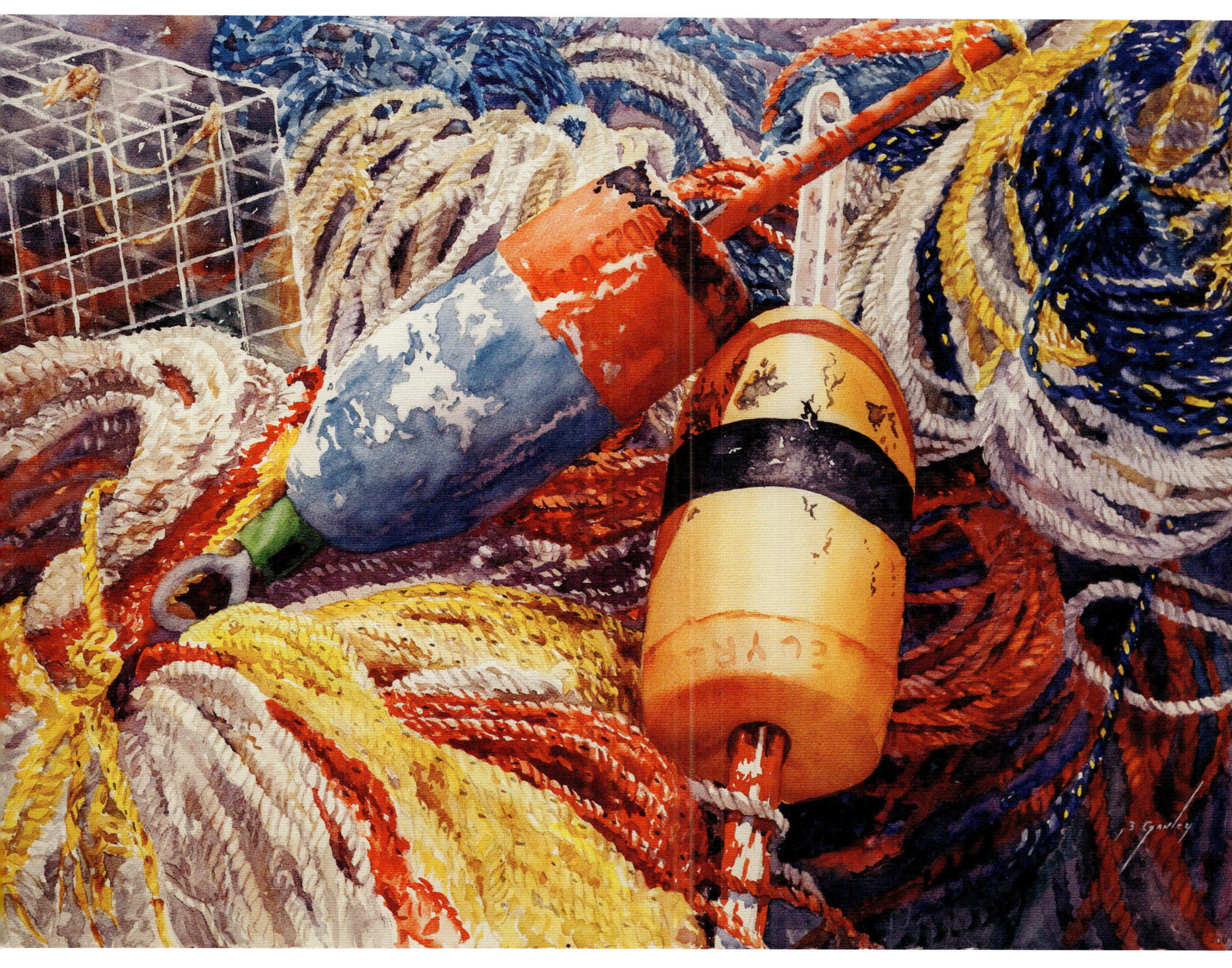

FIXIN' TO GO FISHIN' | Betty Ganley

21½" × 29½" (55cm × 75cm) Watercolor on 140-lb. (300gsm) cold-pressed Arches

I had to figure out how to push partial coils of roping back into the shadows. Note the red coil to the right of the orange buoy. The whole coil was painted with the same value of Scarlet Lake and blotted in a few areas while still damp. When dry, all the sections in shadow were glazed with a thin wash of Cobalt Blue. A second glaze of Cobalt Blue was applied to areas deeper in shadow. Leaving smaller sections here and there without the blue glaze allowed those areas to appear to be lying in dappled light. The addition of neutral-colored roping carefully balanced throughout the painting enhances all the bright colors. For the few areas on the orange buoy that required cast shadows I considered the color of the objects casting those shadows (both red) and added a generous amount of red to the shadows themselves.

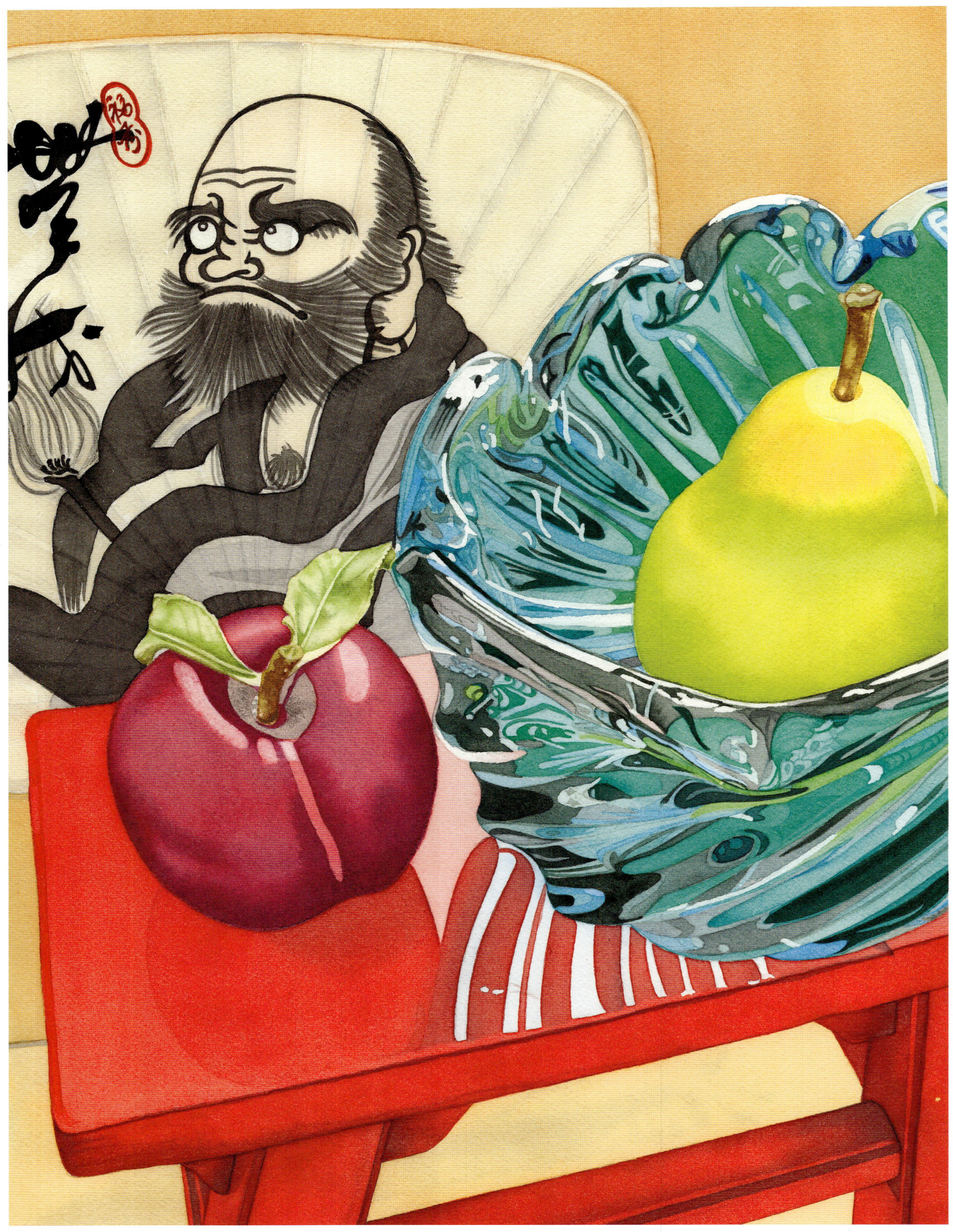

◀ **PERSPICACITY** | Sally Baker
16½" × 12½" (42cm × 32cm) Transparent watercolor on 140-lb. (300gsm) cold-pressed Arches

I begin a painting by arranging and lighting objects that visually appeal to me, have a strong emotional connection or present a challenge. *Perspicacity* includes a multi-faceted, intensely colored crystal vessel. My challenge was to represent this vessel in a specific moment in time. In addition to careful observation of the object, a reference photo enabled me to freeze the light refractions and map how I would approach the painting process. Using a clay shaper tool (available in most art supply stores), I applied masking fluid to my highlights and then slowly built up color intensities in the remaining spaces. I find that the darks always wind up darker than I think they will.

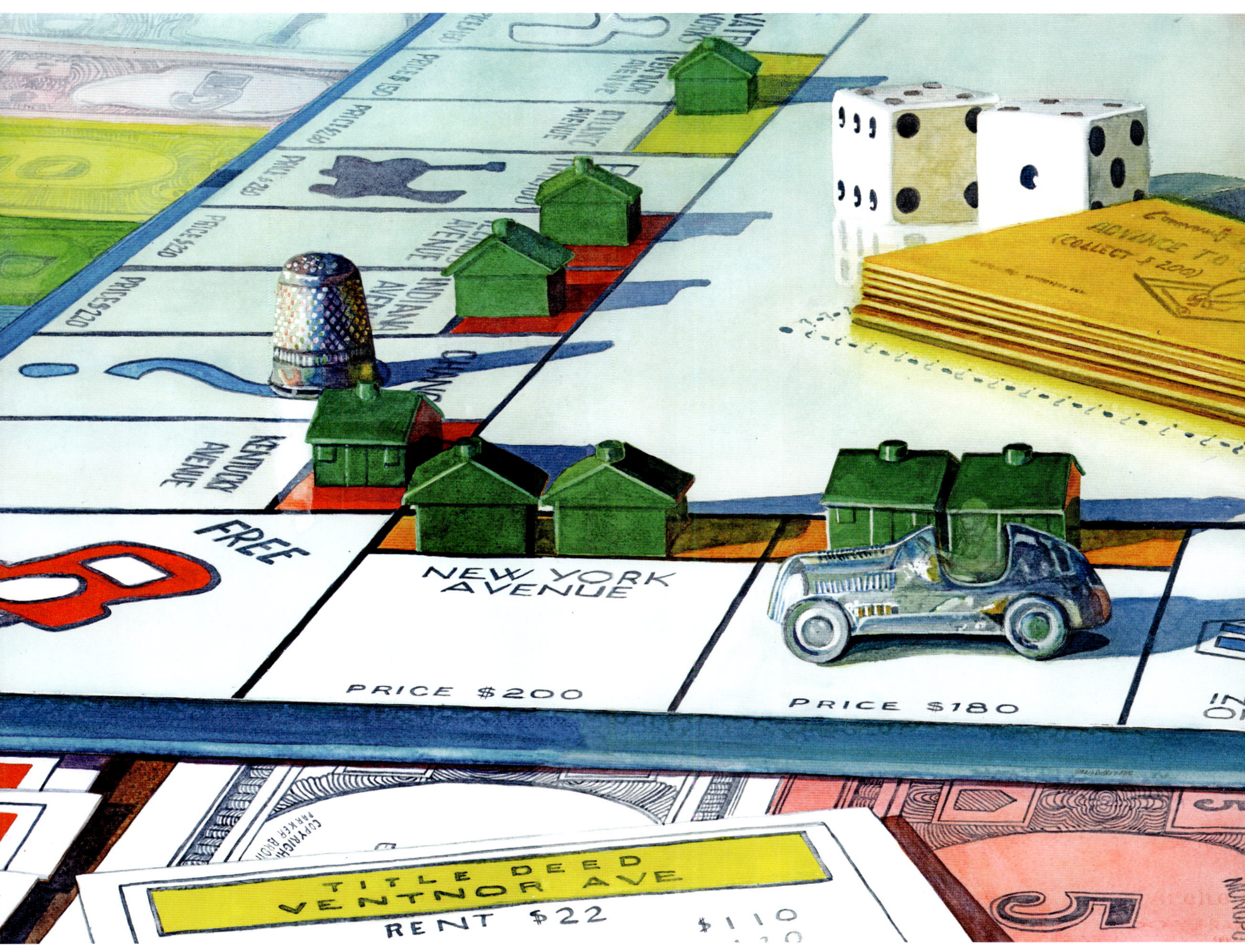

▲ **ADVANCE TO GO** | Janet Mach Dutton
22" × 30" (56cm × 76cm) Transparent watercolor on 140-lb. (300gsm) hot-pressed Arches

The vintage Monopoly board was photographed to get an unusual perspective and drawn from vanishing points far off the paper. After brushing layers of color to achieve depth, fine-tip pens created uniform lines and lettering. My original idea was to paint the car game piece to look like a real 1938 Sprint car with driver, but even after several tries it still didn't work. The aha moment came a few days later when I decided to lift and repaint the car to look like the original game piece and make the driver invisible. That worked! The fun of playing the game had been in pretending that it was real.

"Overlap everything with something; this includes the mat overlapping introduced objects on all four sides."

– CINDY BRABEC-KING

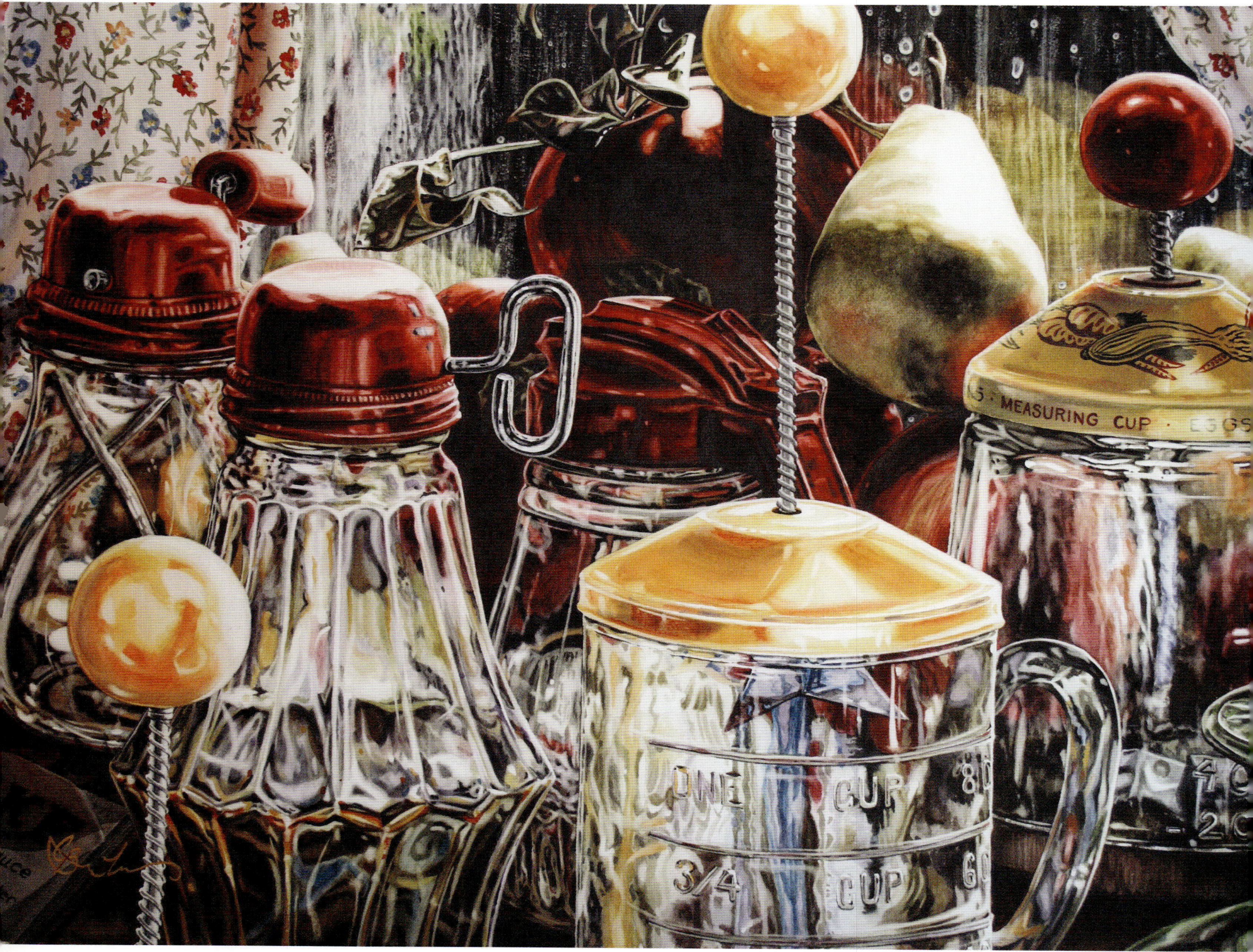

▲ NUTCRACKER SWEET | Cindy Brabec-King
22" × 30" (56cm × 76cm) Transparent watercolor on 300-lb. (640gsm) rough Arches

Solving the puzzle of creating texture seen through the glass jars and windowpane was my challenge in *Nutcracker Sweet*. First, loose strokes were painted in grays and blacks around predrawn white spaces that indicate shine. The use of Sap Green, Naples Yellow and Alizarin Crimson suggests distorted objects in the background. Exaggeration of values and unpredictable linework were the best solution for letting go of the lack of detail in the photos used. Working with flat brushes to create abstract strokes and using less water than color throughout helps the composition as well as solves texture problems.

▶ PAINT BY NUMBERS | Cindy Brabec-King
30" × 22" (76cm × 56cm) Transparent watercolor on 300-lb. (640gsm) rough Arches

Artist studios are complex in a variety of ways, so in order to get *Paint by Numbers* to work it meant even more objects than the original plan. Too simple would have been the mistake. To keep the piece flowing, color choices (mostly of cool tones) had to be reduced. Depth also had to be considered. The theory of thirds was used along with strong dark shadows and lots of overlapping. This hidden interest in the composition keeps the viewer constantly looking for different objects. Fewer color complements were also the answer to helping the pieces blend together.

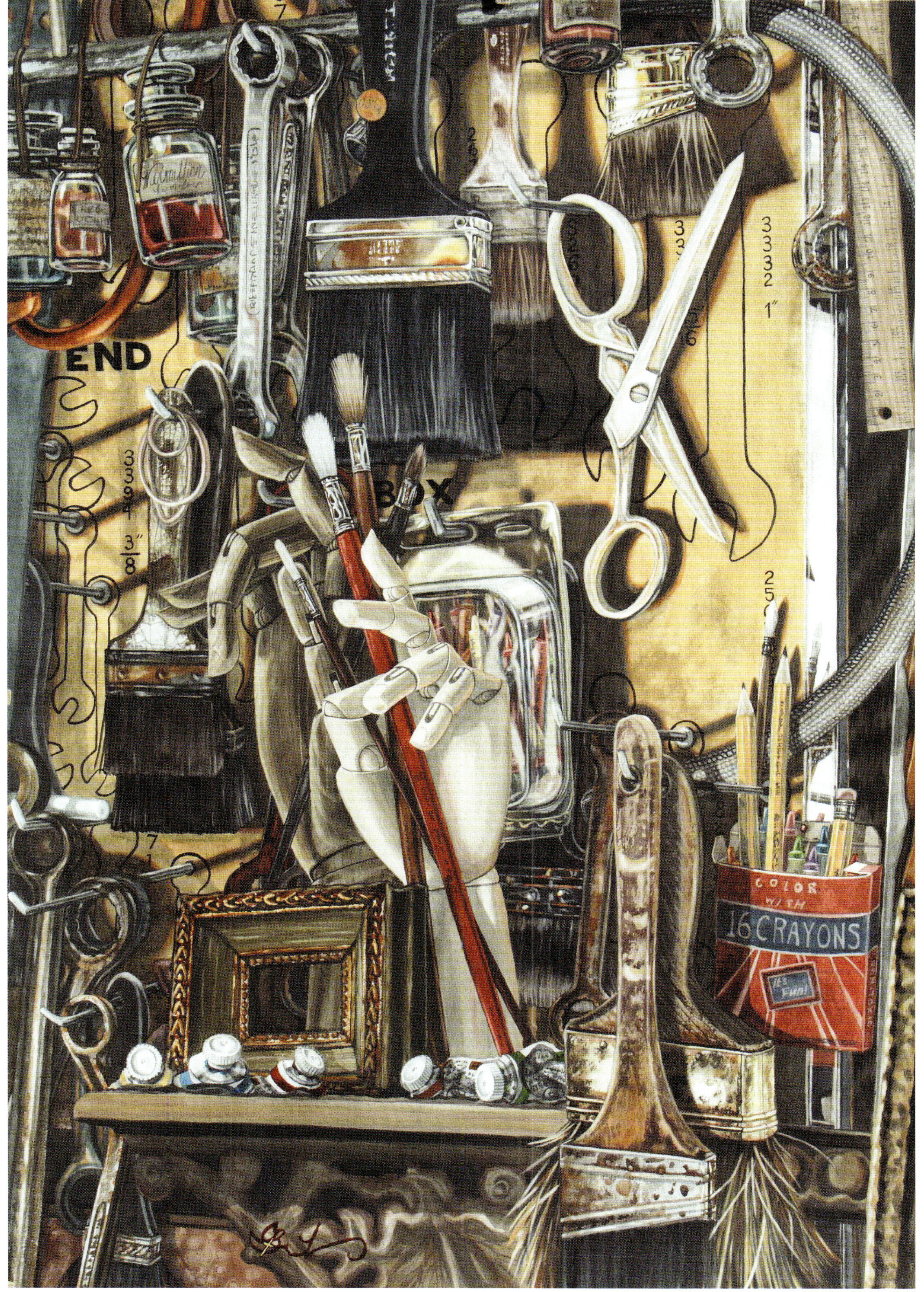
END
BOX
COLOR WITH
16 CRAYONS

TOOLS OF THE TRADE | Laurin McCracken
20" × 28" (51cm × 71cm) Transparent watercolor on 300-lb. (640gsm) soft-pressed Fabriano

The first architect I worked for, a terrific mentor, told me, "Real architects keep their pencils in Dundee Marmalade jars." Over the years I have collected a few and have kept my pencils, drawing instruments and other related items in them. One of the challenges was to get the distinctive typeface on the jars correct. In order to not disturb the white background with my signature, I worked my name into the text of one of the jars. This painting and *Ice Water* were both painted from photographs.

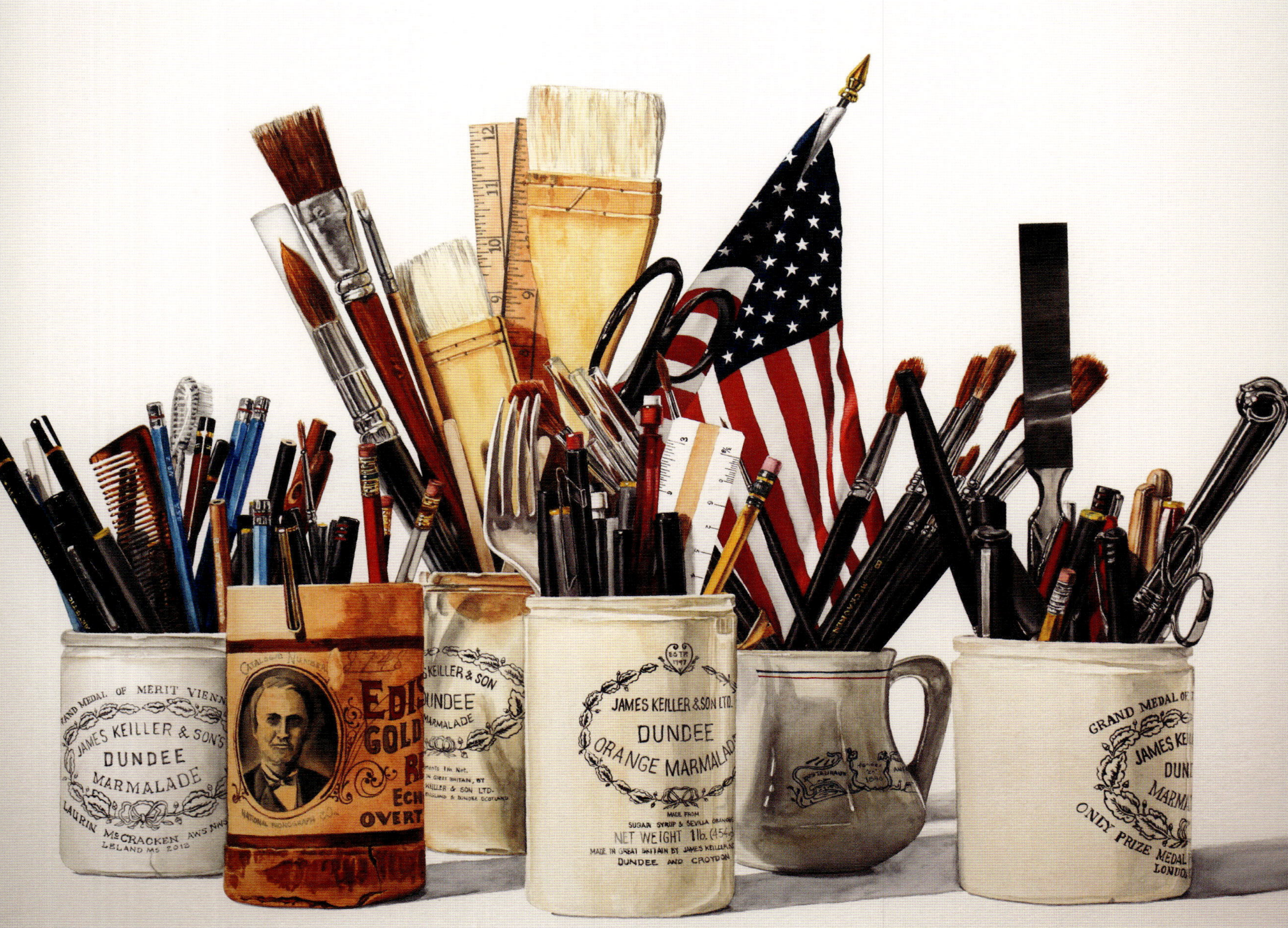

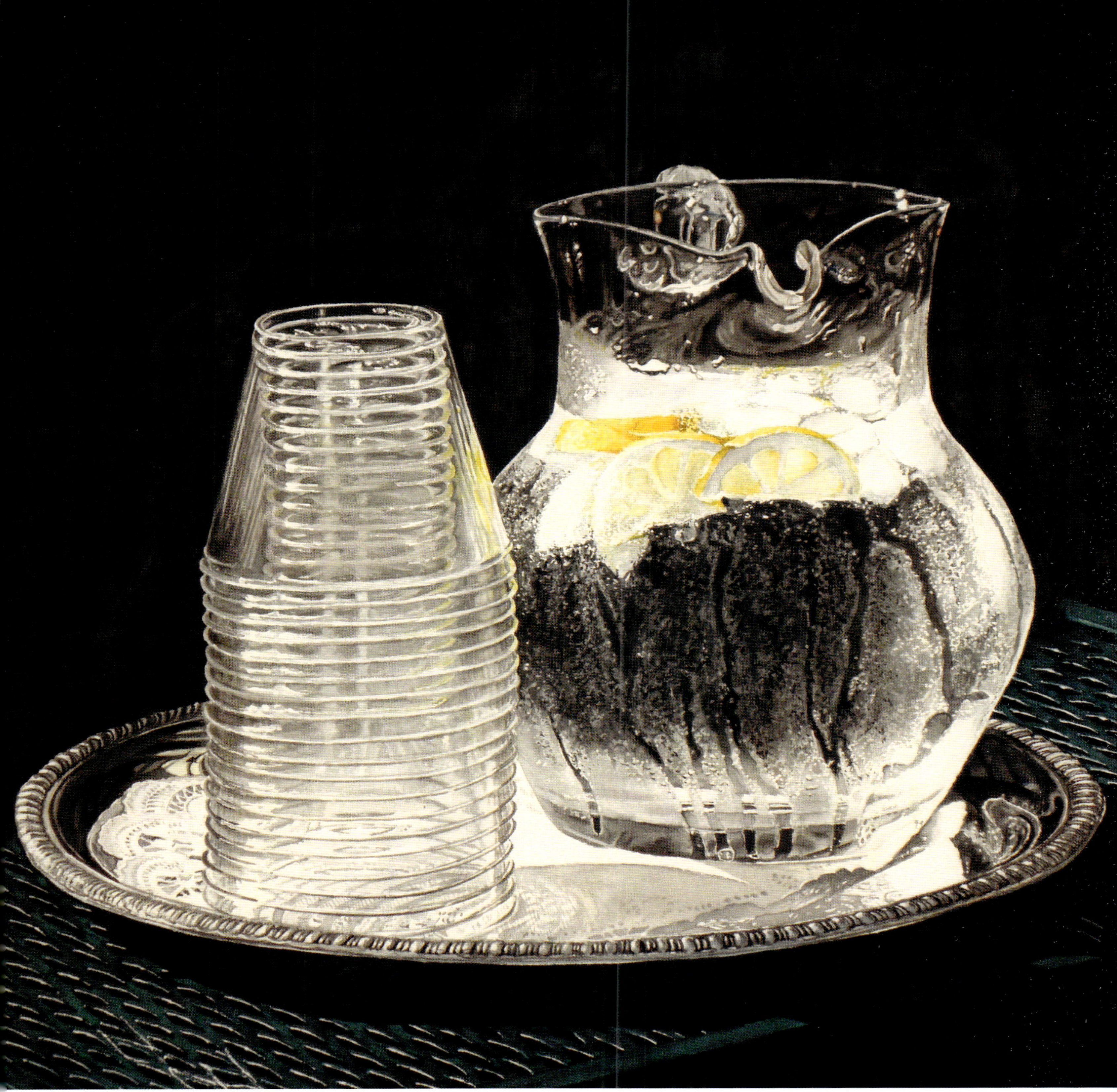

▲ ICE WATER | Laurin McCracken
18" × 18" (46cm × 46cm) Transparent watercolor on 300-lb. (640gsm) soft-pressed Fabriano

After a hot afternoon of touring gardens, we entered a small garden and there sat this pitcher and plastic cups in the bright sun, blacking out all the background—a welcome sight. The first creative challenge was to make the glass of the pitcher and the plastic of the cups look transparent but paint them so that you know one was plastic and the other glass. The other challenge was to paint the ice and the drops of water so that you know the water in the pitcher is really cold. One of the discoveries was the reflection of the lemons down through the plastic cups.

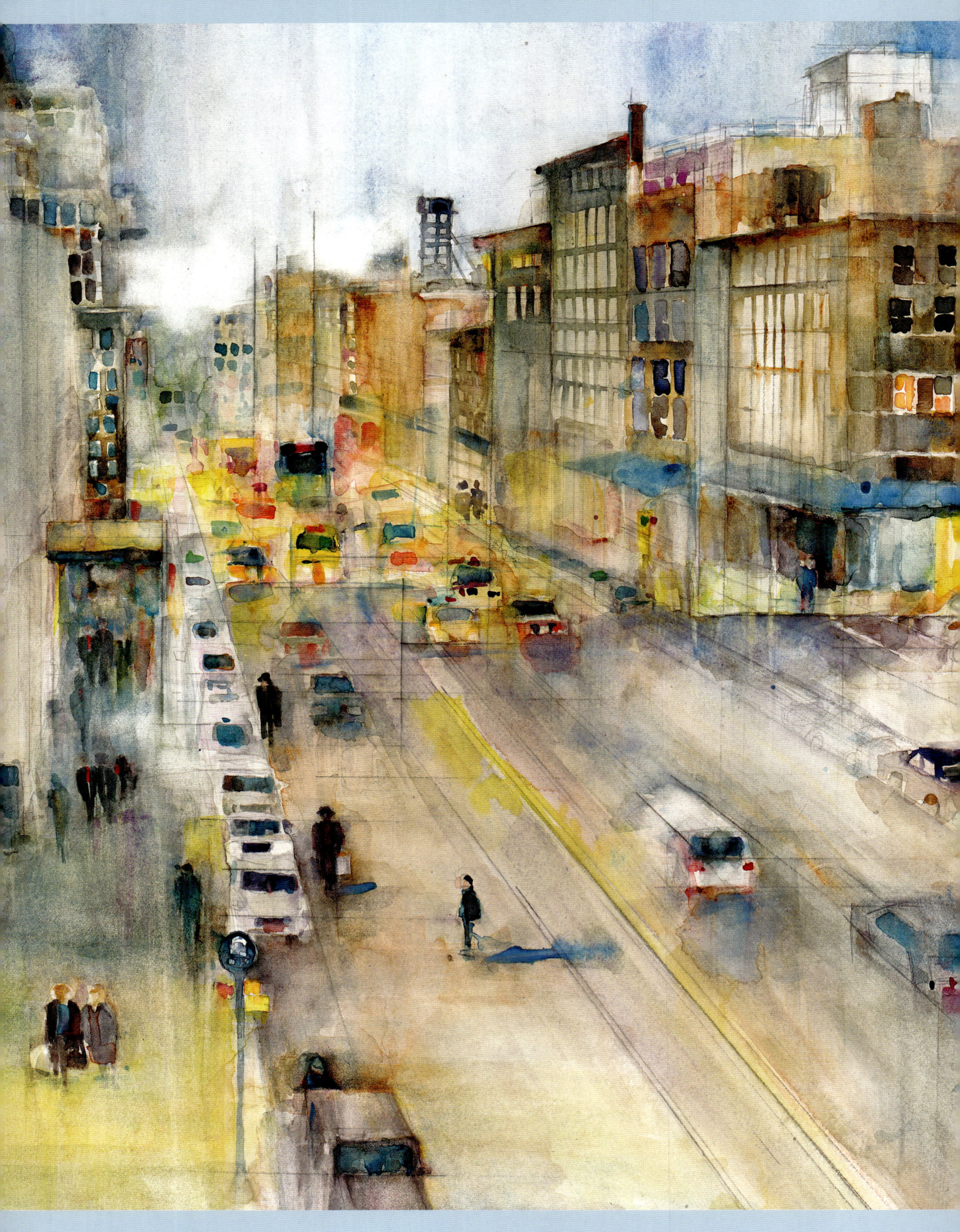

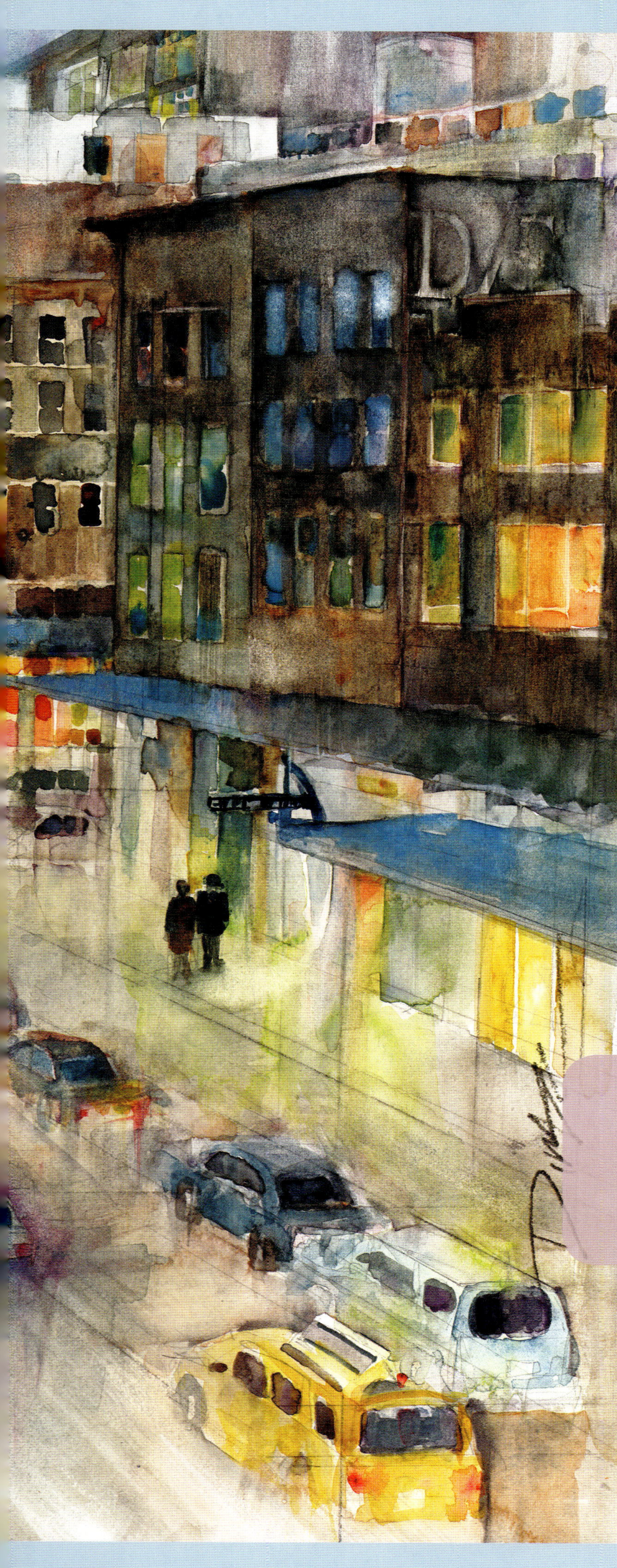

◀ **A VIEW FROM THE HIGHLINE** | Dorrie F. Rifkin
20" × 28" (51cm × 71cm) Transparent watercolor on Strathmore wet media board

I snapped photos during a New York City sunset walk with my husband. In my studio I start with a detailed drawing. Next I add background colors. I should let the paint dry, but instead begin the cars, overworking the painting and making mud puddles and pies. Next I cry. The beauty of watercolor painting is that if one works with and not against it, there is always a solution. Later, the paint dry, I start again, the wiser for the misstep. I use good paper, so it can take a beating, take on water and take to paper towels. I can now remove most of the mud and then slowly add more color.

7 | *City Sights*

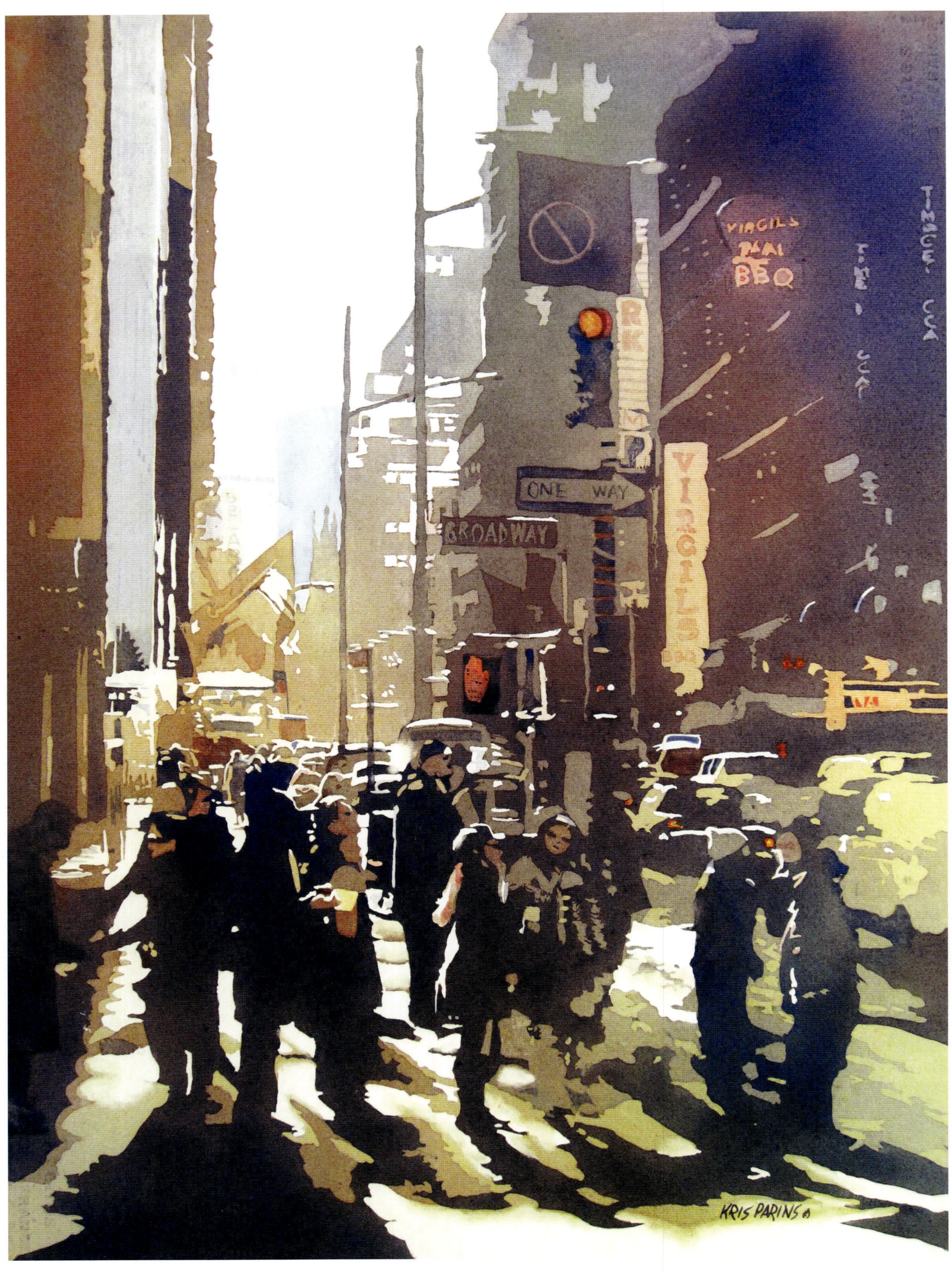
BBQ
ONE WAY
BROADWAY
VIRGILS
KRIS PARINS

◀ CITY LIGHT | Kris Parins
29" × 21" (74cm × 53cm) Transparent watercolor on 140-lb. (300gsm) cold-pressed Arches

Painting in a series presents a unique set of creative challenges (see *Against the Light* on page 39). Another problem is how to keep myself and my audience entertained by injecting variety into the series. To avoid copying myself, I put away each painting after it is done and do not look back as I work on the next piece. As a result, each painting has a unique atmosphere, vantage point and color emphasis. Creating the paintings in the sequential order of the photo references made me mindful of the time passing with the flow of the crowd. The careful observer will see some of the figures repeated as they move from one captured moment to the next.

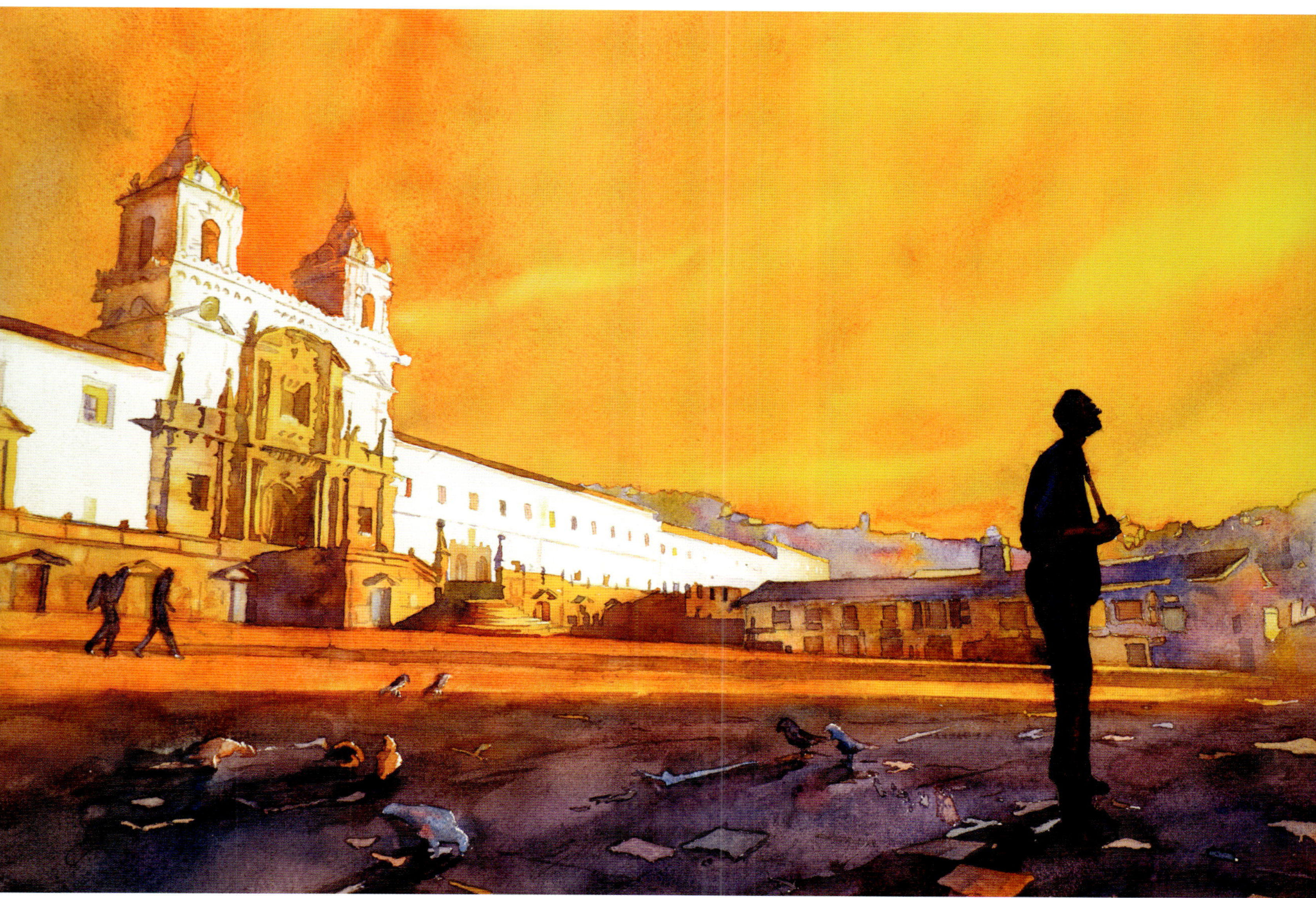

▲ QUITO MONASTERY | Ryan Fox
14" × 21" (36cm × 53cm) Transparent watercolor on 140-lb. (300gsm) cold-pressed Arches

My watercolor paintings are based on my travel photographs. Once the drawing is established, I abandon photo references and rely on intuition. The more creative risks I take, the happier I am with the results. *Quito Monastery* began as a simple drawing with graphic elements added to represent distant buildings, pigeons and the plaza. After painting a sunset from my imagination, I used complementary colors in the foreground. The inherent difficulty of watercolor constantly surprises me and leads to paintings I never envisioned creating. I hope to never fully control watercolor as I am most inspired by the uniqueness of the medium.

AUTUMN AT THE UNION TERRACE | Steven Kozar
14" × 12" (36cm × 30cm) Watercolor on 156-lb. (330gsm) hot-pressed Arches

This watercolor depicts a very popular location on the University of Wisconsin campus. I projected my slides, taken on a cloudy, cool morning, to trace as much of the technical details as I could in pencil but ended up doing a fair amount of freehand drawing as well. Many of the leaves in the foreground were painted freehand, which was the most tedious part. But not much came easily; it was about four months of really hard work. No masking was used; I just painted slowly and carefully, layer by layer and section by section. I really enjoyed portraying the soft, even lighting of that morning. Capturing the feeling or atmosphere of a scene is essential to me; the detail is just the icing on the cake.

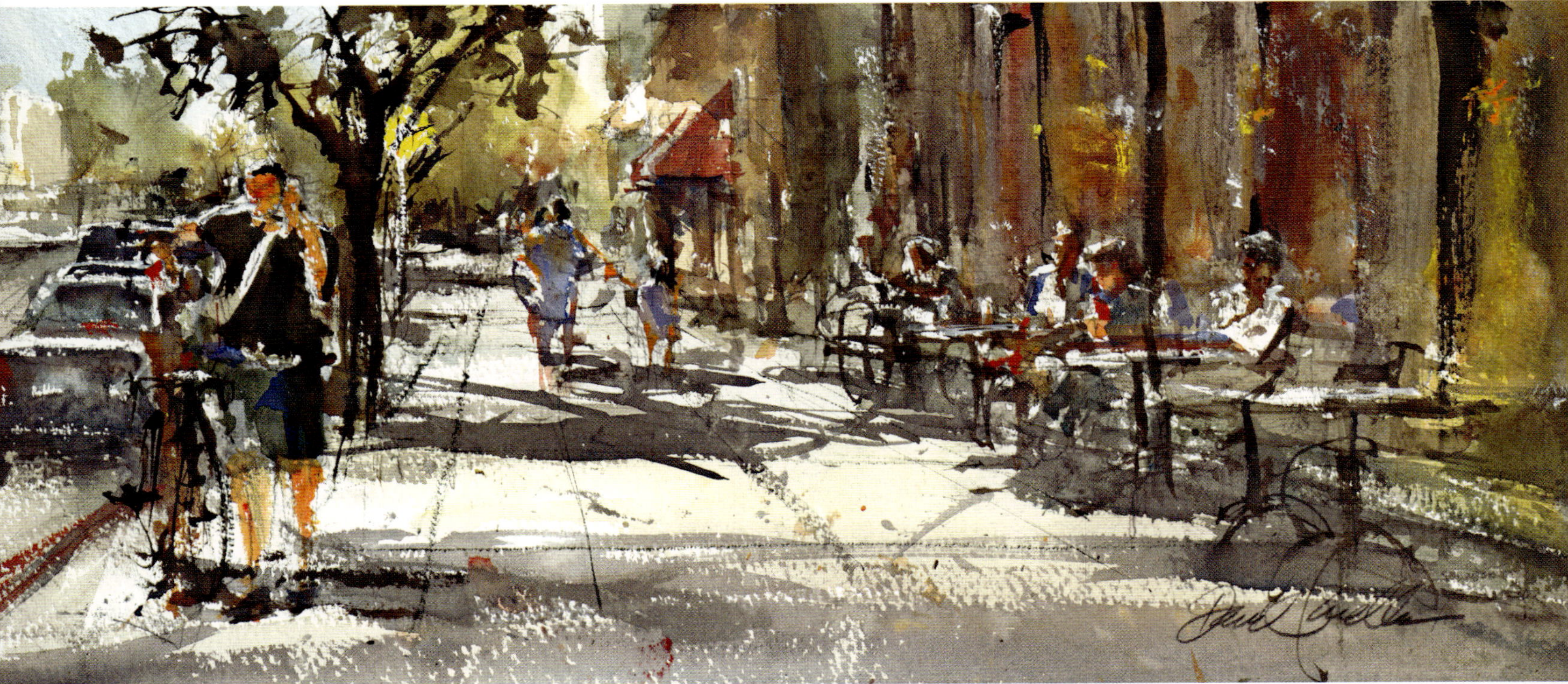

SIDEWALK RHYTHMS | David Savellano
9" × 21" (23cm × 53cm) Watercolor on 140-lb. (300gsm) rough Saunders Waterford

Participating in a two-hour quick-draw as part of a plein air event is a daunting task. I chose a lively street corner with an outdoor café on that overcast day. Once the rough sketch was done, I started painting in the sky, trees and sidewalk. The café's picture window posed a problem because in my toolbox I didn't have what I needed to paint the reflections in the glass. With time running out, I tried applying thick opaque and semiopaque paint. It was a risky move, but instinct told me it might work. I went for it boldly and that passage turned out to be quite successful. When the sun finally came out, it produced strong shadow patterns that I quickly added in one or two minutes, along with a few highlights and details painted with confident brushstrokes to complete the work—with ten minutes to spare! It received two awards that day and was a breakthrough painting because one, I discovered a new technique while trying to solve a technical problem; two, it gave me confidence in an intuitive side of me that up to that point I didn't know existed; and three, I realized I could handle the pressure, focusing completely on the task at hand.

"The rewards of risk can include new confidence in your painting ability."

– DAVID SAVELLANO

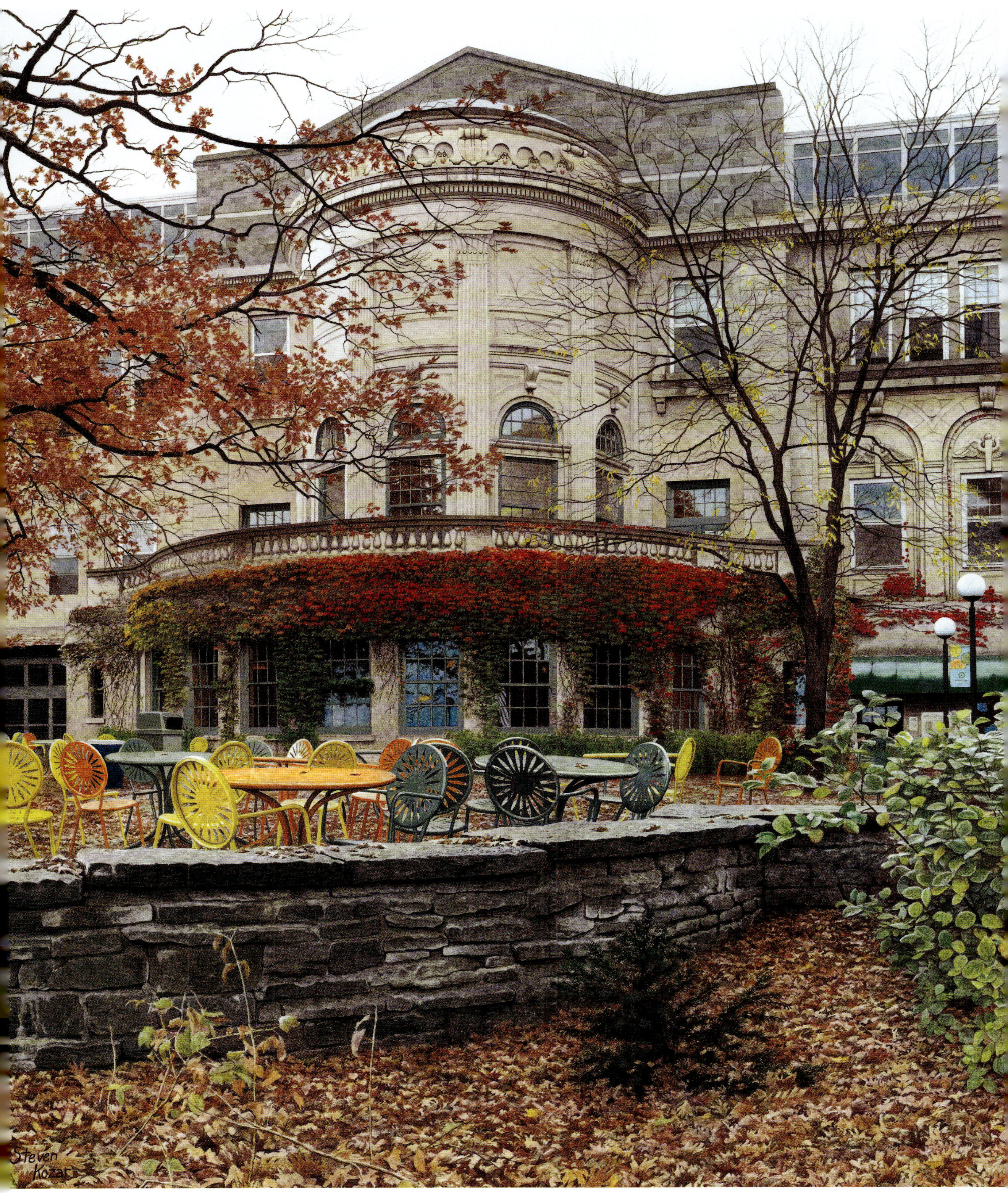
Steven
Kozar

WATER HOUSE | Peng Cao
22" × 30" (56cm × 76cm) Transparent watercolor on 140-lb. (300gsm) cold-pressed Arches

Across the Golden Gate Bridge, just a few miles north of San Francisco, Sausalito is one of my favorite places to sketch. A quiet harbor lined with rows of boathouses, a perfect balance between nature and village charm. The brushstrokes were straightforward to capture the vivid reflection in a serene waterfront.

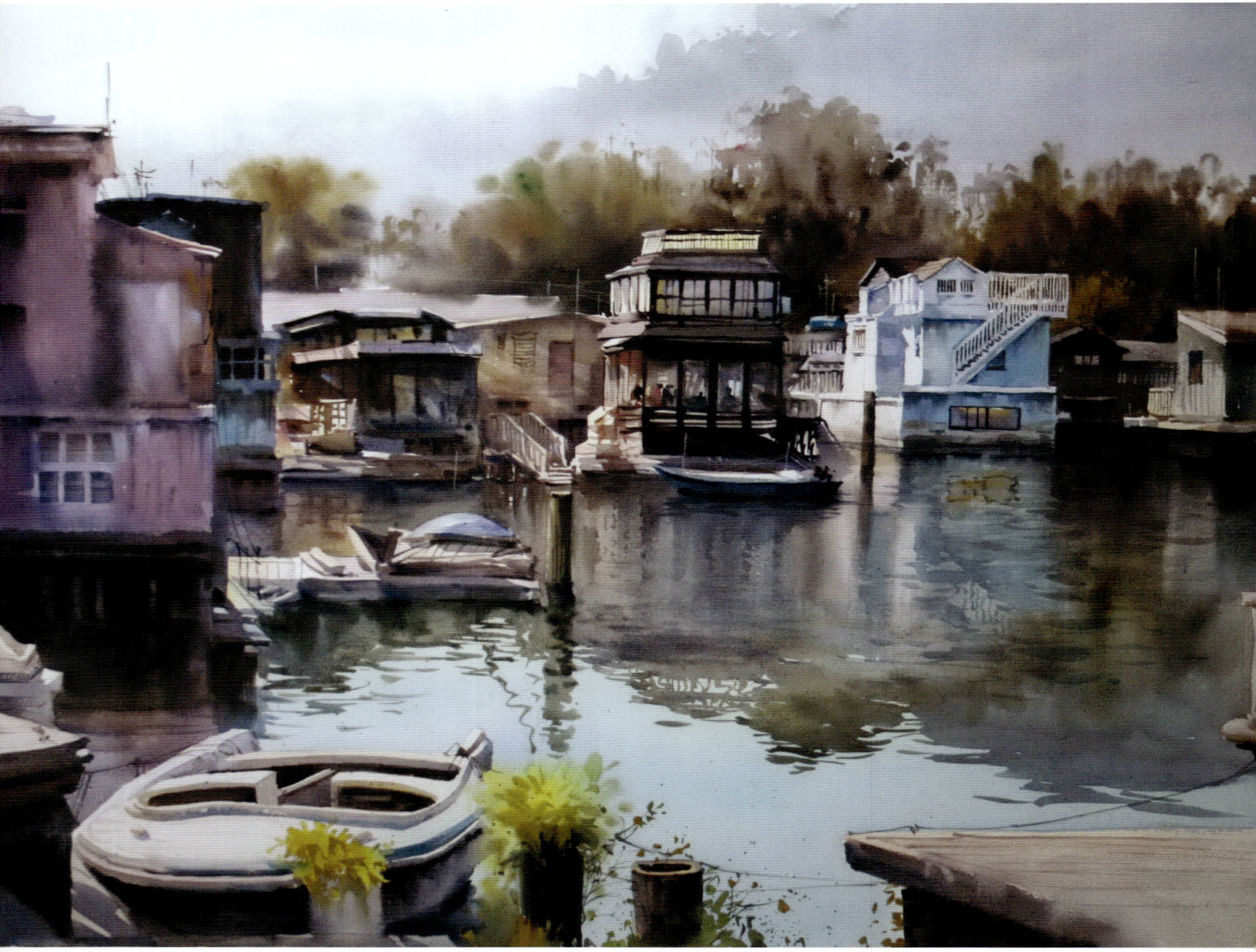

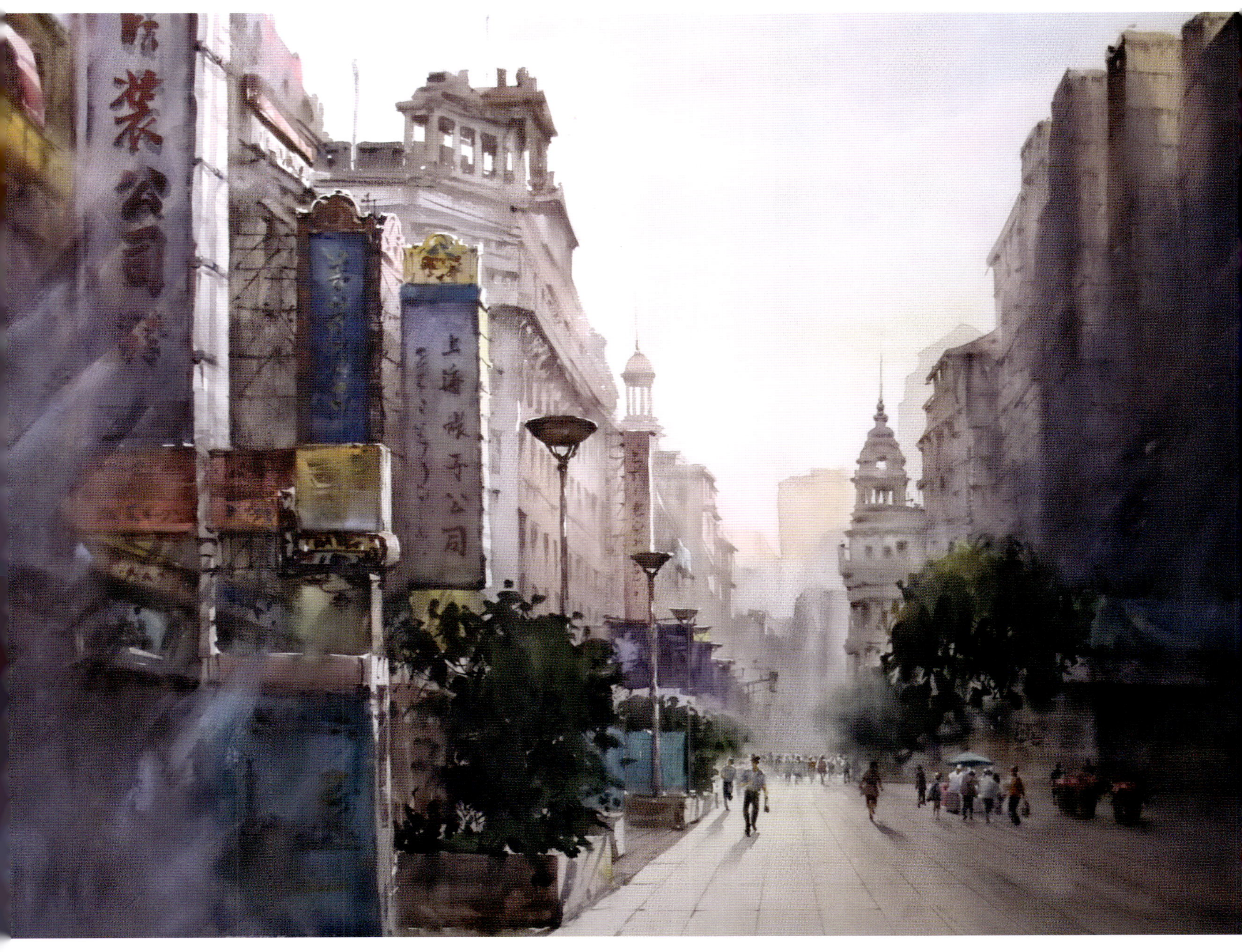

▲ **SHANGHAI MORNING** | Peng Cao
22" × 30" (56cm × 76cm) Transparent watercolor on 140-lb. (300gsm) paper

During my visit to Shanghai, in a splendid dawn morning last summer while walking toward the bustling Nanjing Road, I was touched by the sight of those tall buildings showered in the colorful misty haze: reddish, golden and light gray. Using a large flat brush, I quickly captured the heartfelt feeling in large blocks of colors. When I got home, I outlined the floating feeling of light and shadow, and finished it with mostly wet brushes and minimum brushstrokes.

SHOE BIRD | Ric Dentinger
19" × 29" (48cm × 74cm) Watercolor and gouache on 300-lb. (640gsm) cold-pressed Arches

I was drawn to the sense of isolation evoked by unwanted shoes hanging on a sign in an abandoned warehouse district of San Antonio, Texas. The sparrow watching over the shoes adds a touch of life and hope, while the large shadow adds dimension. I was intrigued by the patterns and geometric shapes created by the bricks, wires and cast shadows. A particular challenge in this painting was making the numerous bricks look varied, interesting and cohesive. I did add gouache to recapture the white of the mortar.

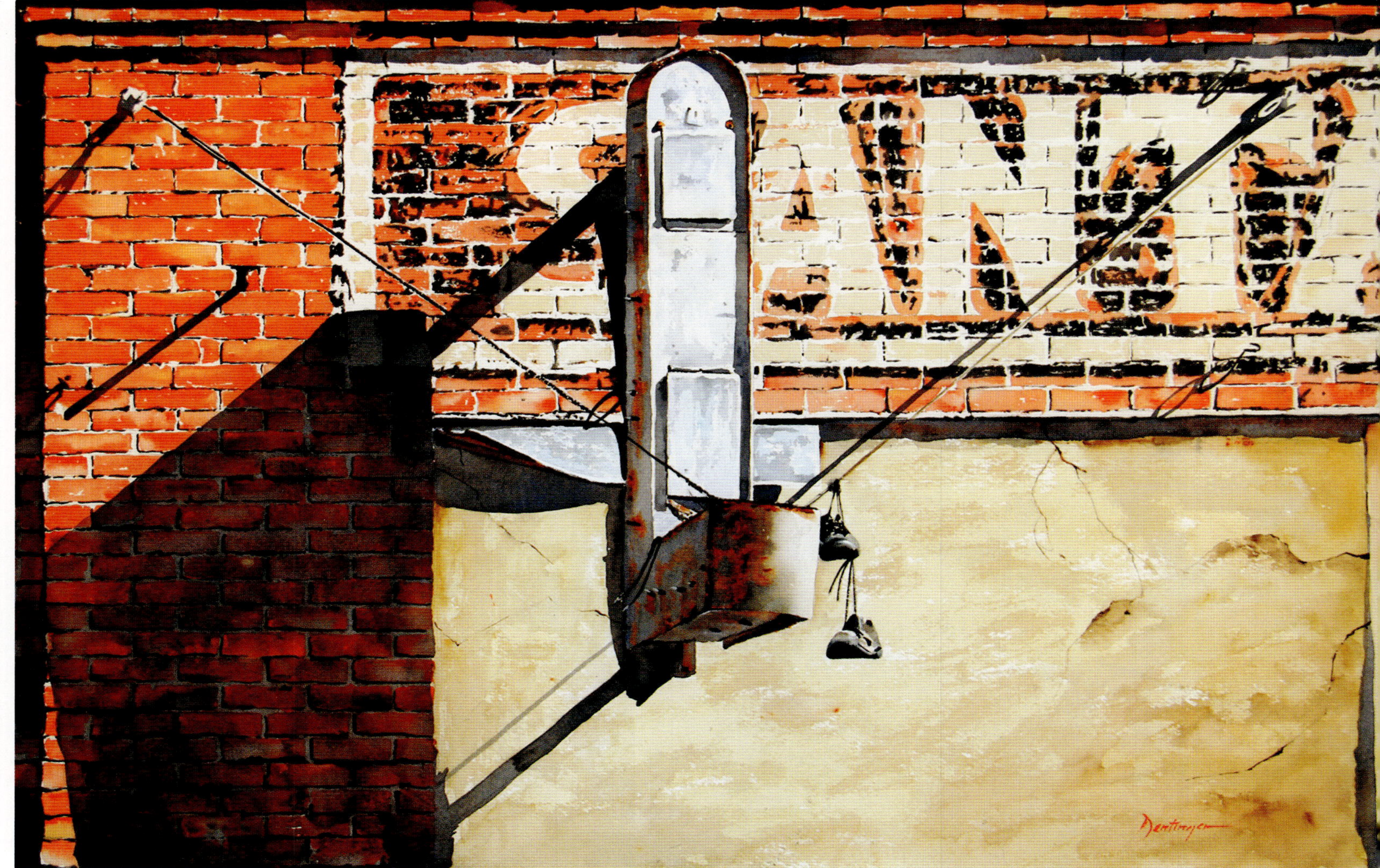

STREET ART CRITIC | Soon Y. Warren
30" × 22" (76cm × 56cm) Transparent watercolor on 300-lb. (640gsm) cold-pressed Winsor & Newton

My challenge with this painting was putting together geometric patterns to create an interesting composition. I was drawn to the vibrant colors of the windows and steps, but the dull gray color of the wall separating the picture plane detracted from the feelings of vibrancy and passion. I changed the gray wall color to bright yellow and introduced the yellow door frame to connect the eye movement of the entire picture frame. To harmonize the colors throughout the entire composition, I glazed the colors until I was satisfied with the result.

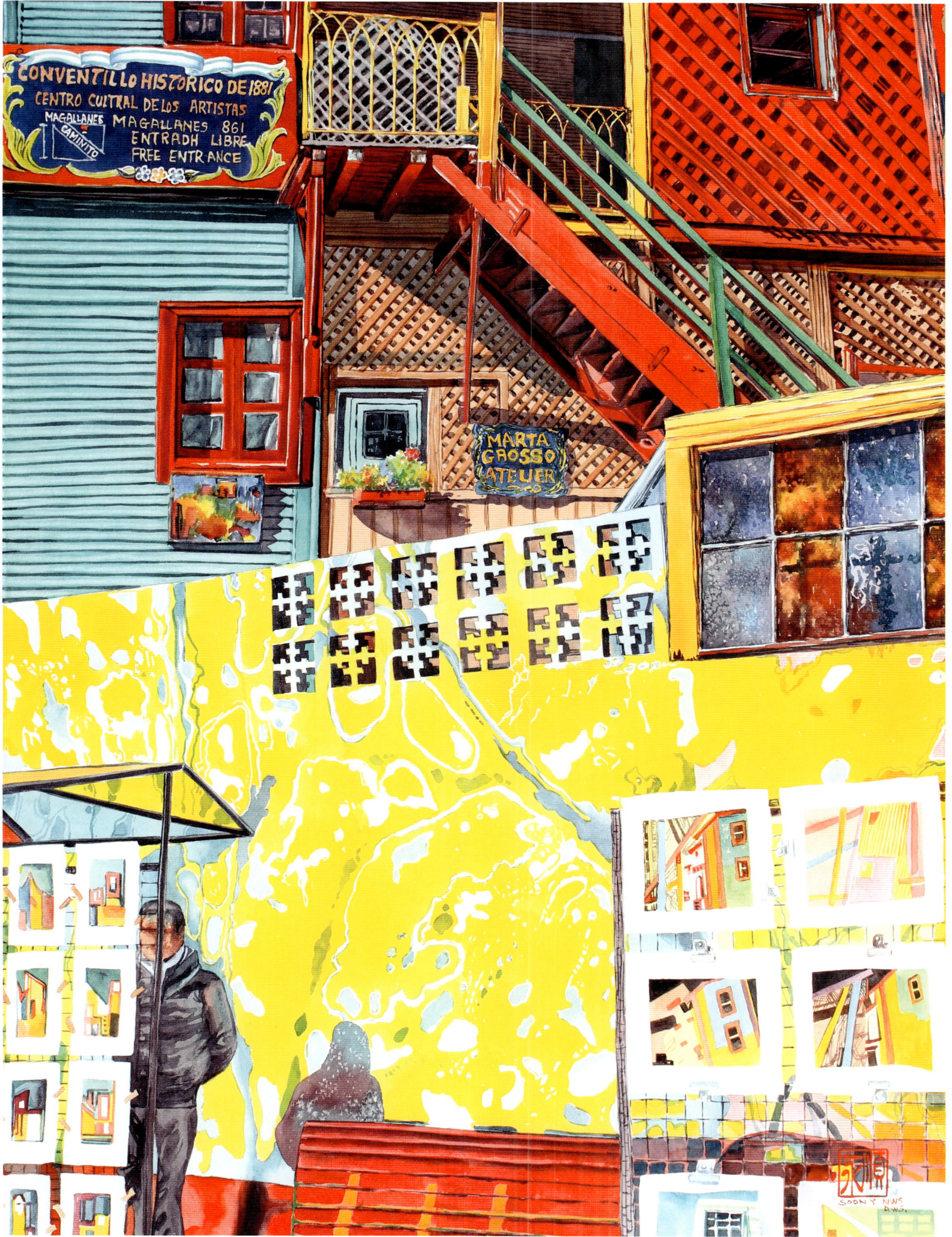
CONVENTILLO HISTORICO DE 1881
CENTRO CULTRAL DE LOS ARTISTAS
MAGALLANES
CAMINITO
MAGALLANES 861
ENTRADH LIBRE
FREE ENTRANCE
MARTA GROSSO ATELIER

SHOPPING IN BARCELONA |
Kristina Jurick
21" × 8" (53cm × 20cm) Transparent watercolor on 300-lb. (640gsm) Saunders Waterford

Reducing the structure on the left and the background building to one shape pops forward the fruit stand as the point of interest. The long vertical format enhances the feeling of high buildings in a city. My reference photo showed the whole scene in shadow, so I made up sunshine and shadows (I love this part!). To find out if a composition and the light in a painting will work, I make preliminary tonal sketches in graphite or sepia watercolor. It makes the painting easier.

"Plan like a turtle and then paint like a rabbit."

– KRISTINA JURICK

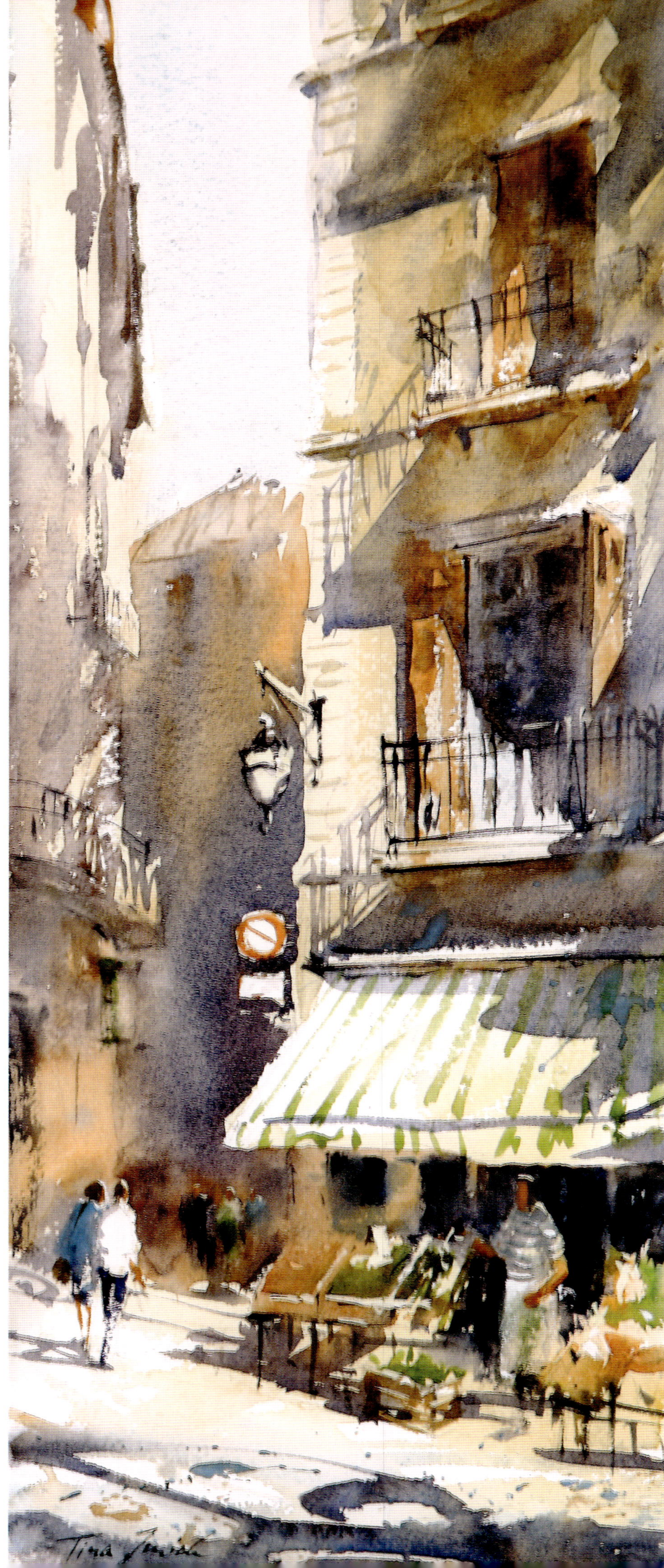

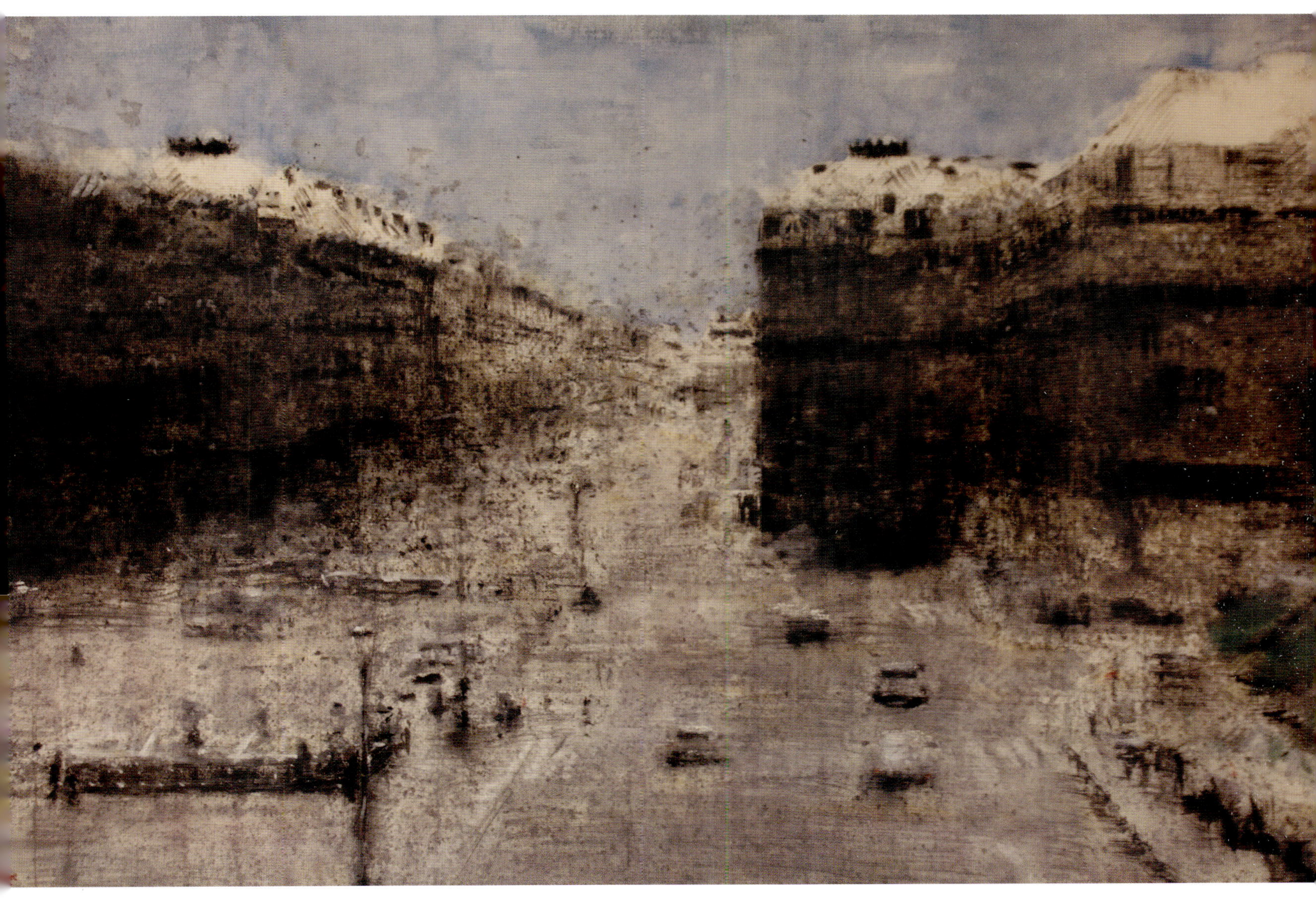

OPERA VIEW II | Kathryn Keller Larkins
30" × 44" (76xcm × 112cm) Watercolor with gouache accents on 140-lb. (300gsm) rough-pressed Arches

I was lucky enough to be in Paris on a grant from the Art Students League of New York City and took the photograph I used as my source from a balcony of the Opera facing out towards the Métro stop. Because I work large, splashing on and spraying off pigment, I paint from photographs in the studio. I used wide housepaint and hake brushes to spatter the paint from the left and right sides of the paper, alternating colors with every layer. Using layers of broken droplets of pigment helped me avoid a static, illustrated look and captured the energy of the light and the city that filled me when I was there.

MORNING RIDE | Antonio Masi
30" × 40" (76cm × 102cm) Watercolor on 300-lb. (640gsm) rough Arches

Every morning I crossed this bridge going to work. I have often been struck by the early morning coolness being penetrated by the warmth of the sun's rays. To achieve this happening, I used cool colors being invaded by warm colors (light into dark, warm into cold). This painting was done from small sketches, photographs and memory. My approach is direct, large brushstrokes, followed by many glazes. I constantly strive to keep the first emotional feeling throughout the process.

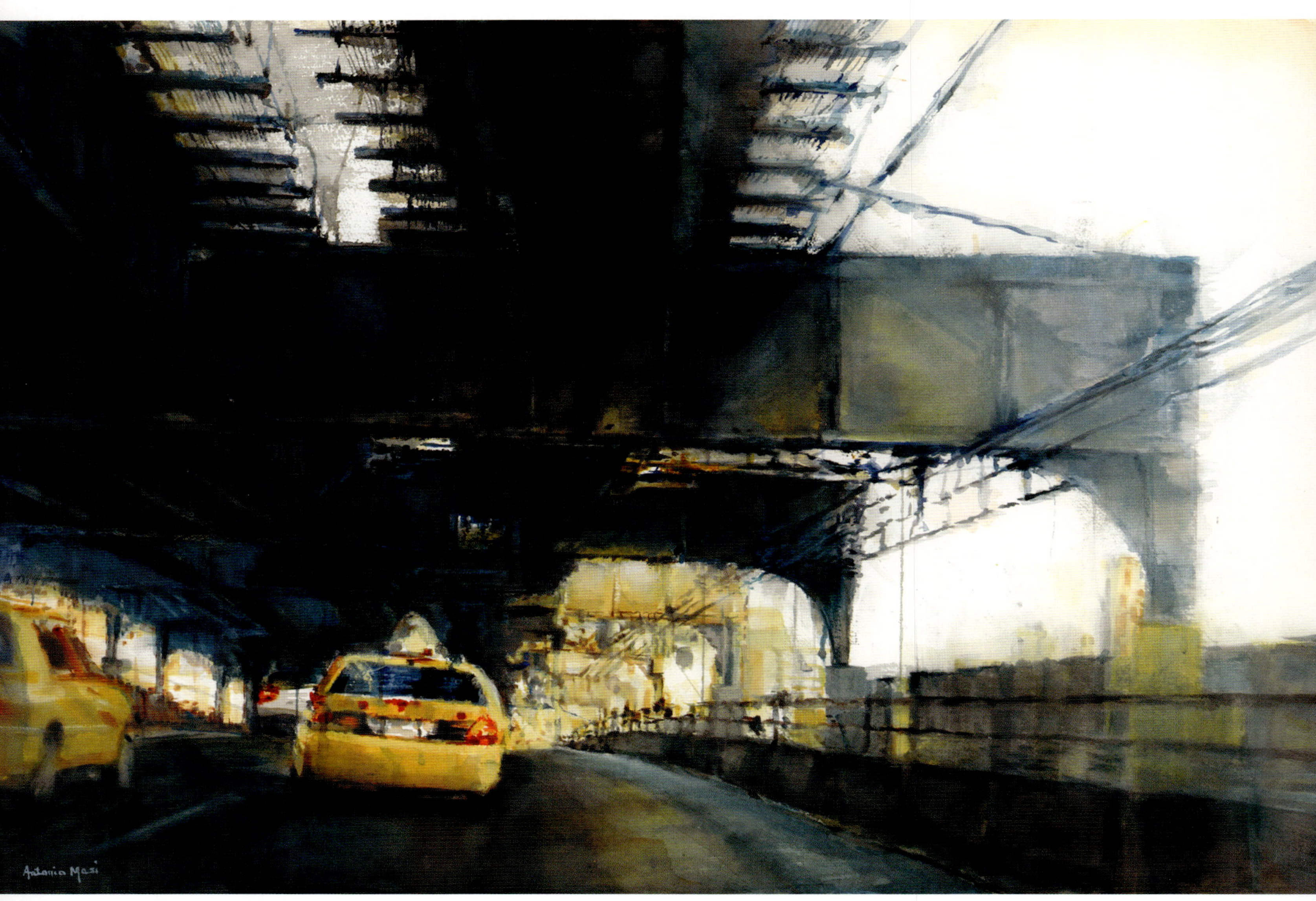

"Without light there is no art."

– ANTONIO MASI

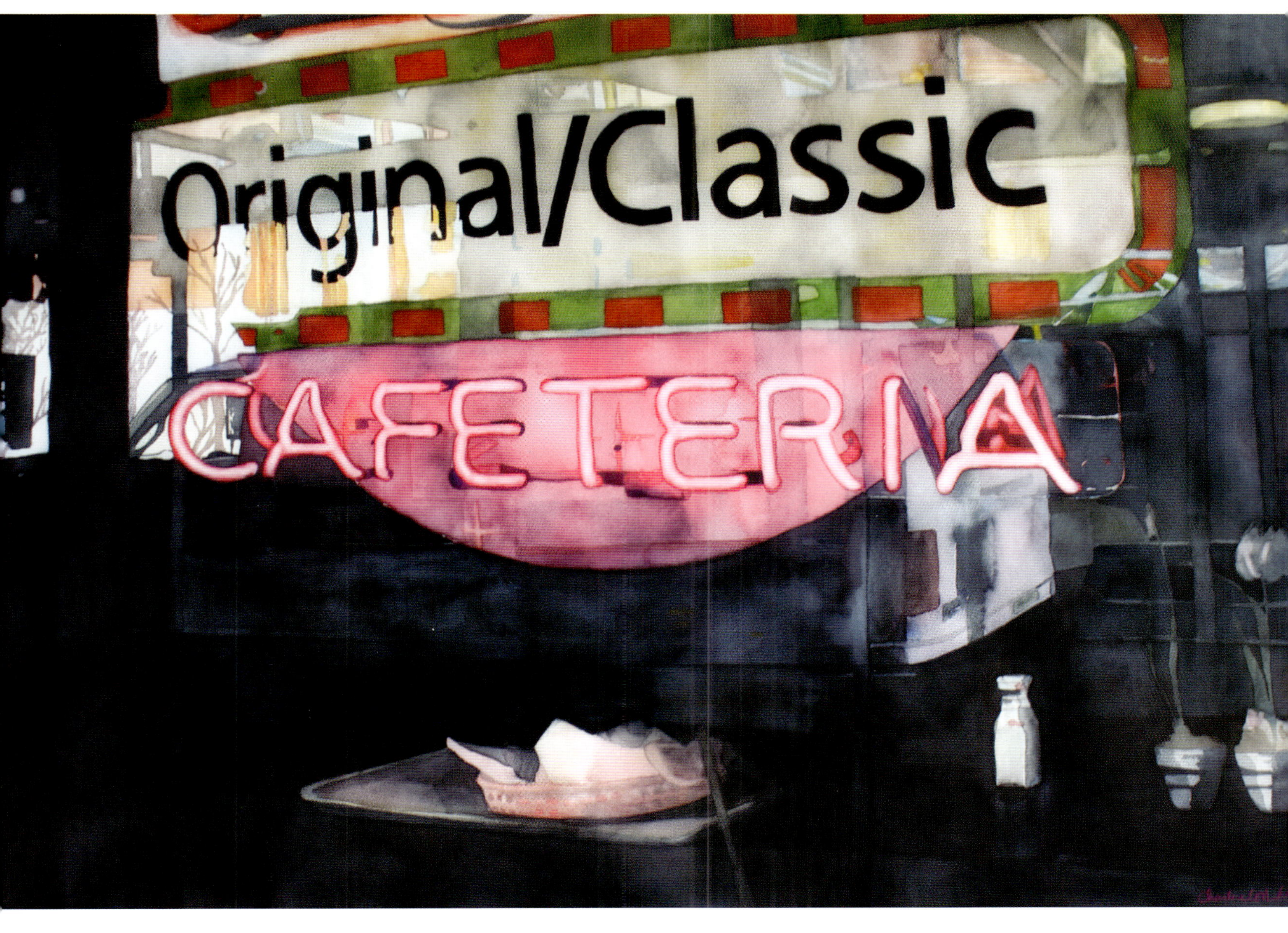

▲ **ORIGINAL CLASSIC CAFETERIA** | Charlene Collins Freeman
24" × 36" (61cm × 91cm) Watercolor on 140-lb. (300gsm) cold-pressed Arches

I am visually intrigued by urban signage, neon and storefront reflections. I shoot multiple digital photographs of these scenes to capture the constant changes in the reflections as traffic and people pass by. When I review the photographs, I consider all the details. The smallest difference between where a person is looking or where a car is frozen in one photo but in not the next becomes very important. I don't think too much about rules of design. Instead I look for a photograph with a strong enough image to hold my interest for the entire process of painting it. Then I draw it on my watercolor surface in great detail. With a strong photograph and detailed drawing, I have a solid foundation on which to paint.

"When becoming too controlling with a painting, find a way to make the painting process exciting again by taking a risk, and let the paint find a life of its own."

– SANDRINE PELISSIER

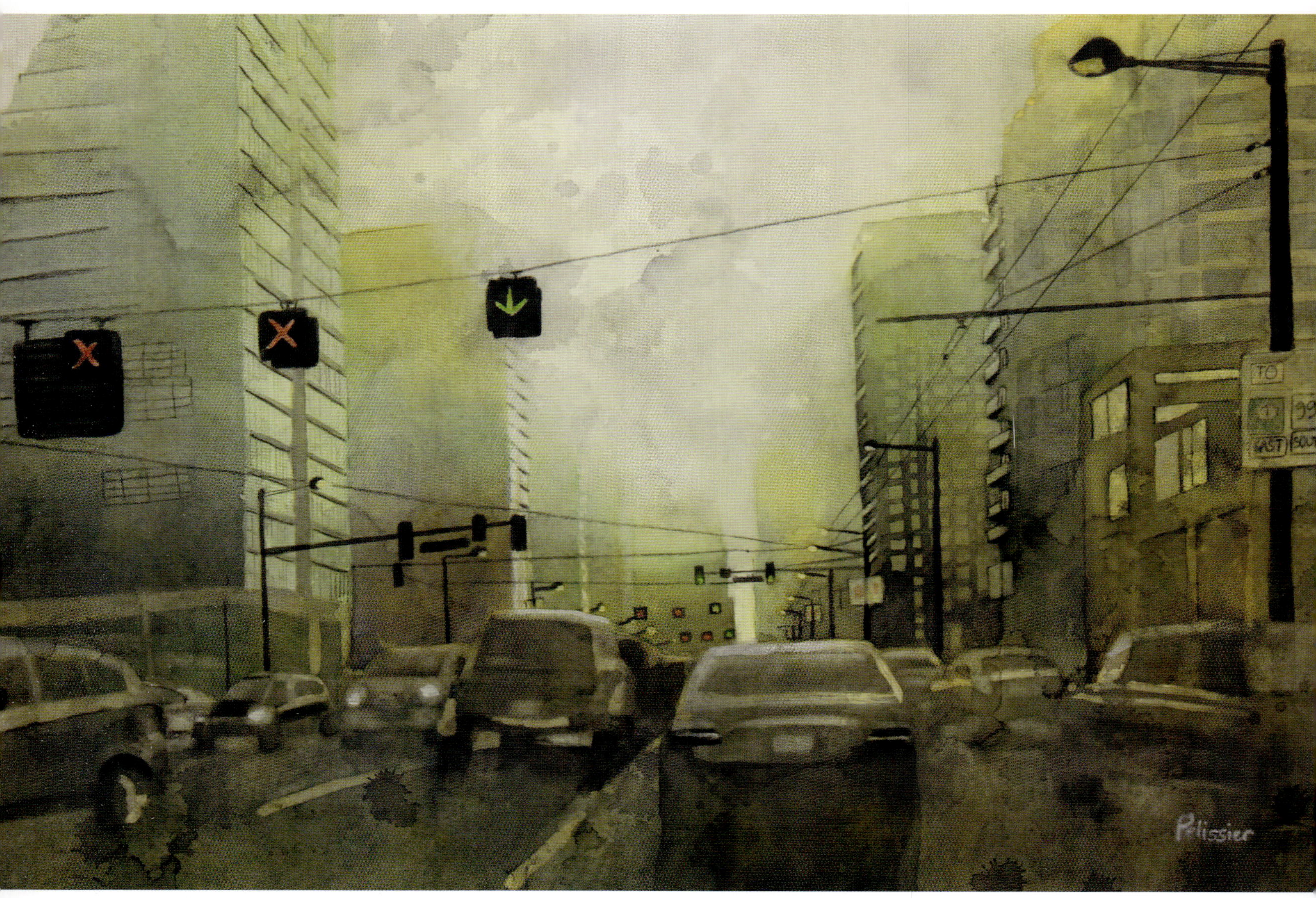

▲ **EARLY THIS MORNING** | Sandrine Pelissier
15" × 22" (38cm × 56cm) Watercolor with gouache and watercolor crayons accent on 140-lb. (300gsm) hot-pressed Arches

When I was painting this cityscape with all the straight lines and details in the buildings, I found myself becoming too controlling and painting too tightly. My challenge was to release some of that control, leave some part to chance and take a risk. I did that by covering the painting once it was done with drips of water and diluted gouache and let the paint do its own thing. I think this technique added to the misty atmosphere of the painting.

▶ **PARK CENTRAL** | Travis Poelle
19" × 13" (48xcm × 33cm) Transparent watercolor on 140-lb. (300gsm) cold-pressed Arches

I enjoy looking at cityscapes, but I often don't like painting them. Yet somehow I'm drawn to keep doing them. There are so many details that it's easy to become overwhelmed both as an artist or as a viewer. I think that's why a cityscape is so pleasing when it works. The only solution is to simplify. Infuse the most important part of the painting with color contrasts and detail work while letting the rest of the piece simmer down. Limit your colors in those areas and combine your adjacent darks. Notice the dark of the foreground car combining into the shadow on the street and also the crowd of background figures. We don't need those extra details, they're just distracting.

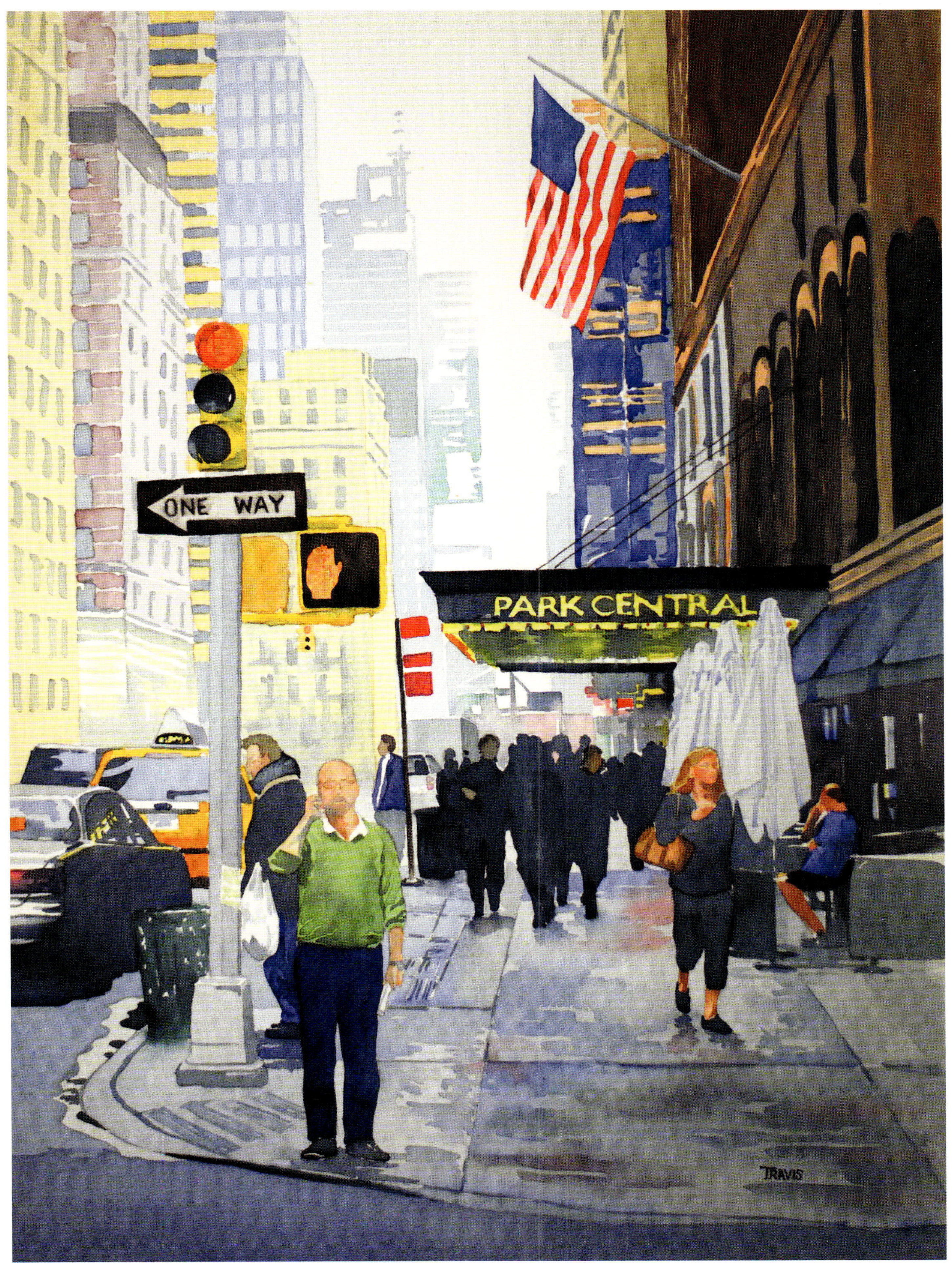

"If your painting isn't working, simplify the areas that aren't your focal point." – TRAVIS POELLE

"If you have a colorful foreground, try then a neutral, softer gray background." – CAROL CARTER

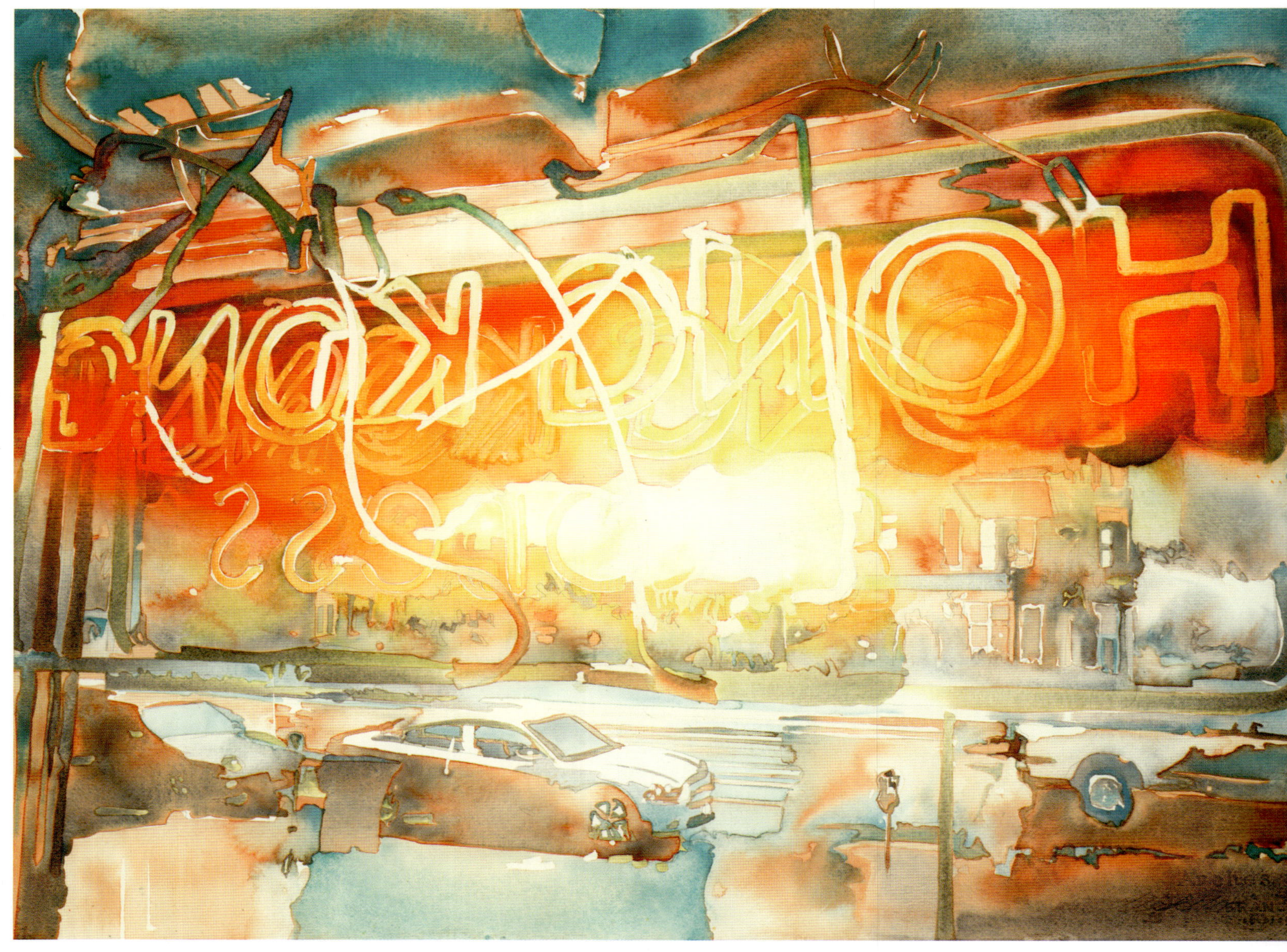

▲ **HONG KONG EXPRESS** | Carol Carter
20" × 30" (51cm × 76cm) Transparent watercolor on 300-lb. (640gsm) cold-pressed Arches

I found this subject at the local Chinese takeout near my studio. I noticed that the scene outdoors was in stark contrast to the neon sign hanging in the window, so I took a photograph. Later translating the image to watercolor, I bumped up the warm colors of the neon and neutralized the background cityscape. I painted the background first using a lovely gray mix of Cobalt Turquoise Light, Burnt Sienna and French Ultramarine Blue to set the stage for the neon sign. I used a liquid mask to keep the neon lettering white. After washes of yellow and red were floated, I removed the mask and painted the letters with warm yellow. Additional light veils of red/yellow soften the transition between the lettering and the glow.

▶ **WERNER AT CRYSTAL BRIDGES** | L.S. Eldridge
28" × 17½" (71cm × 44cm) Watercolor on 300-lb. (640gsm) cold-pressed Arches

My goal with this series was to portray mankind without introducing the literal figure. The question I faced was how to express the myriad aspects of humanity in a fresh way using symbolic imagery. It was while photographing this particular site that I realized I could creatively explore every aspect of life through my construction images! Even so, this painting took months to complete while I struggled to characterize the symbols with color. For me, the beautiful sunlit concrete slabs, representing triumph over obstacles, define the painting. To achieve this bright illusion I adjoined Antwerp Blue to Burnt Sienna and/or Burnt Umber, dropping in Brown Madder and Permanent Rose, finishing with a touch of salt for texture.

"If the rational color choice doesn't work, embrace the irrational."

– L.S. ELDRIDGE

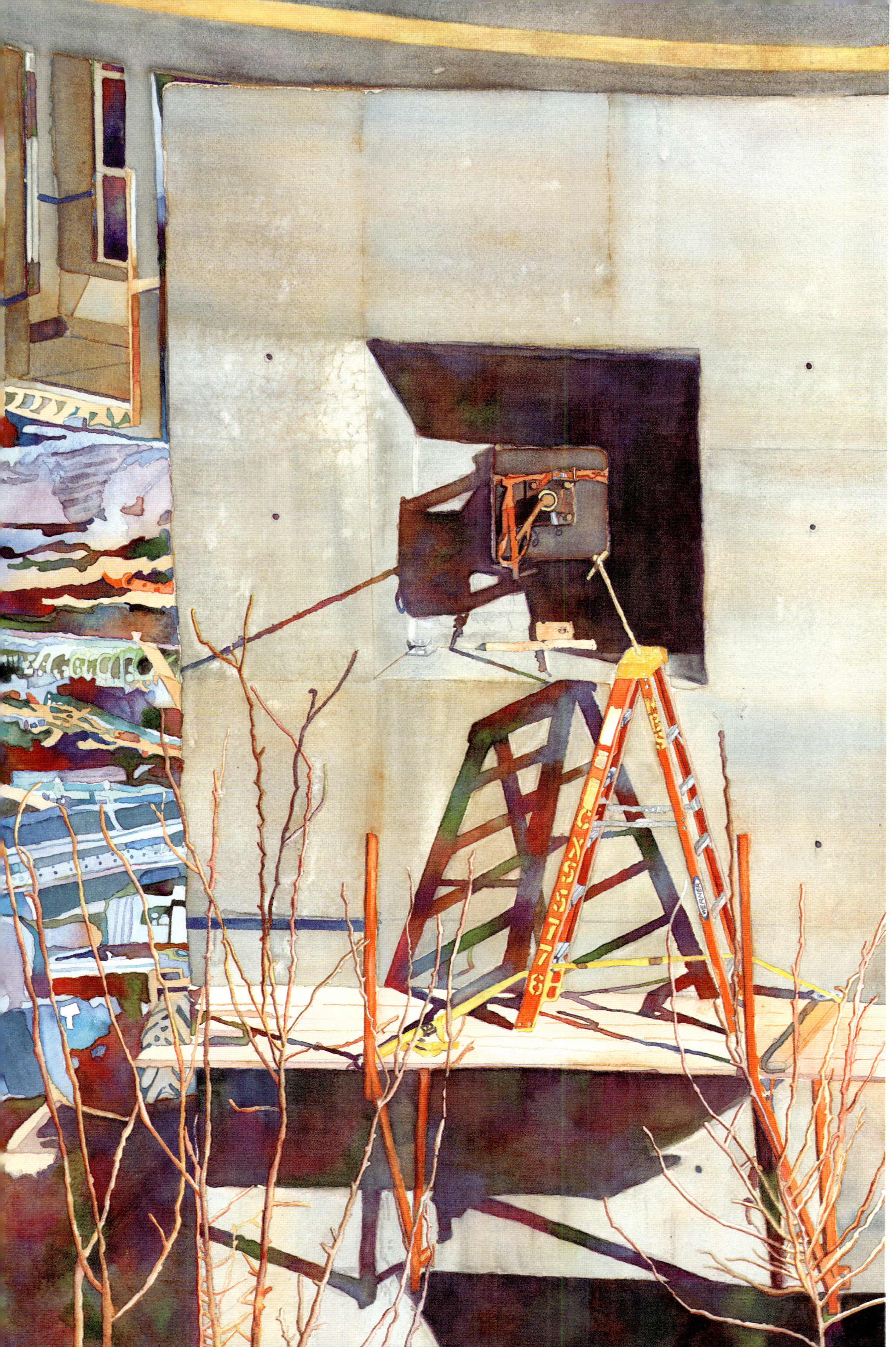

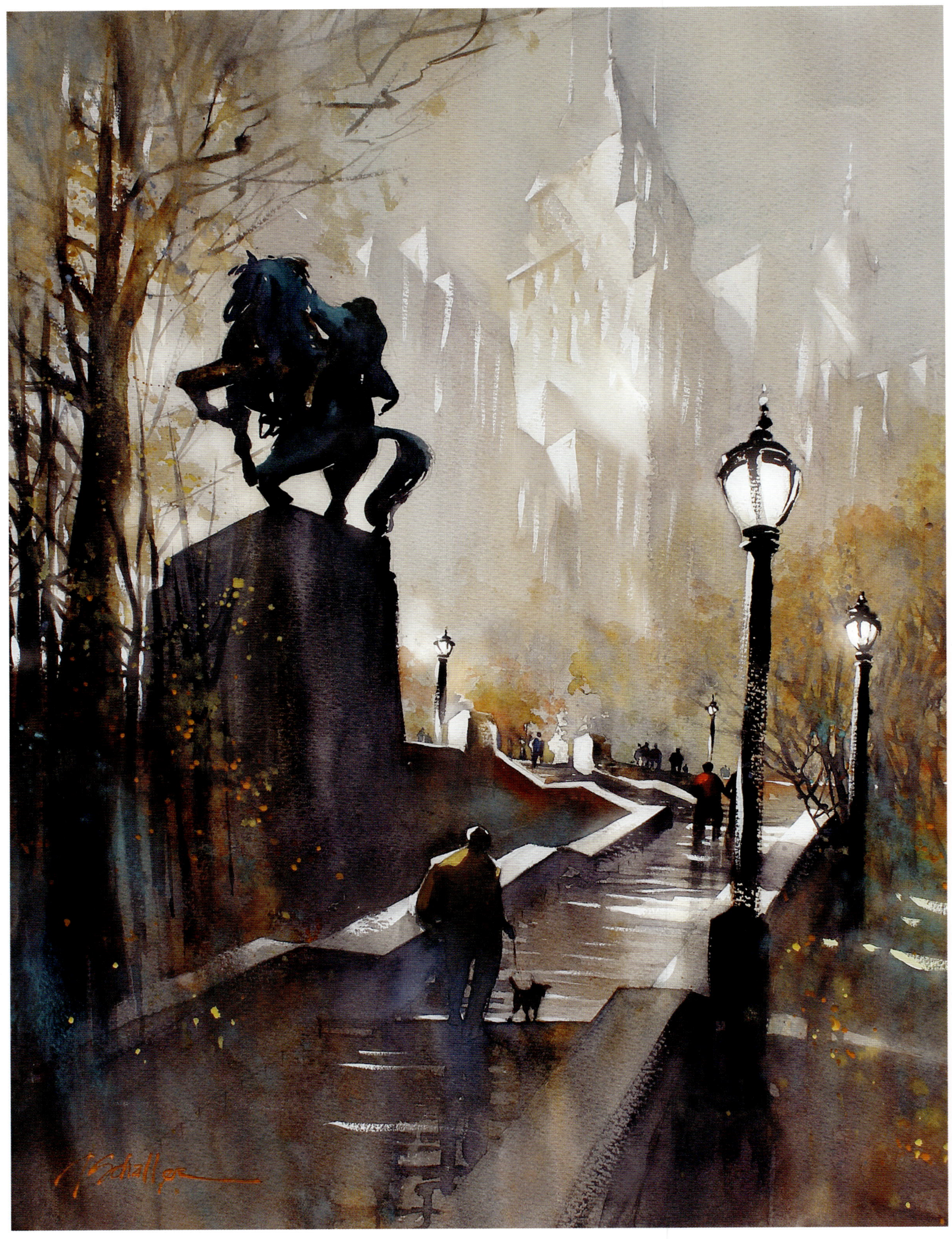

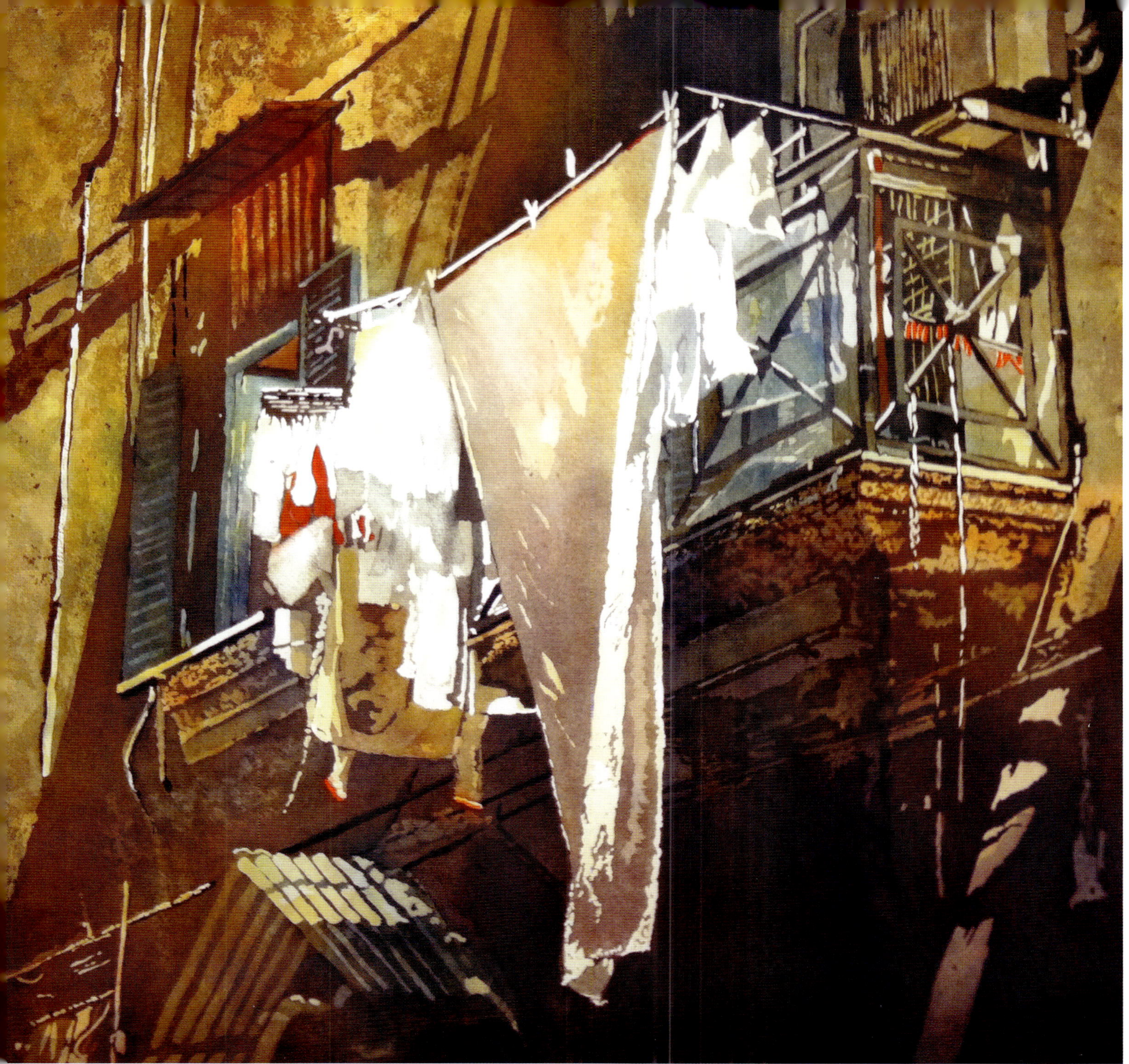

◀ **STEPS TO SIMÓN BOLÍVAR PLAZA – NYC** | Thomas W. Schaller
24" × 18" (61cm × 46cm) Watercolor on 140-lb. (300gsm) rough Saunders

A recurring theme in much of my work is the dialog between the natural and the man-made worlds. So for me, New York's Central Park is an endless source of inspiration. In this painting the staircase out of the great park is meant to act as a sort of visual bridge for the viewer—leading one out of the chaos of nature into the structured grid of the city, its towers rising like ethereal sentries in the distance.

▲ **AFTERNOON BREEZE** | Linda Daly Baker
22" × 22" (56cm × 56cm) Transparent watercolor layered on 300-lb. (640gsm) cold-pressed Arches

Afternoon Breeze is a studio painting taken from a snippet of a photo shot in an urban area. Just this one little portion of the photo struck my creative vision. This painting is created with layer upon layer of transparent watercolor building a patina of texture. The challenge was to make the building look old and textured while keeping the laundry transparent, pristine and with a feeling of movement. I also attempted to add interest by creating a triangle of color with the cool blues to offset the warm dominance in the painting.

"Look beyond the obvious in your photo reference for that unexpected story within a story."

– LINDA DALY BAKER

WARING TEXAS | Ric Dentinger
30" × 22" (76cm × 56cm) Watercolor and gouache on 300-lb. (640gsm) cold-pressed Arches

Waring is a small town in the Texas Hill Country outside of San Antonio. I was drawn to the iconic Texas subject matter: gas pumps, a football and a game of dominoes. I liked the way sunlight fell across the face of the pumps and over the pavement behind them, adding depth to the scene. In my studio I created thumbnail sketches and a detailed drawing from my photograph. I wanted to temper the nostalgia of the subject matter with strong fresh color and dramatic lights and darks. I had to apply my shadow wash very carefully in order not to disturb the intense red color of the pressed tin ceiling. I added gouache for texture on the weathered metal surfaces of the blue gas pump.

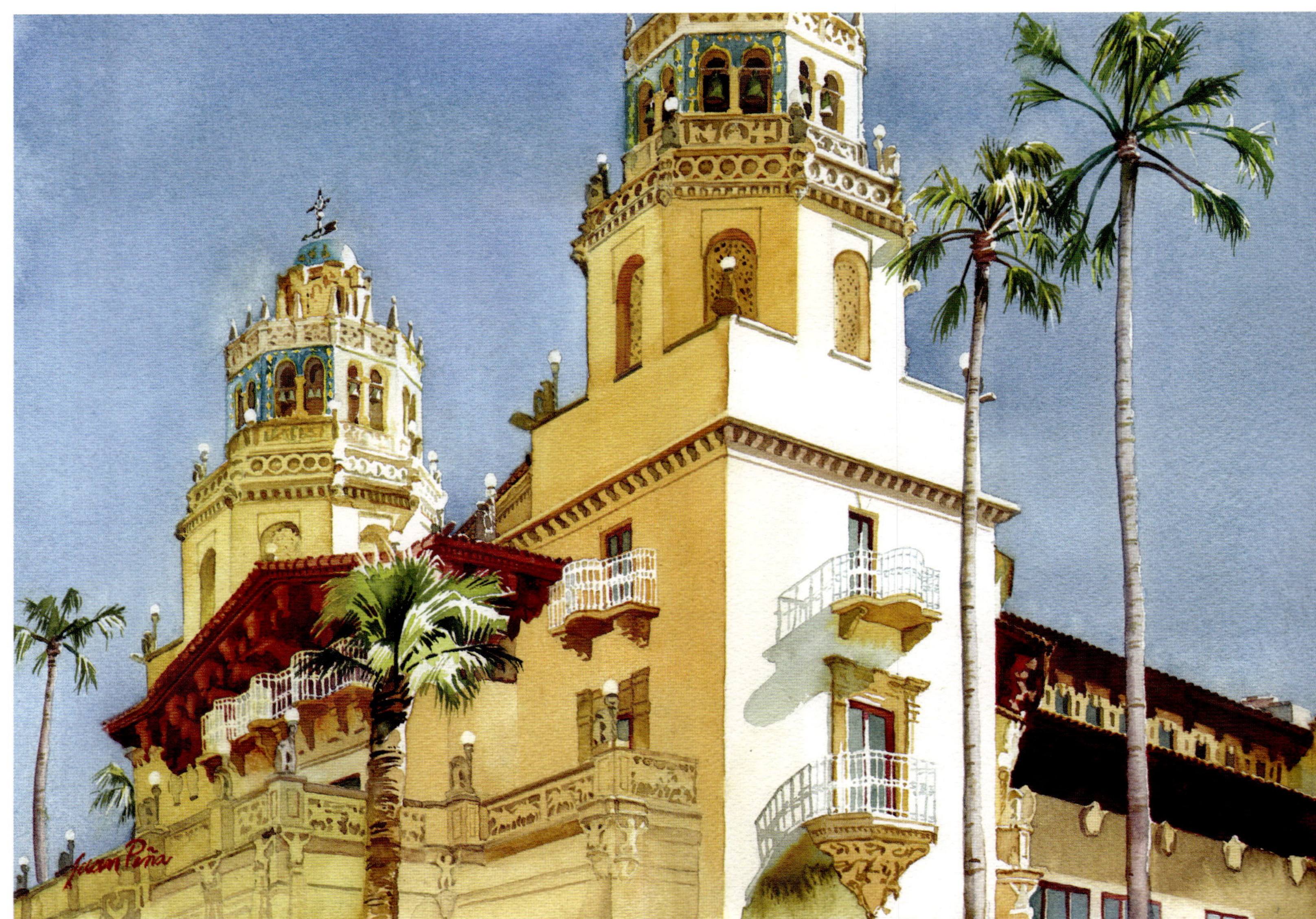

HEARST CASTLE SOUTH TOWER | Juan Peña
19" × 24½" (48cm × 62cm) Transparent watercolor on 300-lb. (640gsm) cold-pressed Arches

Hearst Castle South Tower basks in sunlight often above a layer of coastal fog with the clear blue sky appearing above. Fifty artists were invited to paint on the grounds of Hearst Castle for the third annual fundraiser for the Friends of Hearst Castle. The original painting, done on location, won best of show chosen by those attending. This replica watercolor was painted in my studio using a three-color palette of Winsor Red, Winsor Blue and Holbein's Permanent Yellow Deep. I work almost exclusively with these three colors with the occasional touch of a few others. With this limited palette I'm able to match most of the manufactured colors and mix all of the colors I need for any painting.

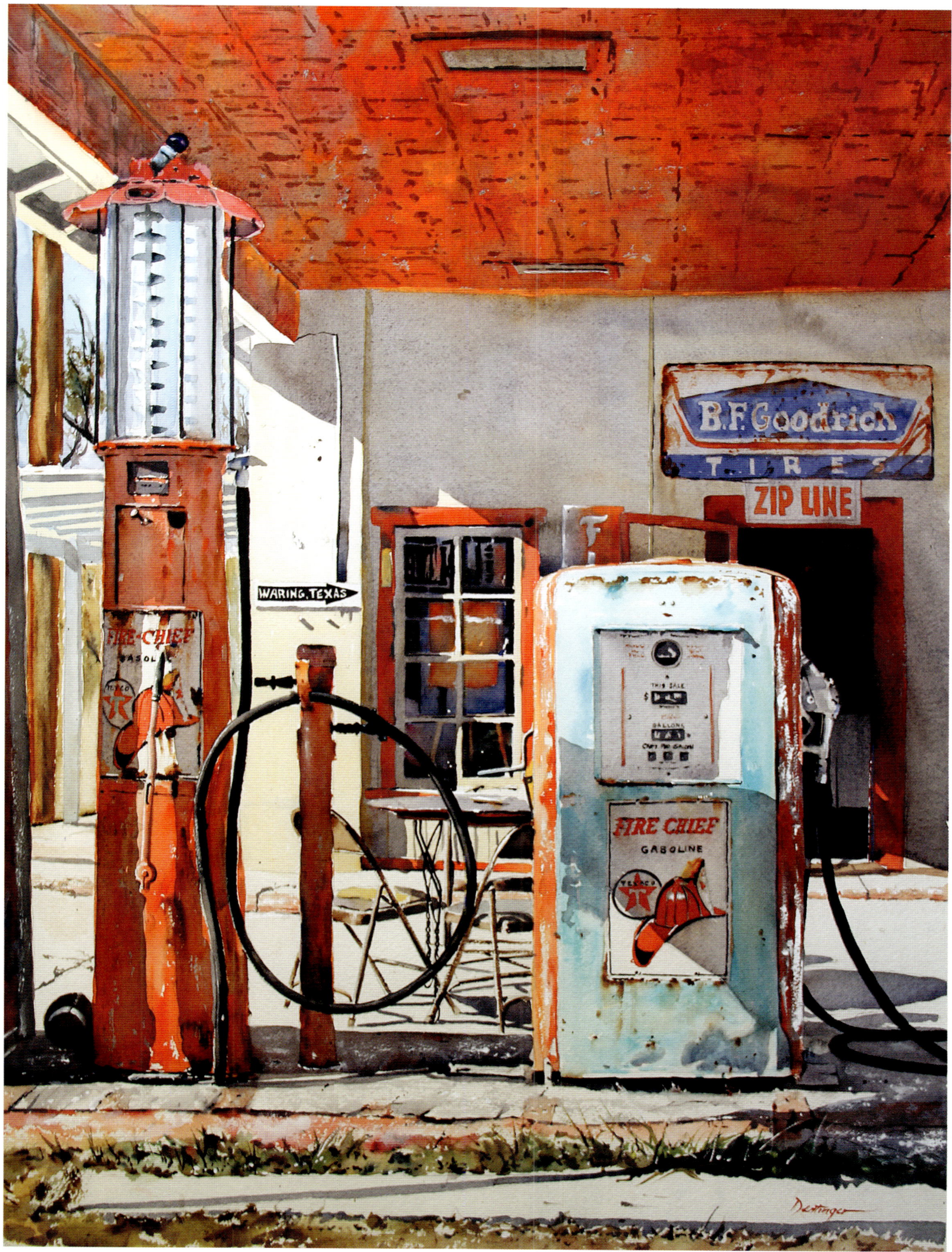
B.F.Goodrich
TIRES
ZIP LINE
WARING, TEXAS
FIRE CHIEF
GASOLINE
TEXACO
FIRE CHIEF
GASOLINE
TEXACO
Dettinger

GULF RIM REFLECTIONS | David L. Stickel
16½" × 22½" (42cm × 57cm) Transparent watercolor on 300-lb. (650gsm) cold-pressed Arches

I love the way the lines of light create movement especially from the light reflected in the windows. I invite these lines into my composition by holding my camera very low when taking my reference photos. This in turn creates the action lines and wonderful drama. The creative process is enhanced by portraying the imagery found in the reflections—the bold orange store name as well as on the other window in reverse. My viewers tell me they're always finding new things in my reflections.

"The elements of wonderful confusion and chaos motivate and excite me as an artist."

– DAVID L. STICKEL

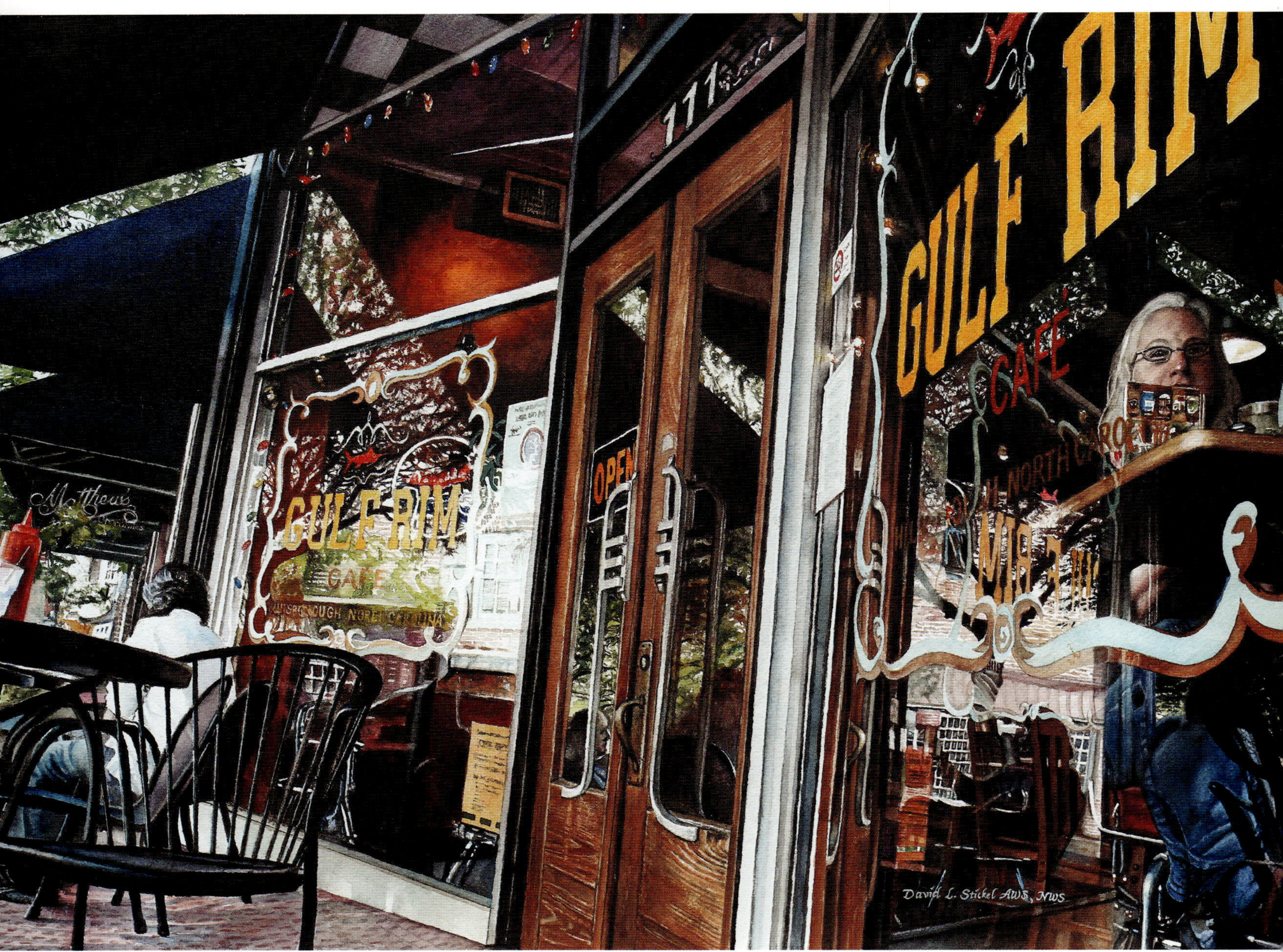

NIGHT LIGHTS OF THE BIG APPLE | David L. Stickel
30" × 22" (76cm × 56cm) Transparent watercolor on 300-lb. (640gsm) cold-pressed Arches

Needless to say, this subject was a challenge to paint—but I love the many ways the lines intersect with each other. To accurately capture the two-point perspective, I assembled cardboard that extended out from my table and secured it so I could establish my vanishing point. The one on the right side extended almost four feet out from my table (longer than the left side). Then I used a long straightedge to record my guidelines with the correct angles from top to bottom. Also, as I was painting—especially the top area of the cube—it was helpful to use sticky notes to block out everything on my reference photo except the small area I was focusing on to paint.

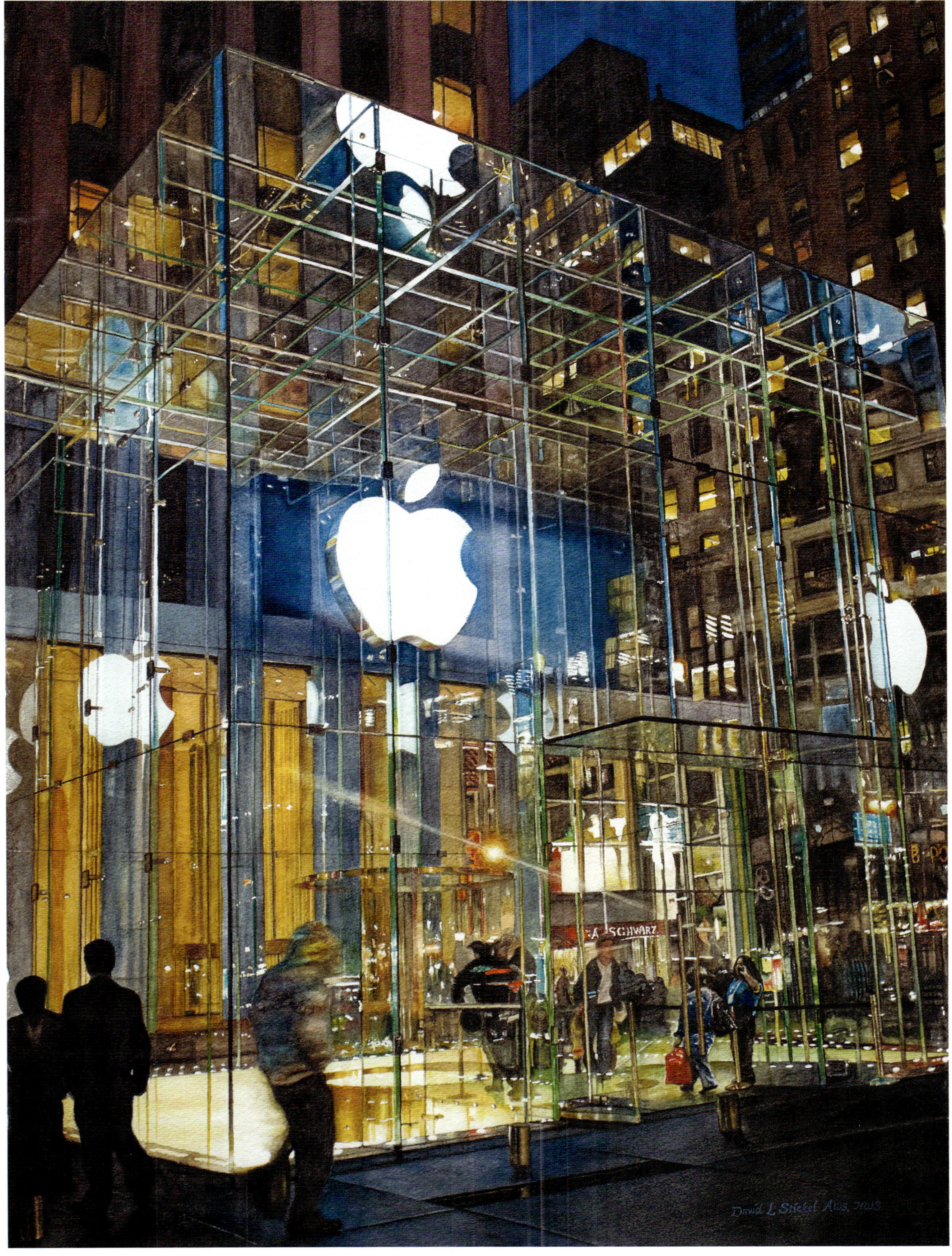
SCHWARZ
David L. Stickel AWS, NWS

Contributors

DEBBIE ABSHEAR
Associate Member of NWS, AWS, WW
15616 Faysmith Ave.
Gardena, CA 90249
310.989.9906
debabshear@att.net
debbieabshear.com
Storm Chasers—Ben and Mary Rabe Award, Watercolor West 2012
p16 *Storm Chasers*

KATHLEEN ALEXANDER
WW, NWWS, NAWA
P.O. Box 300
Pacifica, CA 94044 (July–Dec.)
2645 Alohia Pl. #A
Haiku, HI 96708 ((Jan–June)
studio@kathleenalexanderwatercolors.com
kathleenalexanderwatercolors.com
Village Galleries, Maui
p72 *Hanalei Farmer's Market II*

LISA AMBROSE
Society of Illustrators
616.405.1178
lisamambrose@gmail.com
lisaambrosestudios.com
p44 *New Life for Old Things*
p45 *Forty-Two Hats*

ROBIN SEVESTER AVERY
Watercolor USA Honor Society; Philadelphia Water Color Society; Watercolor Art Society of Houston, Elite Signature Member
14322 Beacon Trace Ct.
Houston, TX 77069
713.410.1075
robinavery47@gmail.com
robinaveryartist.com
Leaving Again?—First Place, Watercolor Art Society of Houston, 2012
p50 *Leaving Again?*

HUGH F. BAKER
California Art Club
310.488.0266
minasirianni@hotmail.com
p64 *At You (Frog)*

LINDA DALY BAKER
AWS, NWS
295 Seven Farms Dr. C222
Charleston, SC 29492
616.846.3453
lindabakerartist@gmail.com
lindabaker.biz
Afternoon Breeze—Edgar Whitney Award, AWS, 2013
p131 *Afternoon Breeze*

SALLY BAKER
Watercolor West, Signature Member
5990 Vine Hill School Rd.
Sebastopol, CA 95472
707.829.0396
krisbaker@yahoo.com
sallybaker.com
Graton Gallery, Graton, CA
p106 *Perspicacity*

CHRIS BECK
NWS, Signature Member; TWSA, Signature Member
P.O. Box 1661, Los Altos, CA 94023
chris@chrisbeckstudio.com
chrisbeckstudio.com
p103 *Hip Hop Bebop*

GRAHAM BERRY
38 Tarragon Dr.
Blackpool, Lancashire
FY2 0WJ, England
01253.592636
grayberry@btopenworld.com
grahamberrystudio.com
p36 *Sat on the Wall*
p37 *Meeting in the Pub*

ANNELEIN BEUKENKAMP
P.O. Box 5774
Burlington, VT 05402
802.864.3840
beukwin@yahoo.com
abwatercolors.com
p89 *Letter Sweater*

PARAG D. BORSE
'Shantai' Bungalow
Dahiwali, Karjat, Raigad
610201, India
+91.2148.223751 (home)
+91.9423375951 (mobile)
paragpaintings@gmail.com
paragborse.com
p27 *Hovering Semblance*

CINDY BRABEC-KING
NWS; TWSA; WCWS, Master Signature Member
3989 Rapid Creek Rd.
Palisade, CO 81526
970.464.4996
cbrabecking@msn.com
Paint by Numbers—Silver Medallion, Adirondacks National Exhibition of American Watercolors, Old Forge, NY, Silver Medallion, 2012; First Place, Colorado Watercolor Society, 2012
p108 *Nutcracker Sweet*
p109 *Paint by Numbers*

FREDERIC S. BRIGGS
AWS, Baltimore Watercolor Society
7 E. Lafayette Ave.
Baltimore, MD 21202
410.685.3568
schulerschool@msn.com
Westmoreland Fair—AWS Award, 2010; Louis J. Kaep Award & The Traveling Show
p32 *Westmoreland Fair*

CHRISTINE MISENCIK BUNN
109 Ebersole Ave.
Fredericktown, OH 43019
740.485.2894
chris.m.bunn@gmail.com
Self-Portrait/Perception—Honorable Mention, Pennsylvania Watercolor Society
p76–77 *Self-Portrait/Perception*

J. HENDERER BURNS
Watercolor Art Society, Signature Member; WAS-H
1401 S. Cross St.
Robinson, IL 62454
jodyhburns@hotmail.com
jhendererburns.com
Illinois State Museum's Southern Illinois Art and Artisans Center at Rend Lake
Squeeze Me—Honorable Mention Watercolor Art Society, Houston, 36th International Exhibition, 2013
p101 *Squeeze Me*

PENG CAO
Asia Arts Society of America
2755 Country Dr. #139
Fremont, CA 94536
510.713.9830
walan1991@hotmail.com
p2–3 *San Francisco Street*
p118 *Water House*
p119 *Shanghai Morning*

CAROL CARTER
St. Louis Artists Guild, Honorary Board Member
3156 Shenandoah Ave.
St. Louis, MO 63104
314.302.5771
carol@carol-carter.com
carol-carter.com
Dolphin Gallery, Maui, HI
p128 *Hong Kong Express*

KATHY COLLINS
NWWS
kathy.collins2@comcast.net
kathycollinswatercolors.com
Tsuga Fine Art, Bothell, WA
p28 *Rainy Day, Bandon*

LAUREL COVINGTON-VOGL
AWS, NWS, RMWMS
212 Meadowlark Ln.
Durango, CO 81303
laurelvogl@gmail.com
Karyn Gabaldon Fine Arts, Durango, CO
p11 *High Tide: Torii Gate at Miyajima*
p24 *Teahouse Umbrella*

LAUREN KELLER DADDONA
PWCS, PWS, BWS
1220 Merrybrook Rd.
Collegeville, PA 19426
lkart@comcast.net
laurendaddona.com
p14 *Southwest Revisited*

SUZANNE K. D'ARCY
Napa Valley Art Association, California Watercolor Association
130 Hidden Glen Ct.
Vacaville, CA 95688
803.389.9099
suzannekdarcy@gmail.com
suzannekdarcyfineart.com
Artists of the Valley Gallery, Napa, CA
p62 *Giraffes*

RIC DENTINGER
TWS, CWA, LWS
15750 IH-10 West
San Antonio, TX 78249
210.260.2508
ric@ricdentinger.com
ricdentinger.com
The Hunt Gallery, San Antonio, TX
p120 *Shoe Bird*
p133 *Waring Texas*

JANET MACH DUTTON
NWS, TWSA, WW
6700 W. Calle de mi Jazmin
Tucson, AZ 85743
520.461.5471
janet@jmachdutton.com
jmachdutton.com
Advance to Go—Strother Printing Award, National Watermedia Exhibition, Blue Ridge, GA, 2013
p107 *Advance to Go*

RICHARD H. DUTTON
14650 N. Barnes School Rd.
Hallsville, MO 65255
573.881.3198
rkdutton60@msn.com
duttonwatercolor.com
Dutton Art Studio
p10 *Sacred Plateau*

ROSE EDIN
NWS; TWSA, Master Status
609 Lakescene Dr.
Venice, FL 34293
941.492.2254; 218.894.2211
roseedin@gmail.com
roseedin.com
Raedeke Art Gallery, Nisswa, MN
p41 *Ravello*

L.S. ELDRIDGE
3507 Mockingbird Ln.
Rogers, AR 72756
479.621.8054
lse123a@gmail.com
lseldridge.com
Werner at Crystal Bridges—Walser S. Greathouse Medal, American Watercolor Society's 145th Annual International Exhibition; Second Place Overall, Artists of Northwest Arkansas 17th Annual Regional Exhibit
p129 *Werner at Crystal Bridges*

SY ELLENS
NWS, MOWS, WW
326 W. Kalamazoo Ave., Suite 321
Kalamazoo, MI 49077
269.342.6326 (studio), 269.353.7078 (home)
syellens@sbcglobal.net
syellens.com
Charlotte Fine Art Gallery, Charlotte, NC
Glorious Day—Jack Richeson & Co. Merchandise Award at the Western Colorado Watercolor Society 20th Rockies West National Annual Exhibition
p15 *Glorious Day*

LINDA ERFLE
2723 Ivy Knoll Dr.
Placeville, CA 95667
erfle@directcon.net
lindaerfle.net
thehighlightgallery.com
p93 *Essential Ingredient*

LYNN FERRIS
NWS, FWS
119 Hickory Hollow Rd.
Berkeley Springs, WV 25411
ferrislynn@yahoo.com
lynnferris.com
p85 *Raining Fish*

MICHAEL FERRIS
Cairns Art Society
21 Kamerunga Rd.
Stratford, Cairns, Queensland 4870 Australia
617.40552544
mfp@ledanet.com.au
michaelferris.com.au
p63 *Hornbill*

RYAN FOX
1928 Jupiter Hills Ct.
Raleigh, NC 27604
919.645.8345
ryan@rfoxphoto.com
rfoxphoto.com
p115 *Quito Monastery*

CHARLENE COLLINS FREEMAN
NWWS
charlene.freeman@me.com
charlenecollinsfreeman.com
Ryan James Gallery
p98 *Second Cocktail*
p125 *Original Classic Cafeteria*

JANI FREIMANN
9240 Horizon Ln. SE
Port Orchard, WA 98367
253.230.8225
janifreimann@msn.com
jani-freimann.artistwebsites.com
Alki Art Gallery, West Seattle
Painted by the Wind—Washington Thoroughbred Publication Award at Emerald Downs Equine Art Show, 2012; Publication on the cover of *Washington Thoroughbred* magazine, August 2012
p59 *Painted by the Wind*

BETTY GANLEY
Great Falls, VA
703.759.4673
bettyganley@hotmail.com
bettyganley.com
p105 Fixin' to Go Fishin'

KATHIE GEORGE
OWS, FWS
kathiegeorge.com
Dovetail Gallery, Egg Harbor, WI
p55 Lunch With the Girls
p66–67 Italian Sunshine
p141 The Grouch

KATHLEEN S. GILES
NFWS, BSA
2336 Hartland Rd.
Gasport, NY 14067
716.795.9368
kgilesstudio@hotmail.com
kgilesstudio.com
Market Street Art Center, Lockport, NY
p95 Grandma's Milk Glass

DOUGLAS F. GREER
CWA, Santa Clara Valley Watercolor Society
1225 Llagas Rd.
Morgan Hill, CA 95037
408.226.1597
dfgreerdll@aol.com
Serengeti Grass—Arizona Watercolor Association National Competition/Exhibition Selection, 2010
p57 Serengeti Grass

JENNIFER C. GRIFFITH
CWA
1003 Bay View Farm Rd. #207
Pinole, CA 94564
jenniepoop@gmail.com
jenniepoop.wix.com/jennieg
p56 Brewtus
p65 Journey

MEL GRUNAU
OWS, Charter Member and Signature Member; ISAP; OPA, Associate Member
mjgrunau@yahoo.com
mjgrunau.com
p97 Red 31

GRACE F. HAVERTY
NWS, TWSA, PSA
11795 N. 95th St.
Scottsdale, AZ 85260
480.657.6210 (home), 602.980.0468 (cell)
gracehaverty@hotmail.com
Snow Geese—Best of Show, Arizona Watercolor Association; Juror's Choice Award, Arizona Watercolor Association
p48 Snow Geese

SUZANNE HETZEL
TWSA, PWS, IWS
25685 Ave. Normandy W
Oak Brook, IL 60523
847.372.5622
suzannehetzel@yahoo.com
dragonflywatercolors.com
p99 Restraint

JOYCE HICKS
AWS
Lantana, TX
jhicks@jhicksfineart.com
jhicksfineart.com
facebook.com/jhicksfineart
p8–9 Pennsylvania Idyll
p18 I Found It in Waldport
p19 A Barn I Saw in Mount Pleasant

LYNN HOSEGOOD
4475 Pleasant View Dr.
Williamsburg, VA 23188
757.564.3098
lynn@lynnhosegoodstudio.com
lynnhosegoodstudio.com
Next Bus to Torremolinos—Frances Nell Storer Memorial Award in AWS 146th Annual Exhibition and selected for the AWS Traveling Exhibition
p34–35 Next Bus to Torremolinos
p38 Mijas Market, Spain

PETER V. JABLOKOW
2457 N. Prairie Ave., #1D
Evanston, IL 60201
847.651.7161
p.jablokow@comcast.net
No. 3 Shaft House Stairs—Founders Award, 36th Transparent Watercolor Society Show; Second Place, 2013 Great Lakes Showcase
p31 No. 3 Shaft House Stairs

PAUL JACKSON
AWS, NWS, MOWS
2918 Bluegrass Ct.
Columbia, MO 65201
573.999.7768
pauljacksonart@gmail.com
pauljackson.com
Suspense—Best of Show, Missouri Watercolor Society Invitational
p80 Suspense

BEV JOZWIAK
AWS, NWS, TWSA
315 W. 23rd St.
Vancouver, WA 98660
paintingjoz@hotmail.com
bevjozwiak.com
Cole Gallery, Edmonds, WA
p87 Sous Chef

KRISTINA JURICK
Hoehenstrasse 12
91227 Leinburg, Germany
jurick-art@web.de
jurick-art.de
p20 Vilassar de Mar
p21 Sono Beach, Brazil
p122 Shopping in Barcelona

DARLENE KAPLAN
Sumi-e Society of America, national and local society (VA-DC); Torpedo Factory Art Center, Art League, Alexandria, VA; Manhattan Arts International, NY
4609 Franconia Rd.
Alexandria, VA 22310
703.922.4175
chineseart@darlenekaplan.com
darlenekaplan.com
Vulcan Gallery
p53 Hey Gorgeous

ONA KINGDON
CSPWC, PWS, NWWS
Richmond Hill, ON, Canada
647.478.6276
ona@onak.ca
onak.ca
p102 Intoxicate-Ted and Inebriate-Ted

STEVEN KOZAR
steve@stevenkozar.com
stevenkozar.com
p117 Autumn at the Union Terrace

MARIE LAMOTHE
Interlochen, MI
mariejoseelamothe@yahoo.com
marielamothe.com
Bier Art Gallery, Charlevoix, MI
p71 A Daylily Dalliance

KATHRYN KELLER LARKINS
372 Manhattan Ave. 3A
New York, NY 10026
rynkeller@yahoo.com
behance.net/kellerlarkins
p123 Opera View II

DOROTHY W. LEE
Valley Watercolor Society
2342 Moreno Dr.
Los Angeles, CA 90039
323.819.8279
dort_lee@yahoo.com
Sorrow—Third Place, Valley Watercolor Society Annual Juried Show
p78 Sorrow

MINDY LIGHTHIPE
American Society of Botanical Artists; Guild of Natural Science Illustrators; Salmagundi Club, Juried Member
1200 NW 94th St.
Gainesville, FL 32606
352.226.0949
mlighthipe@mac.com
botanicalartpainting.com
The Artisans Guild Gallery, Gainesville, FL
Señor Iguana—Silver Medalist, The Horticultural Society of London; President's Award, Salmagundi Club, NYC
p46–47 *Señor Iguana*

TRICIA H. LOVE
NMWS, Signature Member; WAOW, Associate Member; NLAPW
5 Naomi Dr.
Tijeras, NM 87059
505.281.9329
triciahlove@aol.com
jerryandtricialove.com
Old Schoolhouse Gallery, Sandia Park, NM
p60 *The Chicken Coop*

GUY MAGALLANES
620 Taylor Way #2
San Carlos, CA 94070
650.575.9158
guy@guymagallanes.com
guymagallanes.com
p74 *Sun Kissed*

YAEL MAIMON
yael_mai@walla.co.il
yaelmaimon.com
p51 *Yawning*

CLIFF MANN
273 Bellos St.
Prince George, BC, Canada V2M 4W8
250.596.2881
cliffmann25@gmail.com
cliffmann.ca
Frameworks Gallery, Prince George, BC
p90–91 *Timeless View*

GEORGIA MANSUR
AWS, NWS, LPAPA, CAC, KAWA
125 Snake Creek Rd.
Mudgee 2850, NSW, Australia
georgia@georgiamansur.com
georgiamansur.com
passport2paint.com
Randy Higbee Gallery, Costa Mesa, CA
p23 *Rock My World*

ANTONIO MASI
AWS-DF; Allied Artist, Philadelphia Water Color Society
121 Brompton Rd.
Garden City, NY 11530
516.455.6601
antoniofineart@gmail.com
Paul Scott Gallery, Scottsdale, AZ
Morning Ride—Winsor & Newton Award
p124 *Morning Ride*

ANNE MCCARTNEY
CSPWC, NWS
1960 Towne Centre Blvd
Edmonton, AB, T6R 2W3, Canada
780.431.2527
mcanne1960@gmail.com
mccartneyartworks.com
Daffodil Gallery
p13 *Superior Shoreline*

LAURIN MCCRACKEN
AWS, NWS, TWSA
215 N. Deer Creek Dr. W
Leland, MS 38756
817.773.2163
laurinmc@aol.com
lauringallery.com
Greenberg Fine Art, Santa Fe, NM
Tools of the Trade—Totally Transparent Watercolor Award, Tennessee Watercolor Society, 2012
p110 *Tools of the Trade*
p111 *Ice Water*

MARK E. MEHAFFEY
AWS, DF, NWS
5440 Zimmer Rd.
Williamston, MI 48895
517.655.2342
mark@mehaffeygallery.com
mehaffeygallery.com
p70 *Rose Dichotomy*

SANDY MEYER
WHS, TWSA
13434 84th Ave.
Coopersville, MI 49404
homer5@altelco.net
sandymeyerart.com
p104 *Pears and Green Plates*

RAN MU
NWS, Michigan Water Color Society
muran814@hotmail.com
maggiemou.com
p100 *Red Wall Story*

ROBERT J. O'BRIEN
AWS, NWS
2811 Weathersfield Center Rd.
Perkinsville, VT 05151
802.263.9394
robert@robertjobrien.com
robertjobrien.com
p75 *Peony and Chives*

CATHERINE P. O'NEILL
AWS, NWS, TWSA
34 Marengo Ave.
Hamburg, NY 14075
716.648.4852
kconeill@roadrunner.com
catherineponeill.com
p42 *Honor America*
p82 *Aunt Marion*

LISA O'REGAN
St. Hubert, QC, Canada
lisa.oregan@gmail.com
lisaoregan.blogspot.com
p84 *Insignificant Boundaries*

KRIS PARINS
NWS
1508 Pelican Cove Rd., Gr132
Sarasota, FL 34231
kris.parins@gmail.com
krisparins.com
p39 *Against the Light*
p114 *City Light*

DONALD W. PATTERSON
AWS, NWS
108 Ivy Mills Rd.
Glen Mills, PA 19342
610.358.2928
donpatterson1@verizon.net
travisgallery.com
p22 *Spring Rocks*

JEAN PEDERSON
AWS; CSPWC; CWA, Master
4039 Comanche Rd. NW
Calgary, AB, T2L 0N9, Canada
403.289.6106
artform@telus.net
jeanpederson.com
Diana Paul Galleries
p86 *The Library*

SANDRINE PELISSIER
AFCA, NWWS, SDWS
171 W. Kings Rd.
N. Vancouver, BC, V7N 267, Canada
sandrine@watercolorpainting.ca
watercolorpainting.ca
p126 *Early This Morning*

JUAN PEÑA
720 Hi Pines Ranch Rd.
Colfax, CA 95713
530.637.5250
juan@paintingsbyjuanpena.com
paintingsbyjuanpena.com
High-Hand Art Gallery, Loomis, CA
p30 *Dark Sands Beach*
p132 *Hearst Castle South Tower*

TRAVIS POELLE
150 Bennett Ave., Apt. 3H
New York, NY 10040
323.428.3669
tpoelle@gmail.com
travispoelle.com
p127 Park Central

JENNIFER POLNASZEK
TWS; Coppini Academy of Fine Arts, San Antonio; Gentileschi Aegis Gallery Association, San Antonio
100 San Miniato St.
Georgetown, TX 78628
210.896.7459
jenniferpolnaszek@yahoo.com
Still Life With Quilt—Best in Watercolor and Brad Braune Watercolor Award, Coppini Academy of Fine Art Members Juried Exhibition, San Antonio, 2012
p94 Still Life With Quilt

KRIS PRESLAN
AWS; NWS, Signature Member; TWSA, Signature Member
17841 Lake Haven Dr.
Lake Oswego, OR 97035
971.285.0918
krispreslan@mac.com
preslanart.com
p73 Under the Arch
p83 Rice Paddy

DORRIE RIFKIN
TWSA, NEWS, BWS
31 Regency Cir.
Englewood, NJ 07631
201.567.6336 (home), 201.913.1140 (cell)
drifkin@dorrierifkin.com
dorrierifkin.com
A View From the Highline—Loew-Cornell Art Brushes Award, 35th International Show, North East Watercolor Society Exhibition; Best in Show, 2013 CAA Members' Show
p112–113 A View From the Highline

CLAUDIA RUTHERFORD
Arts Council of Anne Arundel County
2595 Golfers Ridge Rd.
Annapolis, MD 21401
410.212.9837
Guess Who Came to Dinner—Award of Distinction; Best in Show
p61 Guess Who Came to Dinner

DAVID SAVELLANO
NWS, CWA
1328 Eastshore Dr.
Alameda, CA 94501
eastshoreart@comcast.net
davidsavellano.com
Sidewalk Rhythms—Artists Choice Award, Best Watercolor at Frank Bette Plein Air Paintout
p116 Sidewalk Rhythms

PRAFULL B. SAWANT
Art Society of India; Bombay Art Society
31, Chitrangan Bungalow, Shiv Colony, Vanvaibhav, Indira Nager, Nasik - 422009, (MS), India
+91-9860745385 , 9766311965
prafullsawant79@gmail.com
prafullsawant@rediffmail.com
prafullsawant.com
p25 Evening at Banaras Ghat

THOMAS W. SCHALLER
4080 Glencoe Ave. #201
Marina del Rey, CA 90292
310.390.4630
tom@twschaller.com
thomasschaller.com
p33 Fairmount Road – Ohio
p96 Carousel, Central Park – NYC
p130 Steps to Simón Bolívar Plaza, Central Park – NYC

THERESA SHEPHERD
VWS, Artist Member; James River Art League
5204 Watercrest Pl.
Midlothian, VA 23112
804.739.1692 (home), 804.338.4830 (cell)
tshepherd1491@verizon.net
p52 Unfurled Devotion

DUNCAN SIMMONS
NWS, TWSA, RMWM
16306 DeLozier St.
Houston, TX 77040
713.466.6841 (home), 713.562.2915 (cell)
duncansimmonsartist@yahoo.com
2collaborationgartists.com
Harris Gallery, Houston, TX
Destination for Peace of Mind—Juror's Merit Award, 15th Annual Rio Brazos Art Exhibition
p26 Destination for Peace of Mind

HAROLD DEAN SMITH
231 Aspen Cir.
Lincoln, MA 01773-4921
781.259.9142
ehsmith1@yahoo.com
p29 Old Farm Building, Portugal

ROBERT STEINMETZ
AWS, NWS, NEWS
93 Island Ave.
Spruce Head, ME 04859
207.594.2974
patashton@me.com
Haynes Galleries, Nashville TN and Thomaston, ME
p81 Riposo

TUVA PAGE STEPHENS
SW, WSA, KWS
190 David Ct.
McKenzie, TN 38201
731.352.5852
tuvart@charter.net
tuvastephens.com
Court Square Art and Antiques, Trenton, TN
Tiggy!—Tennessee Art Associations Award, TWS, 2012; Best of Show, Southern Expressions Art Show, Bolivar, TN
p58 Tiggy!

IAIN STEWART
stewartwatercolors.com
p6 Thursday on Decatur – New Orleans
p12 St. Andrews Boatyard – Scotland

DAVID L. STICKEL
AWS, NWS, WSNC
1201 Hatch Rd.
Chapel Hill, NC 27516
919.942.3900
dlstickel@juno.com
davidstickel.com; waverlyartistsgroup.com
Gulf Rim Reflections—First Place, NC State Fair
p134 Gulf Rim Reflections
p135 Night Lights of the Big Apple

RON SUMNER
9785 Montego Ct.
Windsor, CA 95492
707.838.8616
sonomron@pacbell.net
localcolorgallery.com
p54 Red-Tailed Hawk

ROBERT N. TALBERT
Baltimore Watercolor Society
12504 Gravenhurst Ln.
Darnestown, MD 20878
rob@talbertfineart.com
talbertfineart.com
Under Her Parasol—Jack Richeson Award, 2012 Mid-Atlantic Regional Watercolor Exhibit
p88 Under Her Parasol

DANIEL K. TENNANT
1977Delphi Rd.
New Woodstock, NY 13122
315.662.7263
dktennant1@juno.com
danielktennant.com
M.A. Doran Gallery, Tulsa, OK
p92 Still Life With Blueberry Muffin

FERNAND THIENPONDT
Aquarelinstituut van België; Vlaamse Aquarel- en Tekenschool; Aquarellistes en Nord, France
Kunsthuis Gir-Art, JerusalemSt. 18
8000 Bruges, Belgium
0032.50.34.5822
aquathien@hotmail.com
vlaamseaquarel-tekenschool.be
Ready to Fly—Art Prize, Musée Hyogo, Kobé, Japan
p17 Ready to Fly

SUSAN WEBB TREGAY
NWS, WHS, TWSA
57 Skyline Dr. Ext.
Hendersonville, NC 28791
828.693.0553
susan@tregay.com
tregay.com, susanwebbtregay.com
Wickwire Fine Art / Folk Art, Hendersonville, NC
Monday People—Accepted nto 2013 AWS Exhibition
p43 *Monday People*

ROBIN VAN DEN BARSELAAR
AWSSA, HAWSSA
15 Arbroath Rd.
Bedfordview, South Africa 2007
0027116166430 or 0027827792360
African Singers – Simphiwe Dana and Busi Mhlongo—Highly commended at 84th National Exhibition, South Africa; Viewers' Choice Award
p79 *African Singers – Simphiwe Dana and Busi Mhlongo*

WEN-CONG WANG
1F., No. 43, Ln. 120, Zhong 3rd St., Xizhi Dist.
New Taipei City 22153, Taiwan (R.O.C.)
886.2.8646.2688
wencong.w@gmail.com
wangwencong.com
p40 *Morning Migration*

SOON Y. WARREN
AWS, NWS, TWSA
4062 Hildring Dr. W
Fort Worth, TX 76109
817.923.1586
soonywarren@gmail.com
soonwarren.com
Your Private Collection Art Gallery, Granbury, TX
p49 *Koi Pond – Yellow Leaves*
p121 *Street Art Critic*

KEIKO YASUOKA
AWS, NWS, TWAS
23 Litchfield Ln.
Houston, TX 77024
713.973.2739
keiko_yasuoka@hotmail.com
2collaboratingartists.com
Harris Gallery, Houston, TX
Romance Is in the Air—Merit Award, Louisiana Watercolor Society 42nd International Exhibition
p68 *In the Spotlight*
p69 *Romance Is in the Air*

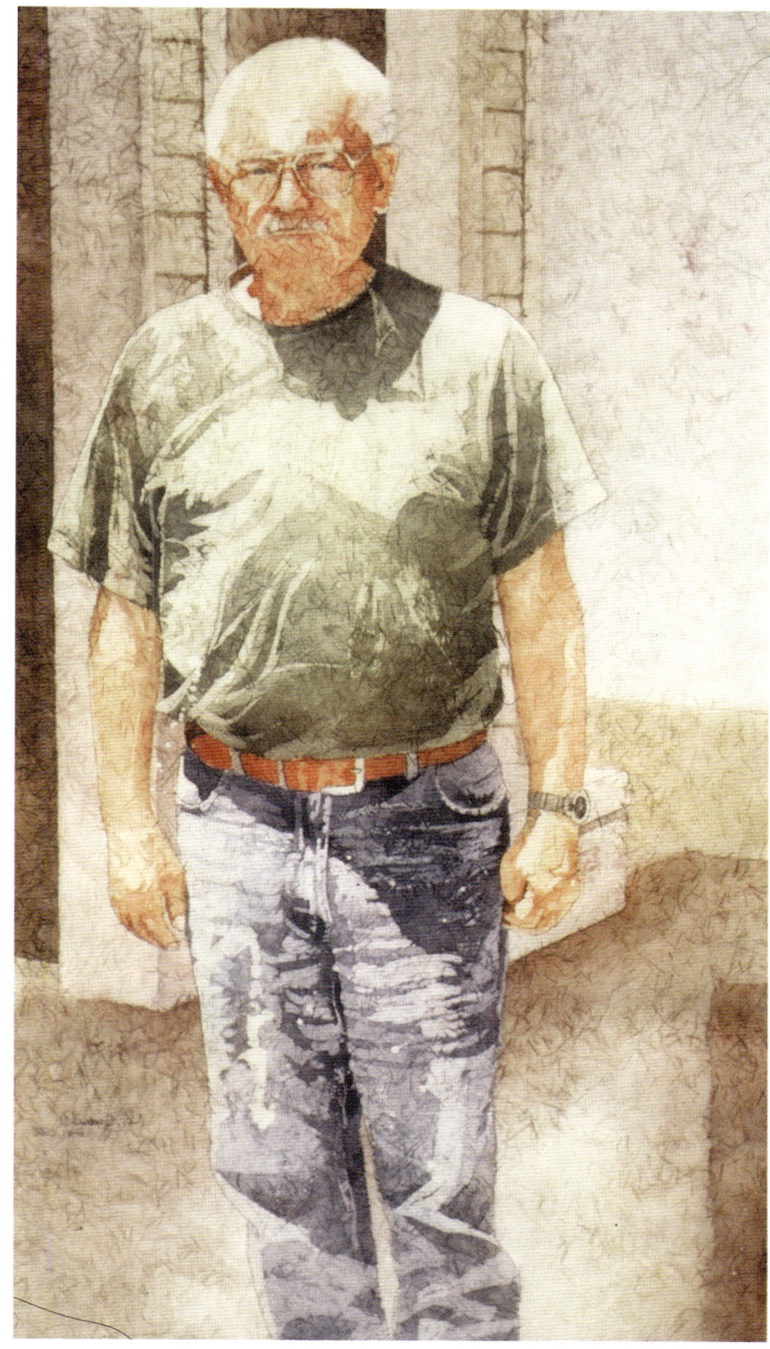

▲ **THE GROUCH** | Kathie George
37" × 22" (94cm × 56cm) Watercolor batik on rice paper

This is a portrait of my father and it was a long time coming. He wanted me to paint him for so long but was continually joking that I'd probably paint him with three eyes in Picasso-like fashion. The truth is I was a very realistic painter. When I began this painting, the portrait came easily. The background was a different story. Being used to painting everything as I saw it, the realistic background was taking too much attention away from the figure. So I gulped and took my first try at simplifying and abstracting the background, which included that very scary dark rectangle in the bottom right corner. To my surprise, it won an award in the OWS show. Sometimes you need to follow an instinct and take a chance.

Index

Published by North Light Books, an imprint of F+W Media, Inc., 10151 Carver Road, Suite 200, Blue Ash, OH 45242. (800) 289-0963. First Edition.

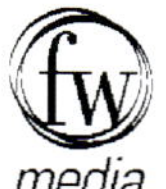

Other fine North Light Books are available from your favorite bookstore, art supply store or online supplier. Visit our website at fwmedia.com.

18 17 16 15 14 5 4 3 2 1

Distributed in Canada by Fraser Direct
100 Armstrong Avenue
Georgetown, ON, Canada L7G 5S4
Tel: (905) 877-4411

Distributed in the U.K. and Europe
by F&W Media International LTD
Brunel House, Forde Close, Newton Abbot, TQ12 4PU, UK
Tel: (+44) 1626 323200, Fax: (+44) 1626 323319
Email: enquiries@fwmedia.com

Distributed in Australia by Capricorn Link
P.O. Box 704, S. Windsor NSW, 2756 Australia
Tel: (02) 4560 1600; Fax: (02) 4577 5288
Email: books@capricornlink.com.au

Production edited by Sarah Laichas
Designed by Clare Finney
Production coordinated by Mark Griffin

ISBN: 978-1-4403-2040-8

METRIC CONVERSION CHART

To convert	*to*	*multiply by*
Inches	Centimeters	2.54
Centimeters	Inches	0.4
Feet	Centimeters	30.5
Centimeters	Feet	0.03
Yards	Meters	0.9
Meters	Yards	1.1

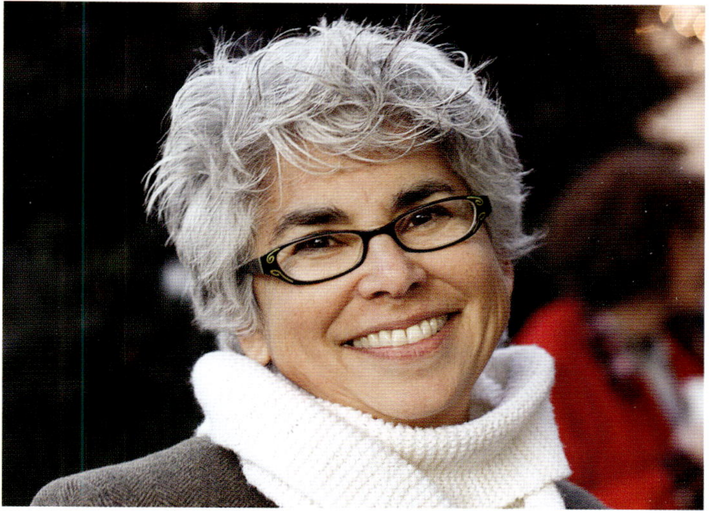

ABOUT THE EDITOR

Rachel Rubin Wolf is a freelance editor and artist. She has edited and written many fine art books for North Light Books, including *Watercolor Secrets*; the *Splash: The Best of Watercolor* series; the *Strokes of Genius: Best of Drawing* series; *The Best of Wildlife Art* (editions 1 and 2); *The Best of Portrait Painting*; *Best of Flower Painting 2*; *The Acrylic Painter's Book of Styles and Techniques*; *Painting Ships, Shores and the Sea*; and *Painting the Many Moods of Light*. She also has acquired numerous fine art book projects for North Light Books and has contributed to magazines such as *Fine Art Connoisseur* and *Wildlife Art*.

ACKNOWLEDGMENTS

We could not produce *Splash* without the editors, designers and staff at North Light Books who attend to the many thankless details needed to make this into a beautiful finished book, including designer Clare Finney and production coordinator Mark Griffin. Special thanks as always to my *Splash* partner, production editor Sarah Laichas, who does more things than I know how to count up to.

My gratitude also goes to all of the artists in this book, who I trust find creative solutions in their lives as well as in their art! You are wonderful creative people! Thank you for sharing your techniques and your advice with us. I am appreciative of the time (and money) spent in getting the properly formatted digital photos to us. We certainly couldn't do it without you!

Cover image: **KOI POND – YELLOW LEAVES**, Soon Y. Warren, p49

Back cover image: **DESTINATION FOR PEACE OF MIND**, Duncan Simmons, p26

Ideas. Instruction. Inspiration.

Receive FREE downloadable bonus materials when you sign up for our free newsletter at artistsnetwork.com/newsletter_thanks.

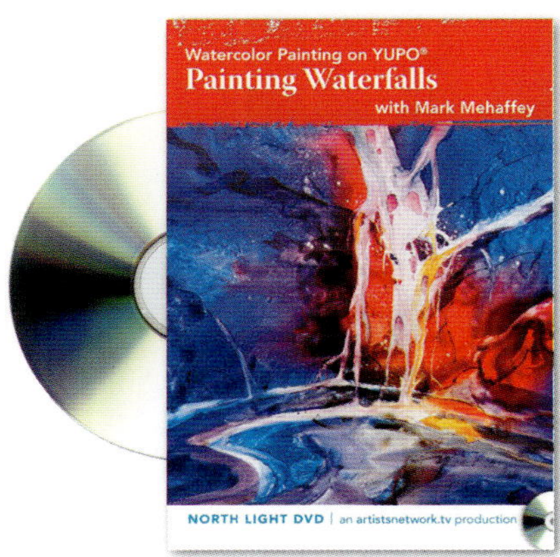

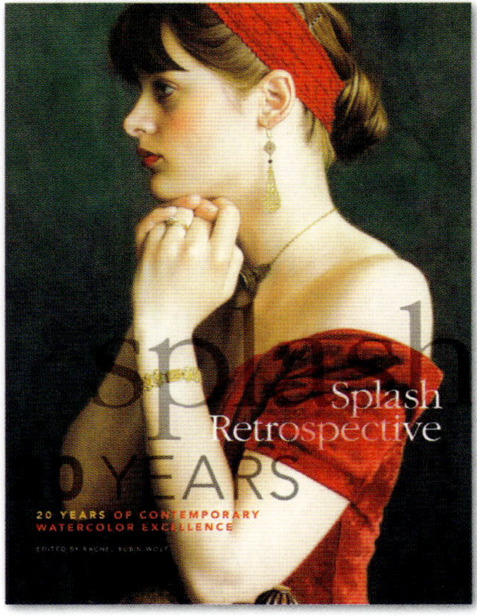

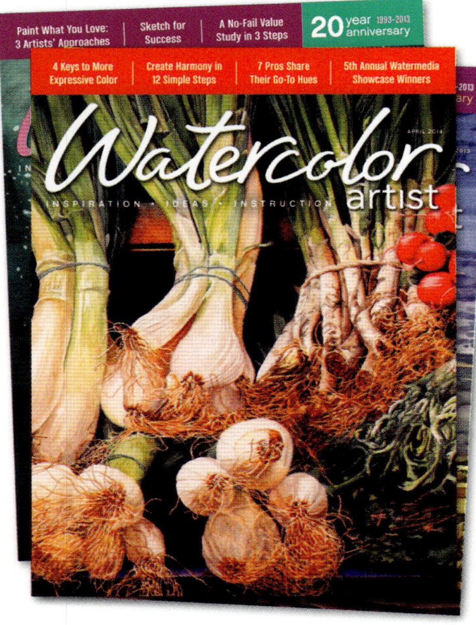

Find the latest issues of *Watercolor Artist* on newsstands, or visit artistsnetwork.com.

These and other fine North Light products are available at your favorite art & craft retailer, bookstore or online supplier. Visit our websites at artistsnetwork.com and artistsnetwork.tv.

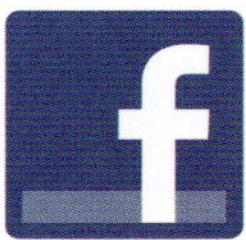

Follow Artist's Network for the latest news, free wallpapers, free demos and chances to win FREE BOOKS!

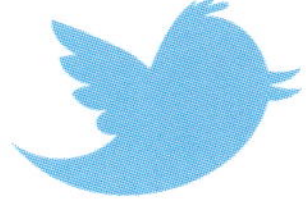

@artistsnetwork

Get your art in print!

Visit artistsnetwork.com/splashwatercolor for up-to-date information on Splash and other North Light competitions.

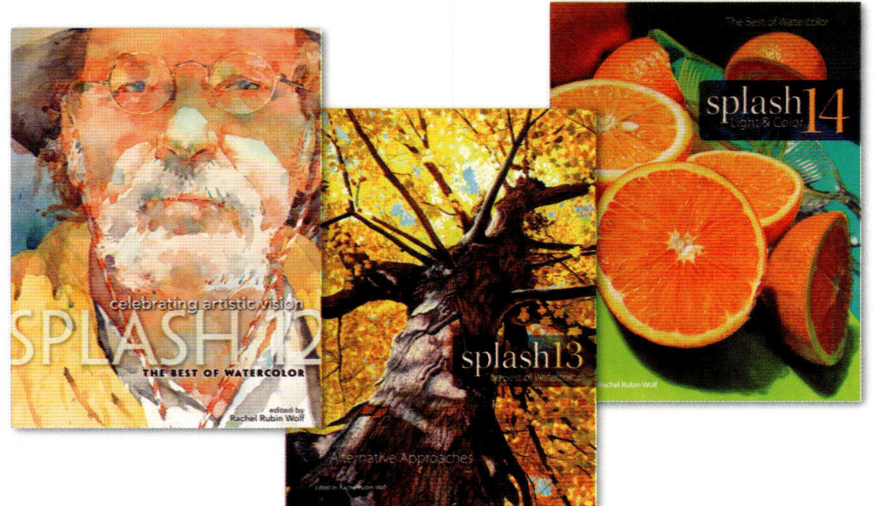